The F
and the C

The Hero's Quest and the Cycles of Nature

An Ecological Interpretation of World Mythology

RACHEL S. MCCOPPIN

McFarland & Company, Inc., Publishers
Jefferson, North Carolina

LIBRARY OF CONGRESS CATALOGUING-IN-PUBLICATION DATA

Names: McCoppin, Rachel S., 1977– author.
Title: The hero's quest and the cycles of nature : an ecological
    interpretation of world mythology / Rachel S. McCoppin.
Description: Jefferson, North Carolina : McFarland & Company, Inc.,
    Publishers, 2016. | Includes bibliographical references and index.
Identifiers: LCCN 2016041366 | ISBN 9781476662015 (softcover : acid
    free paper) ∞
Subjects: LCSH: Nature—Mythology | Heroes. | Mythology. | Heroes—
    Mythology.
Classification: LCC BL435 .M328 2016 | DDC 202/.13—dc23
LC record available at https://lccn.loc.gov/2016041366

BRITISH LIBRARY CATALOGUING DATA ARE AVAILABLE

ISBN (print) 978-1-4766-6201-5
ISBN (ebook) 978-1-4766-2575-1

Cover photograph of Buddha head in tree roots © 2016 Yothind/iStock

Printed in the United States of America

McFarland & Company, Inc., Publishers
    Box 611, Jefferson, North Carolina 28640
    www.mcfarlandpub.com

To Landon
and Season

Table of Contents

Preface

This book explores myths from around the world that involve the hero, but unlike many other discussions of the mythic hero, this book strives to portray the hero in terms of a personification of nature.

Myriad world myths connect the lives of human beings with the natural world. For instance, numerous creation myths portray humans as directly coming from natural elements, and multiple cultures envision pantheons of divine beings who personify components found in nature. In connecting mythic beings to nature, a message is revealed to audiences that reminds us that we will always be firmly bound to the demands of the environment. This acknowledgment carries over into some of the world's most popular heroic myths, often showing that if mythic heroes embrace their tie to nature, there are spiritual promises of renewal.

Mythic heroic journeys have long been analyzed by many scholars; this book looks towards this scholarship for guidance of heroic archetypes, yet it strives to carry the analysis of the mythic hero to a new level with a discussion of a special kind of hero, which I call the "botanical hero," because he or she serves as a representation of nature and its cycles. Therefore, this book analyzes the most renowned mythic heroes to find natural themes within their heroic quests that serve to mark them as following the same seasonal cycles found in the environment.

Multiculturalism is a direct focus of this book, as heroic characters from many world myths are analyzed. It should be stated that this book does look towards themes that connect global heroes together as botanical representations, but there is no intention to claim that all mythic heroes, social practices, or philosophical and religious beliefs from the cultures discussed are identical or especially interconnected. Instead, this book strives to show the archetypes of the hero in terms of natural patterns in an effort to acknowledge the vital role nature plays in our most treasured heroic myths from around the world.

1

This book is important because myths, though sometimes associated in contemporary times as outdated, are in fact evidence of a people's attempt to find meaning to mankind's most timeless of questions, particularly surrounding life and death. In contemporary times, mythic heroes are either overlooked or misrepresented through popular renditions found in comic books, films, or television—take for example the contemporary superhero. The superhero of popular culture is represented often as better than the average person because he or she possesses a superhuman skill or attribute, but in presenting a hero as superhuman, a disservice is committed to the integrity of mythology. Myths of the hero are for the education of the audience. The audience of heroic myth must relate to the hero, so that the wisdom the hero gains is embraced by the audience. Moreover, this book contends that the wisdom audiences can receive from botanical heroes educates them on the necessity of embracing one's role within nature. Given the current state of environmental destruction found in our times, it is imperative that humanity remembers their tie to the earth.

I would like to thank the people who helped this book come to fruition. My kids' ceaseless wonderment of heroic myths from around the world inspired me, and my family's willingness to travel to far-away places and share in my excitement of ancient ruins, enabled me to write this book, so it is to them I would like to express my extreme gratitude. I would also like to thank Ioannis Kiourtsoglou and Constantinos Sfikas for making Greek and Roman mythology come alive for me. And finally, I would like to acknowledge James Aasen for inspiring me towards the natural nuances of Celtic mythology.

Introduction

"I wonder if the snow loves the trees and fields, that it kisses them so gently?
And then it covers them up snug, you know, with a white quilt; and perhaps
it says 'Go to sleep, darlings, till the summer comes again.'"—Lewis Carroll

"Yesterday is ashes; tomorrow wood. Only today the fire shines brightly."—
Inuit Proverb

Slowly stepping through the passage tunnel of Newgrange, a Neolithic
tomb and/or ceremonial monument in the Boyne Valley of Ireland, provokes
trepidation. It feels uncomfortable, even slightly terrifying, to squeeze the
human body against cold rock walls to journey into the dark earth. Though
archeologists do not know the full purpose of Newgrange to its Neolithic
builders, it was most likely connected in some way to death as remnants of
human remains were discovered inside. When I first visited Newgrange and
passed through the entrance tunnel, after a few claustrophobic tourists opted
not to, I too felt hesitant, even a bit fearful. Once inside the constructed inner
chamber, though, I was overcome with the beauty of the place. The circular
shape, the high ceiling, the intricately carved designs, and the perfect view of
the entrance tunnel soon induced in me a sense of peace.

Knowing that in some way its builders constructed it to be connected to
death, I felt that the experience of proceeding into this chamber provided a
message to whoever journeyed into it. To me, the experience represented the
process one goes through upon death, as the entrance tunnel seemed to be created to be purposefully terrifying, but once inside, it also equally seemed that
the beauty of the inner realm was created to evoke serenity. The inner chamber
of Newgrange looked like it was intentionally constructed to represent the
womb of the earth. Once within the inner chamber, the archeologist leading
the tour began a simulation of what happens to the structure on each winter

3

solstice; the lights within the chamber were turned off, so one could see what happens on the winter solstice when a single shaft of light pierces through the entrance tunnel and illuminates the darkness of the inner chamber. A tomb or ceremonial monument connected to death that incorporates a chamber that becomes annually illuminated seemed to me to contradict a message of the finality of death.

The experience within Newgrange made me think that its agriculturally focused builders perhaps believed that death for human beings was connected to the death of botanical elements within the natural environment. Creating a place where humans could enter into the dark recesses of the earth, a place that was constructed in a circular, womb-like fashion, perhaps delivered a message that like a decayed or dormant plant, humans too died and decayed back into the earth. But perhaps the light of the winter solstice, that illuminates the inner chamber of Newgrange, symbolized a belief that deceased humans would also, like a plant that regrows annually, be naturally reborn.

Standing in the silent inner chamber of Newgrange as it passed from dark to light, and then slowly walking once more through the passage tunnel to emerge back into the light of day, able to see, perhaps more clearly now, the magnificent view of the Irish countryside all around Newgrange, solidified for me the same process found in the hero's journey of many world myths. Myths involving the heroic quest in many ways mimics the process of entering into and emerging out of Newgrange or other Neolithic passage tombs found throughout the world, such as Maeshowe in Orkney, Scotland. Myriad tales showcase heroes who must crawl through mythic tunnels, enter mysterious caves, and journey into sad and horrific underworlds that house the dead, so that they may symbolically resurrect after their respective ordeals having been transformed into the status of hero. It is believed that many of our most beloved world myths were in some way related to stories from our nature-dependent ancestors, and so perhaps the archeological structures, like Newgrange and Maeshowe, as well as the belief systems of nature-dependent cultures can provide insight into the mythic archetypes that continually ask heroes to face death in order to be symbolically reborn, resembling the process of botanical agents within the environment.

Mythic Beliefs of Nature-Dependent Cultures

People in many nature-dependent cultures, from the Paleolithic (c. 2,000,000–10,000 BCE) and Neolithic (c. 10,000–4,000 BCE) periods into contemporary times, revered the land as sacred because nature affected all aspects of life for human beings. Paleolithic people imagined that the earth was "an all-giving Mother from whose womb all life emerges and to which, like the cycles of vegetation, it returns after death to be again reborn" (Eisler xvi).[1] Neolithic communities envisioned an Earth Goddess who, as a representation of nature, presided over all aspects of the essential harvest. Many nature dependent cultures, like those of the American Indians and Aboriginal Australians, embraced the concept that the earth and its elements were divine.

Many nature-dependent cultures believed that humans were only one part of the greater natural order, not at all superior to any other natural element. Humans, animals, plants, and all living organisms were accepted as part of a necessary and structured eco-system. Many cultures imagined that the earth, whether it was conceived of as a Paleolithic Great Mother, Neolithic Earth Goddess, or natural element embedded with divinity, like the Egyptian god of the sun Rê, expected people to operate in accordance to a system where they both benefited from the earth's resources as well as readily gave back to the earth what they could. Death became understood as the means for all living beings to return to the earth what it gave to its inhabitants.

In Paleolithic imaginings the interior of the earth was the womb of the Great Mother. Living beings were viewed as birthed from the earth itself, and therefore upon death, they returned there to allow for the growth of the next generation. Similarly, the Neolithic myths of the male consort and the Earth Goddess that arose out of the Near and Middle East repeatedly discussed a male consort willingly dying in an acknowledgement that his death was needed to continue the natural cycles of the vital harvest. Many nature-dependent cultures narrated tales where divine beings were also called upon to sacrifice themselves for the preservation of the eco-system. The American Indian Penobscot Corn Mother, for instance, instructs her family to murder her, so that her body can nourish the soil in order for the much needed staple crop of corn to grow. It is significant to understand, though, that the Corn Mother's resurrection as corn, as the death of the Neolithic male consort for the propagation of the harvest or the return of Paleolithic people into the womb of the earth to ensure the rebirth of the next generation, displays a belief within these nature-dependent cultures that death is not final.

Many nature-dependent cultures did not conceive of time in linear terms; "Paleolithic people believed in timeless, repetitive cycles of life, a wheel of birth and rebirth, perhaps modeled on the analogy of the seasons" (Oelschlaeger 21). Brown and Cousins state that for many American Indian cultures even today "time tends to be experienced as cyclical and rhythmic, rather than linear and progress oriented" (9). This conception of time as cyclical carries over into a philosophical view meant to explain the life cycle of living beings;

because the cyclical patterns of time "continue to revolve, there is always an opportunity for life cycles to be renewed.... Winter leads to another spring, the death of a deer leads to the continued life of a human family, a harvest renders more seeds for planting" (Brown & Cousins 10). In looking at the patterns of nature, human beings' conceptions of life and death became interconnected with nature's cycles; therefore, many myths coming from nature-dependent cultures teach audiences that there is no ultimate death for humans, as there appears to be no lasting death in nature.

Ritual, the Initiate and the Hero

Enactment in sacred rituals was an essential component of many nature-dependent civilizations. Ancient societies around the world took part in mock battles, shamanistic rituals, and rites of passage that allowed audiences to psychologically undergo experiences that were at times confusing and terrifying, but also enlightening. For example, many cultures around the world, in Africa, Asia, Europe, North and South America, imagined caves, or their man-made counterparts like the Neolithic rock structures found throughout Europe, to be the entrances to the realm of death and used them in ritualistic behavior in order to allow initiates to gain spiritual wisdom. By ritualistically facing the terrifying elements that are symbolic of death, like entering a cave meant to be the entrance of the underworld, the initiate was able to move beyond the fear of death towards psychological apotheosis. Though this process of facing mortality to obtain wisdom originated in myths from nature-dependent cultures, we still see these patterns presented in the heroic tales of later periods. The shamanic journey, related in many nature-dependent communities perhaps as far back as the Paleolithic period, also presents patterns that are similar to the elements of the mythic heroic journey of later periods, as the shaman also ventures into otherworlds or the underworld in order to achieve knowledge.

Though death seems to be the focus of many myths and rituals from nature-dependent cultures, the vital element one must grasp is that the message of these stories and ritualistic enactments was not focused on death, but upon the value of life. The myths and rituals meant to portray death do so with an intention of stripping the fear of death away, showcasing it as natural, and therefore, not an end but as a beginning.

Nature Demoted, Humanity Elevated

Many nature-dependent cultures throughout the world at some point, despite the reason, experienced a modification of cultural beliefs as they transitioned away from hunter/gatherer or Neolithic values and practices. For instance, over centuries Indo-European invaders in the late Neolithic and Iron Ages modified the belief systems of many nature-dependent cultures, spurring the mythology of many Neolithic cultures to become transformed into tales that held human beings, particularly males, in more prominent roles, which often meant dispelling Neolithic Earth Goddesses of their supreme roles. Statuettes and artwork of this transformative period also began to show human beings as singularly important, as artistic depictions of some of the first human faces emerged, presenting a psychological shift towards the value of one human life. This "self-awareness" (Cauvin 133) becomes crucial in the shifting concepts of the perceived supremacy of human beings within the eco-system and thus the belief that one individual life is singularly important.

Also, as civilizations advanced in the Neolithic period, agriculturalists began to make the realization that humankind could be an agent of environmental change. As civilizations advanced, the loss of a close relationship with the land caused many spiritual views to become modified. For example, Oelschlaeger looks towards the Hebrew belief in Yahwism (c. 1400–1050 BCE) as an "evolution in ... ecological transition" (42), as "the Hebrews rejected not only nature gods and mythology but also natural place as having any basic importance.... Yahweh was not a nature god but a god above nature who had designed the world expressly for his chosen people" (Oelschlaeger 42–3). Once the shift away from a value of nature as sacred occurs within a culture, then the messages of the regenerative value of nature become altered or omitted from their mythology.

One of the most telling shifts in values, apparent in many cultures after moving away from a strict dependence upon nature, comes from the altered conception of time as linear instead of cyclical. This shift in the perception of time redefined conceptions of the life cycles of human beings—the most marked change occurred in the conception of death. When time is conceived by humans as linear and not cyclical, then death is conceived as an end, not another beginning. Once perception of time shifts to linear terms, then death becomes a substantial concern, and subsequently the sacred beliefs of a people must change to accommodate this concern, often resulting in the creation of concepts such as an afterlife with a singular identity, often defined as the soul of a person, living on after the physical death of the individual.

As many civilizations became more technologically dependent and lost direct connection with the natural world, many myths began to be created to stress the importance of the individuality of a person. No longer was an individual simply one part of a larger, natural pattern, dependent upon ceaseless deaths for ceaseless births; with the conception of time as linear, individuals began to be viewed as fighting against a timeframe that would ultimately run out. The conception of individual identity became something that must be embraced as highly valuable. Portrayals of heroes began to mythically emerge as examples of how to live an exemplary, singular life, no longer serving as agents to show how to only accept death as necessary and natural.

Yet this book contends that the archetypes of many of these later myths, most especially the myths of the hero's journey, still remain firmly tied to the cycles of nature. This book looks towards the hero's journey in many historical eras as still a representation of the cycles of nature, asserting that like the plant that grows from a seedling, lives fully in the sun, decays in the autumn, and nourishes the soil so that new growth can emerge, so too does the hero, or more precisely as coined in this book, the botanical hero, follow this pattern. Like the cycles of nature demands, the botanical hero must learn that death is unavoidable, so that the audience of the myth can come to terms with this harshest of life lessons. Yet in the hero's acceptance of mortality, there often comes a mythic message to the audience that presents the wisdom of nature— that in nature, death is only one part of a ceaseless cycle, making rebirth imminent.

Defining the Hero's Journey

Literary analysis of the mythic heroic journey has been discussed and debated in academic circles for quite some time. For instance, Otto Rank's *Myth of the Birth of a Hero* (1914) and Lord Raglan's *The Hero: A Study in Tradition, Myth, and Drama* (1936) were among the first texts to identify common archetypes found within what came to be identified as the heroic journey. Rank and others like Sigmund Freud, D. E. Oppenheim, Carl Jung, and Carl Abraham also used heroic myths to identify patterns that to them seemed to be elements within the human psyche. In addition, Jung used the myths of the hero's journey to represent "'the process of individual development'" towards self-actualization (Lefkowitz 432).

Joseph Campbell, author of *The Hero with a Thousand Faces* (1949) and other important texts that focus on the mythic hero's journey, also described the heroic journey using archetypal elements that can be traced in some of the most famous myths of the hero. He articulated the stages of the heroic quest as follows: first heroes are called to leave the comfort of their familiar surroundings. Heroes then face a stage that Campbell terms the "Belly of the Whale," where they find themselves in a realm that is completely unfamiliar to them; this experience of the unknown can take many forms, but often it culminates to a journey to the mythic otherworld and an experience of "Meeting with the Goddess" that eventually leads the hero to experience the mythic underworld, where he or she faces his or her fears, coined by Campbell as "Atonement with the Father." Campbell states that the mythic underworld allows the hero to psychologically face the elements that restrict the hero from self-actualizing, which most succinctly is the fear of mortality. After leaving the underworld, the mythic hero is usually transformed spiritually into a state of "Apotheosis," where he or she gains a sense of inner enlightenment precisely because the hero has "died to his personal ego" and no longer fears death (Campbell, *Hero*, 243). Though quite renowned in popular culture, Campbell has often been criticized within academic circles[2] for not displaying a deep cultural understanding of the myths he references (Trubshaw 10).

David Leeming, author of *Mythology: The Voyage of the Hero* (1998), Jake Page, who with David Lemming published *God: Myths of the Male Divine* (1996), *Goddess: Myths of the Female Divine* (1994), and Karen Armstrong, author of *A Short History of Myth* (2005) and *The Great Transformation: The Beginning of Our Religious Traditions* (2006) support Campbell in identifying common archetypal patterns in heroic myths from around the world, but often Leeming, Page, and K. Armstrong additionally focus on the cultural and historical background of each heroic myth to a greater degree than perhaps some of Campbell's scholarship. In addition, Leeming, Page, and K. Armstrong repeatedly point towards the cultural views of nature in relation to the respective heroic myths they are analyzing, often conceding that the values existent in many nature-dependent communities that created the myths play a key role in identifying meaning within that culture's representation of the heroic journey.

Therefore, without maintaining a declaration that all world myths of the heroic journey present similar patterns, or that these patterns hold identical meaning in different cultures, this book will also trace heroic archetypes as defined by Campbell, Leeming, Page, and K. Armstrong throughout myriad world myths of the hero in order to define heroes as botanical heroes, by revealing the natural messages inherent in many of the archetypes.

The Format of the Botanical Heroic Quest

As stated, many myths of the hero tend to follow archetypal patterns, but arguably the archetypes of the most well-known heroic tales repeatedly reveal a connection to the most basic laws of nature, marking some of the most famous heroes as botanical heroes, and it is these initial components of the botanical heroic quest that will be discussed in chapter 1 of this book, "From Seeds and

Sprouts to Branching Out." For instance, as acknowledged by Rank, Raglan, and Campbell, frequently the hero is removed from his or her home environment as a child to be reared elsewhere, but what is often not discussed at length is the importance of this time of development, which quite often takes place within the natural environment. Also, archetypically young heroes often find an adventure outside of their childhood home, often within the deep wilderness; this book claims that botanical heroes learn important lessons in this initial stage. Another heroic archetype early within the quests of many heroes is the mythic otherworld. The mythic otherworld if often portrayed with an abundance of natural resources and beauty, and because of this it often allows botanical heroes to separate from their former identification of self with the aid of these natural elements.

Archetypically, the hero after journeying through unknown environments must often enter a mythic underworld, portrayed as either a psychological experience that symbolically represents death, or an actual place where the dead reside, which is usually within the earth. This experience often forces the archetypal hero to face the reality of his or her own mortality. The botanical hero must also face the reality of death in order to fully embrace the cycles of nature. The botanical hero learns, as a result of the underworld, that singularity in life is ridiculous—that ambitions in life, longings, beliefs in an identity-driven eternal soul, are all elements that are ego-driven. Therefore, in the underworld the botanical hero faces the same process that initiates of ancient rituals or shamans from nature-dependent cultures experienced, which teaches the botanical hero that the loss of his or her identity and impending demise are necessary parts of nature; this mythic stage will be the focus of chapter 2, "Caves and the Underworld."

The act of sacrifice in many nature-dependent cultures was a sacred activity that was thought to ensure the renewal of the land's resources. Often when mythic characters from nature-dependent myths died, or faced a symbolic death, they were serving as a symbolic sacrifice to the people, but, the sacrifice was often not presented as a grandiose affair; it was instead like that of an American Indian hunter who believed that an animal willingly died in the hunt because it was one part of an unending cycle of natural death and regeneration. From the necessity to sacrifice for the survival of the people, narratives of the heroic quest arose. Therefore, when the botanical hero succumbs to the reality of death, he or she is educating the audience of the myth on the necessity of conceding that death is natural and inevitable, and by only embracing this can the botanical hero achieve a symbolic resurrection. These elements will be discussed in chapter 3 of this book, "Death and Sacrifice."

Campbell identifies the mark of a true hero with a state of apotheosis, where the hero finishes the journey having attained enlightenment. The apotheosis of the botanical hero is dependent upon him or her embracing death as a natural part of life. Botanical heroes let go of the need to believe that their singular identity supersedes that of the most basic patterns of nature. Centuries of teachings attempt to prove humans as superior to nature, but the botanical hero strips all of this away and learns that nothing is lost in realizing one is merely a part of nature; instead, a cyclical promise of everlasting life, where no element fully disappears, is realized. Thus, the vital message the botanical hero provides to audiences is not to dwell on death but to embrace the majesty of ceaseless life; this will be the focus of the final chapter of this book, "Natural Apotheosis and the Resurrection of the Botanical Hero."

Being mindful of one's connection to the earth and its cycles can be a hard lesson for humanity to grasp; this is why we have myths that continually show a shaman, male consort, divine being, or hero struggling to reconcile the laws of nature within their psyche. These myths teach both ancient and contemporary audiences that believing one is separate from nature is folly; it causes disappointment and disillusionment when imaginings of self-importance inevitably fall short. Myths of the botanical hero teach audiences that it is dangerous to view human beings as separate from nature, for if we forget the vital lesson of these myths—that nature will always dominate, and thus that the hero within the myth must always understand that he or she is, and always has been, merely a part of the land—then we abuse the earth, and thus abuse ourselves.

CHAPTER 1

From Seeds and Sprouts to Branching Out

"I like it when a flower or a little tuft of grass grows through a crack in the concrete. It's so fuckin' heroic."—George Carlin

"Show me a hero, and I'll write you a tragedy."—F. Scott Fitzgerald

"As you get older it is harder to have heroes, but it is sort of necessary."— Ernest Hemingway

The start of the botanical hero's journey presents heroes in seed-like fashion; the heroes sprout and grow in the initial stages of the quest into strong and able-bodied specimens as they gain knowledge connected with the environment, but, in order for botanical heroes to reach apotheosis, they must realize that the stage of summer-like growth will soon fade into symbolic periods of autumn and winter where they will have to contend with the natural fact of death and the loss of their identity.

The botanical heroic quest often shows the hero leaving his or her community behind to enter a place that is teeming with natural abundance, and this initial stage is vital to the education of the botanical hero because it teaches the hero to embrace the laws of the environment. Often the hero must enter myriad unknown, wild, or otherworldly environments during these initial stages of the heroic quest and contend with elements in these locales, such as monstrous beasts, merciless hurricanes, or enchanted divinities, that challenge and often disorient the hero into moving beyond preconceived notions of selfhood. It is precisely the natural components of these experiences that shape the hero into realizing botanical heroism.

Often heroes encounter helpers along their quests. The helpers are sometimes divine, and sometimes they are just people or animals at the right time and place. Occasionally, helpers to the mythic hero appear as hindrances, but to achieve the actual goal of the quest, not necessarily the goal the hero thinks he or she must accomplish, both the helpers and apparent hindrances aid the hero upon his or her true journey towards knowledge. Again, nature plays a prominent role in this archetype of the helper for the botanical hero.

Many times, if the myth centers on a male hero, which is common, female characters still tend to play a large role in instructing the hero during his quest. As discussed in the introduction, women since Paleolithic times have been worshipped in many nature-dependent cultures as the givers of life in their Great Mother and Earth Goddess variants, still maintaining roles of significance in pantheons of later male-dominant belief systems, such as the Greek Demeter's essential role as goddess of the harvest. Therefore, the depictions of women in the heroic myths of later periods still hold great significance, even if their societal positions may have been demoted as ideologies shifted throughout history. Quite often women in heroic myth are portrayed as possessing mystical agents that aid the hero on his quest, and largely, this mysticism is connected to the natural world, showing that often female characters within later myths of the hero's journey may be remnants of older, nature-dependent belief systems. In many heroic myths female characters may at times appear to counter the efforts of the hero; they may even appear sinister, like Grendel's mother in the Anglo-Saxon poem *Beowulf*, causing destruction and death, but if viewed in terms of a representation of nature, as they often were in more traditional mythologies coming from the Neolithic period for instance, then many female mythic characters can be seen as often serving the function of nature itself, forcing the male hero to admit his own insignificance in the face of the greater natural order. Women also often appear to the hero at important transitional moments, such as leading the hero into mythic otherworlds; for example, Celtic myth is ripe with tales of otherworldly women meeting male heroes in lands meant to confound and ultimately spiritually elevate the hero. Therefore, though many myths from around the world may appear to most often promote heroic myths of male heroes, the female mythic characters in these myths arguably hold some of the most important messages in reminding audiences of nature's dominance.

The Shamanic Journey of Manabozho

Henry R. Schoolcraft's recorded tales of Manabozho[1] (1839) are said to come from his interaction with the Lake Superior Algonquin/Ojibwe tribes from his time as an Indian agent from 1822–1841. The representation provided by Schoolcraft, and later embellished by Henry Wadsworth Longfellow in his

Song of Hiawatha (1855), allows readers a glimpse into the mythic Manabozho as an example of a botanical hero, though of course it should be acknowledged that Schoolcraft, and especially Longfellow, undoubtedly used artistic license to tell a tale that originated outside of the realm of their own culture. Schoolcraft, unlike Longfellow who wrote his poem for artistic purposes, stated that he tried to maintain the integrity of the oral recitations he received from American Indian storytellers when capturing the various myths he recorded. However, because of a lack of communication, as well as Schoolcraft's lack of the generational wisdom behind the stories, they are undoubtedly filled with misrepresentations and flaws. Still, the legends surrounding Manabozho, despite Schoolcraft's possible misrepresentations in recoding some of them, present valuable glimpses into a mythic hero who relies upon nature for all aspects of his quest.

Central to the myths of Manabozho is that, though he is connected to the Great Spirit, he is portrayed as accomplishing tasks that a mortal could feasibly do; he may be stronger and wiser than the average man, but his abilities are always feasible, and it is this aspect of Manabozho that makes him an appealing hero. Manabozho remains a lasting hero because he must rely on his human elements, such as bravery when he very often feels fear, his intellect when his strength cannot accomplish a needed task, and his sense of humor when life delivers him unexpected sorrows or challenges.

Manabozho's birth is tied to the natural elements of the earth, making him a good heroic representation of a botanical hero. His grandmother is the daughter of the moon; his mother was slyly impregnated by the wind, and therefore, central to the myth of Manabozho is his natural connection to elemental forces. Schoolcraft states that not much is known about Manabozho's childhood, but what is mythically portrayed is that the young Manabozho loved to be immersed within wild environments watching nature intently. Living with his grandmother, Manabozho would go into the wilderness and observe animals of every kind:

> He ... saw exhibitions of divine power in the sweeping tempests, in the thunder and lightning, and the various shades of light and darkness, which form a never-ending scene of observation. Every new sight he beheld ... was a subject of remark; every new animal or bird an object of deep interest; and every new sound uttered by the animal creation a new lesson, which he was expected to learn. He often trembled at what he heard or saw [Schoolcraft 28].

This time as a child allowed Manabozho to become a botanical hero because it helped him realize his connection to the natural world, especially his relation to the animal realm; "he deemed himself related to them, and invariably addressed them by the term 'my brother'" (Schoolcraft 27).

The epic of Manabozho continues with his quest to find his father, the North Wind, who impregnated his mother, causing her death upon giving birth to Manabozho. This onset of his journey to overpower his elemental father clearly ties Manabozho to mythic heroic archetypes. As stated, often the mythic hero will undergo a journey away from the safe confines of his or her home to face any force that holds the hero back psychologically or spiritually, and quite often this is represented by a mythic father-figure. Campbell[2] discusses the heroic archetype of the necessity of the hero to face his or her father-figure, which can be mythically portrayed as the hero's actual father, as it is here with Manabozho, or it can be a symbolic father-figure representing a dominant conception that may be holding the hero back from psychologically self-actualizing. When Manabozho must face his father, he attains the status of hero according to Clasby because he matches himself "against forces no one can reasonably hope to overcome" (585), but his bravery at this moment is not the only reason Manabozho becomes a botanical hero; in fact, his botanical heroism in this aspect of the myth is more tied to his willingness to self-destruct because of this interaction with his father. A botanical hero's willingness to self-annihilate is a part of multiple myths, and often, it is connected to mythical episodes of the hero facing his or her father. The facing and attempted defeat of the elder father is a necessary stage for the archetypal hero attempting self-actualization because it reveals that the hero is no longer willing to be held back by any element, even if it spells his or her death. The facing of the father in myth often represents conflicted psychic elements within the hero, like feeling that he or she is not good enough, or it may represent perceptions of societal expectations about what the hero thinks others want him or her to do in life. The hero upon his or her journey must move beyond this stage in physically or symbolically killing the father, thus enabling the hero to psychically grow up. Many mythic scenes follow this archetype; for instance in Greek myth the younger generation often must defeat the older generation, often portrayed as a son fighting a father, like Cronus did with his father Uranus, and Zeus then did with his father Cronus.

Manabozho in seeking out his estranged father in order to defeat him because of his perceived wrong in impregnating his mother is experiencing the integral heroic archetype, discussed by Campbell, of defeating the father's psychic hold on the hero. But, interestingly Manabozho learns that he cannot defeat his father because his father is a natural element, and it is this tenet that marks Manabozho as a botanical hero. Mythically Manabozho must face his father, because for Manabozho, his father represents to him a view of the world where he has the power to right a perceived wrong, but this type of belief keeps Manabozho child-like. Manabozho must learn from his father, the North Wind, that life, especially within nature, is not this simple. Manabozho meets his father, but does not possess the power to overcome the elemental force of his father; instead, he must learn that he can only gain wisdom from the experience of attempting to defeat his father. The wind is a symbol of change, bringing in essential weather fronts that initiate new growth or spread natural events such as wildfire. Manabozho in this episode must realize that he cannot overcome this element, and by learning this, he also must accept that there was no wrong done in his father's impregnation of his mother, as the action becomes understood as merely natural. The wind is unharnessed and unpredictable; it will always be this way, and as a natural element, it always must be this way. Manabozho realizes that one cannot hold nature, or his father, to human levels of understanding. Therefore, Manabozho from this experience grows from childhood into adulthood because he gains a realistic view of life as it exists in nature, and in doing so, he puts aside the power his father holds upon his psyche and becomes more like his father, thus tying Manabozho more directly to botanical heroism.

The next significant moment upon Manabozho's journey is that while fishing he is swallowed by a giant fish, known as the King of the Fish. This stage connects him to another of Campbell's heroic archetypes, the stage defined as the "Belly of the Whale," where the hero upon leaving his or her safe community enters into a realm of utter confusion that forces the hero to face components of reality that he or she never could have conceived of before beginning the journey. In this stage the mythic hero usually must begin a process of stripping away his or her former identity, and here too Manabozho meets this archetype while inside the belly of the King of the Fish by conceding that he again, like he learned with the episode with his father, is not all powerful. However, Manabozho has not yet learned the essential quality of the botanical hero, which is humility—a willingness to let go of selfhood in order to unite with nature. This scene could display transformative aspects of the mythic underworld within the psychic development of Manabozho, similar to the shamanic journey portrayed in the tales of nature-dependent cultures, because Manabozho dies a symbolic death by being consumed by a greater predator. For instance, many legends of the shamanic journey relate shamans as delving into the environment of an animal in order to gain wisdom; they learn upon these journeys that they must fully become like the animal in order to gain the knowledge they seek. One such tale is presented by the Tikigaq of northwest Alaska that tells of a shaman, Aquppak, who made a journey to live with whales for a winter in order to try and save his people from starvation by convincing the whales to come back to his people, so they could hunt them.[3] Aquppak's soul was said to have taken the shape of a whale, as his body lay motionless back in his homeland, and as a whale, he watched the ways of the whales closely. He learned that when the hunters come for the whales, the whales actually willingly go to meet them. After months of living as a whale, Aquppak eventually learned that he must himself return in whale form and allow his own people to kill him. The sacrifice of Aquppak in this legend is not presented as bringing him grandiose recognition; instead, it is presented as showing Aquppak as understanding that he and his people are not superior to the whales. Aquppak, by dying at the hands of his own people as a whale, sees what the whales have always done for his people. But the tale doesn't end here; the story continues to show Aquppak, after having died in his whale form, returning back to his people once more as a shaman, having attained the wisdom he sought—which was in essence his understanding to let go of his own autonomy. Aquppak, as a whale, went towards his advancing people and offered himself to them; "they rejoiced at the catch although they did not know the whale contained Aquppak's soul. When they brought the whale back to land and cut up its flesh, his soul was released and entered his body again. Aquppak recovered and found that he now had shamanic powers" (Allan, Phillips, & Kerrigan 77). In Aquppak returning upon death back to his shaman form, a message is delivered that speaks towards natural regeneration. The whales teach Aquppak to face death as they have done for his people for generations, but they also teach him that there indeed is no death within nature, as Aquppak simply transfers from man, to whale, to man again, so that death is related in this story as only a momentary experience for Aquppak, revealing a cultural view of time as cyclical. Aquppak learns from the whales that they are cognizant of the time that his people will come hunting them, and they have always willingly come in for their own slaughter because they understand that they are part of an essential eco-system where everything is equal and connected, and in thus preserving the people, the whales preserve the system—the same natural system that promises constant renewal upon death, thus eradicating singular death. However, the myth of Manabozho does not portray him as internalizing the necessity of such events within the eco-system. Manabozho does experience a type of resurrection from death by hitting the King of the Fish in the heart with a club and sailing out of its mouth with his canoe that was initially swallowed with him, but at this point in the myth, his escape is portrayed as just that, an escape, instead of a rebirth in shamanic terms. This is evidenced by the fact that after this point in the myth, Manabozho only increases his tie to an ego-driven identity by believing that he can defeat or overcome any "adversary." Therefore, he has not yet fully learned that there is nothing for him to defeat in nature; instead, like he learned from his father, he must concede to the laws of nature as necessary in order to find the psychic means towards apotheosis.

Manabozho resumes his quest, overcoming more mythic creatures, like the fiery serpents who guard the Manitou of Wealth who killed his grandfather, and then finally the Great Manitou himself. After these accomplishments, Manabozho grows boastful and over-confident; "he felt himself urged by the consciousness of his power to new trials of bravery, skill, and necromantic prowess" (Schoolcraft 36). This stage of over-confidence is common for heroes of world myth; it is also an essential stage for botanical heroes to experience, as it shows them fully embracing their youthful vigor when they have it; in other words, it is their symbolic stage of summer. This is also the stage that many popular, contemporary versions of myths become stuck in their portrayals, but moving beyond this stage is crucial to the enlightenment of the botanical hero. And so, Manabozho, as a botanical hero, moves beyond this stage of self-importance into the next stage of his heroic quest.

Manabozho grows tired of his false state of over-confidence and falls into a period where he must now begin to learn. The myth presents him coming upon a shaman in the appearance of an old wolf. Upon meeting him, Manabozho asks to also be transformed into this new form. The shaman transforms Manabozho into an average wolf, but upon seeing this, still in an early stage of his heroic quest, Manabozho mistakenly feels he should become a bigger and more ferocious wolf. This is mythically portrayed as a misunderstanding from Manabozho about the importance of the average wolf. To learn this lesson he is changed into the mythic wolf he thinks he wants to embody, giant and fierce, but the myth proves this state as false, not an accurate or natural state, so Manabozho soon realizes that he should be transformed again into an average wolf. Then Manabozho undergoes more and more challenges against his preconceived ideas about life, learning every step of the way from the old wolf shaman that a life of simplicity in the natural world is a wise life. This process of stripping the hero from his or her belief in self-importance is an essential component of the botanical heroic quest; it preps the botanical hero for the final annihilation of his or her illusion that he or she is somehow distinct or better than the natural world.

The myth continues to strip Manabozho from his belief in self-importance when the old wolf shaman leaves him; the myth states that "Manabozho was disenchanted and again returned to his mortal shape" (Schoolcraft 40). However, the old wolf shaman left him with a young wolf, and soon Manabozho regarded this pup as his own grandchild. This element within the myth, of showing Manabozho first becoming and living as a wolf, and then coming to love a wolf as his own grandson, returns him to his childlike respect for nature, yet his depiction now is not as wanting to overpower nature, and this is significant.

As often happens, the archetypal hero in his or her quest must face hardship and death, and so this young wolf, who Manabozho has grown to love, dies by being swallowed by a giant serpent, and this initiates Manabozho to go in search of him, beginning the heroic archetype of the hero's descent into the underworld, which can be a physical place associated with death, or a psychological state where the botanical hero learns to let go of his identity; this stage will be discussed at length in the next chapter. Manabozho makes his way to a lake filled with giant serpents, and representative of him as a botanical hero, he transforms himself into the stump of an oak tree and hides this way on the beach waiting for the serpents to come out of the water to sun themselves. Once they do this, Manabozho transforms back into his own form and kills the Prince of Serpents, the one who killed his grandson. The remaining serpents chase Manabozho, causing a great flood, but Manabozho speaks to a tree he has climbed to escape and asks it to grow, so that he may rise above the impending flood. The tree grows, and Manabozho asks the animals and birds around him to attempt to dive down and recover a piece of dirt, so that a new earth can be created. Clasby states, "Manabozho, hanging from the limbs of his tree, is like the seed of the tree ... carrying within himself all the regenerative forms" (588–9). But life in this new world, that the tree and the animals helped Manabozho create, proves hard for Manabozho, and soon he finds himself fully stripped of his former identity; "after Manabozho had killed the Prince of Serpents, he was living in a state of great want, completely deserted by his powers as a deity, and not able to procure the ordinary means of sustenance.... He was miserably poor" (Schoolcraft 45). Living with now a wife and children, he finds that he cannot even support himself or his family.

The myth moves on to its vital message that ties Manabozho to the natural cycle that must be understood by the botanical hero. Manabozho, who is now starving and concerned that his family, the next generation, will also starve, sees a male moose feeding his own family by carving a piece of flesh directly off the body of his moose wife and feeding it to their children, only to see the flesh immediately grow back on the body of the female moose. Manabozho tries this act on his own wife, but not yet knowing its true significance, he only causes his wife to almost die from the loss of blood. The moose sees Manabozho misrepresent the sacred act, so the moose restores Manabozho's wife back to health. Manabozho is utterly confounded and distraught, and just as his experience as a wolf taught him to humbly reconnect with the natural world as it really was, he now recognizes that he has much to learn. So Manabozho retreats alone to a cave, fasts, and begs to be shown the lesson that will enable him to ensure the survival of his children. After this experience, Manabozho, now connected to the shamans of many nature-dependent cultures, is said to gain the wisdom he sought, so that he may finally provide for his offspring. This portion of Manabozho's myth is similar to the tale of Aquppak and the whales, because Manabozho, in a shamanistic portrayal, like Aquppak, learns from the animals that death is an illusion in nature. Just as Aquppak could die as a whale and become a man once again, so too can the flesh of the moose wife be cut off and then immediately grow back. Both tales show their respective shamans that death and destruction are only momentary experiences when viewed according to nature's cyclical and regenerative terms.

Manabozho's myth showcases the necessity of the natural world and its cycles; it also presents wisdom as something that comes with recognizing nature's patterns. Manabozho is a botanical hero because he "must pass through the underworld before rising again" (Clasby 584), and this he does through a series of steps where he learns to accept death by letting go of his loved ones and also shedding his grandiose ideas of self-importance. Manabozho gains humility instead of overcoming any great foe; he learns about the cycles of nature, which operate without any action on his part. He learns, when he is finally humble enough to recognize the power of nature, that death and life are connected as part of a never-ending natural cycle. Clasby concurs by defining the myth as sacred, because it presents the "sacrificial rite of death and resurrection" (584). Manabozho is consistently demoted within his myth, so that he can come to understand the importance of the act of giving oneself over to ensure the survival of the next generation, just as the moose mother is portrayed as willingly doing.

The moose mother does not die from her injuries because she represents the greater natural pattern of willing sacrifice leading to constant renewal; therefore, through her, Manabozho learns, and subsequently teaches audiences, that death in nature is only one small part of an eternal process. He is therefore not a hero who is better than the audience for his superhuman feats; instead, he is a botanical hero because he acknowledged that nature is supreme.

Svyatogor and the Superiority of Nature

The early Baltic Slavs, dependent on nature for survival, created many heroic myths that teach the important lesson of respecting the natural environment. One such myth shows the hero, Svyatogor, learning a fatal lesson that revealed his place in relation to nature.[4] Svyatogor was revered by his people for his strength and bravery as a warrior and fine hunter; "when peasants looked up to see him pounding the plains on his tall horse, they saw a fearless warrior, a leader of men—almost a god" (Phillips & Kerrigan 34). Svyatogor knew this too; he took pride in his appearance making sure that his gear and saddle sparkled with the best jewels one could find. One day he partook on a heroic quest through the steppes, confident as he always was in his success: "On the plains the sun was warm and the wind swept briskly over the long grasses. Svyatogor felt full of life. Far away he spotted a wild boar and clenched his hands on the reins, feeling the power of his own strength—so great that it was like a weight that he carried around. He laughed as he looked across the immense plain and shouted a boast that he was strong enough to lift the entire Earth in his bare hands" (Phillips & Kerrigan 34). This final utterance, though, proved to be his downfall. Though Svyatogor was rivaled by no man in hunting and battle, his proclamation that he was superior to nature immediately caused his undoing.

After uttering his pompous remark, Svyatogor spotted a saddle bag in his path; he dismounted his horse to investigate, but surprisingly found that he could not lift it from the ground. After just shouting out that he could carry the weight of the earth itself, he laughed out loud because he realized that this was a divine challenge, so he attempted to lift the saddle bag again, putting all of his strength into the endeavor, but he was horrified to see that he still could not even budge it. Growing more defiant, he was now determined to lift the saddle bag no matter what the cost. He tried again and again, but when he paused from his fit of shame and rage in his useless effort to lift the bag, he found that he had begun to sink "deep into the earth.... Red drops splashed onto his arms—for tears of blood were pouring from his eyes" (Phillips & Kerrigan 34). Panicked now, as clearly this supernatural test challenged his utmost capabilities, he conceded that he must give up his attempt at trying to lift the mystical saddle bag. Now, he put all of his efforts into attempting to free himself from the clutches of the earth. But, his early pomposity of feeling above the powers of nature was too great an offense, and he found that he was thoroughly trapped. Svyatogor's heroic quest, as many heroic journeys do, reduced him fully from the status he imagined he once held, as by the end of his journey, "he howled with rage and yelped for help" (Phillips & Kerrigan 34). No one, however, heard his pleas, as true to the heroic quest, Svyatogor was utterly alone in the vast steppes, so he had to finally accept that this was to be his death.

After days of solitude, entrenched within the earth, knowing that he would soon die, he saw that nature produced a group of wild horses to entice even his own trusted horse to leave him. Svyatogor spent his last days forced to only look out at the vast and unrelenting land around him as he still remained firmly encased within nature's embrace until, in death, he became truly a part of the land once more. This myth shows that even the best of heroes must fully acknowledge the power of nature. The botanical hero does not feel superior to nature, but comes to realize, through the heroic quest, that he or she is only one small part of the environment, and perhaps in his final moments Svyatogar realized this goal of the botanical heroic quest. This myth provides a pattern found in many myths of the hero—showing that arrogance is the first trait to be dispelled upon the botanical heroic quest, because knowledge of the workings of nature, not acclaim, must be the boon.

Rama and the Earth Mother

Valmiki's *Ramayana,* written approximately in the 5th–4th century BCE, is a highly popular Indian epic that presents multiple representations of the heroic quest. The protagonist, Rama, is said to be one of four parts of the divine god Vishnu, who came to earth within the epic in the form of four princely sons. Though he is the central protagonist, Rama only represents one part of the divinity of Vishnu, and this detail is important to the message of the epic. In showing that Rama is semi-divine, it reveals to audiences the possibility that they too are inextricably connected to the divine, as central to Hinduism is the belief that all beings equally connect to Brahman, because Brahman as creator of the universe is said to encapsulate all. The plot of the *Ramayana* articulates many components of the quest of the botanical hero. Rama, as son of king Dasharatha, is recognized as being the justifiable successor to the throne, but due to a pact that Dasharatha made to his youngest wife, Kaikeyi, her son, Bharata, instead of Rama, becomes the next king. Kaikeyi then demands that Rama be exiled within the deep wilderness of India for fourteen years.

As discussed, the archetypal heroic quest often signals the necessity of the hero to leave behind his or her known environment to enter into an unknown realm. Oftentimes in myth, this leaving the known existence thrusts the hero into an opportunity to re-conceptualize one's sense of identity, as it did for Manabozho. In the *Ramayana,* after enduring the slight of his rightful throne, Rama leaves behind a life of pleasure and opulence to enter his demoted exile into the natural environment of the deep forest. This time of the epic is crucial to Rama's potential identification as a botanical hero, as it indicates that he is leaving the environment that formerly helped him to identify within his community and within himself. The forest becomes central to his botanical heroic quest, as it provides Rama spiritual guidance. In Hinduism, a member of the Brahmin class, after serving the community and raising a family, can choose renunciation, often into the wilderness, to seek enlightenment. Here too, Rama in entering into the forest for fourteen years offers audiences a mythic example towards botanical spirituality.

During his forest exile with his wife Sita and his brother Lakshmana, who both volunteer to accompany Rama on his exile, Rama learns that life holds more importance than just the occurrences of kingly affairs:

> Doffing then their royal garments Rama and his brother bold
> Coats of bark and matted tresses wore like anchorites of old [Valmiki, 3.6].

The botanical hero must often leave behind his or her defined existence to enter into a stage of confusion in an otherworldly environment, and Rama does this during his exile. The otherworld in myth often presents the archetypal hero with an environment that is unfamiliar to his or her frame of reference. The otherworld quintessentially is used as a mythic device to confound the hero, asserting its reality against all preconceived beliefs the hero once held. The mythic otherworld is also often portrayed as being directly tied with nature, as frequently the hero finds that the otherworld is teeming with abundant natural resources, or even seasons of perpetual growth. The mythic otherworld often serves to remove the botanical hero from a life where the belief systems of civilization dominate. The mythic otherworld that is presented as overtly natural, thus, in being decidedly different to the "civilized" hero's frame of reference, usually propels the botanical hero to see error in believing tenets associated with civilization as ideal. Instead, the natural otherworld, teaches the botanical hero to begin to see what exists in nature as valuable, thus seeing the demands of society as unnatural. In Rama living within his otherworld of the forest for fourteen years among the ascetics of the forest, he is forced to learn a new lifestyle without worldly pleasures, question his former persona, face incredible adversaries, and finally confront elements that force him to question his own sense of identity.

It is significant that the whole time that Rama is on his heroic quest his wife Sita is by his side. Sita is an avatar of the divine Lakshmi, and also the daughter of the Mother Earth Goddess, Bhūmi. In the *Ramayana,* Sita at her birth is depicted as rising directly from the soil in order to be paired with Rama. Therefore, Sita is connected to nature throughout the epic, and it is her consistent connection to the environment that arguably teaches Rama important lessons attached to his journey towards botanical heroism. As Rama, Sita, and Lakshmana roam the wilderness in their exile, Sita is repeatedly displayed as paying reverence to nature as divine. For instance, before the three cross myriad rivers, Sita always pays homage to the goddess of each particular river before asking for safe passage. In Rama consistently viewing Sita's respect and devotion to the natural environment, it appears that he is able to accomplish various components of his quest as it culminates into his psychological descent into the heroic archetype of the symbolic underworld. Rama's mythic underworld, arguably, is when he must face a process that further forces him to lose his connection to his self-identified life by losing the love of his life, Sita. Sita is presented in the epic as a model wife for the period, but the symbolism of her character as a representation of nature portrays her as more than just a model wife. While residing in the wilderness, Sita finds a mystical deer, and wishing Rama to hunt the deer, she falls for a trap set up by Ravana, depicted as the demon king of Lanka. This point in the text serves to reveal more of Sita's role within the *Ramayana.*

Rama is of course distraught when Sita is captured. His pain at the loss of his wife immediately reveals to audiences that this is his worst fear, thus making this the symbolic underworld for Rama. Rama must conceive of the likelihood that he has lost Sita forever, and thus contemplate life without her; this analyzing forces him to face the transitory nature of life, which is a requirement of the mythic underworld upon the botanical heroic journey, as the underworld compels the botanical hero to accept the fact of mortality. However, it is important to understand that Rama and Sita are divine; they are only presented in the epic as living in human form. This scene of pain for the avatar of Vishnu suggests that even in divine form, Vishnu, as Rama, must concede that all life, and love within life, is transitory in order to teach audiences the same message. Sita, as a representation of nature, though, will teach Rama, and audiences of the myth, that nature provides a cycle that is not transitory.

Rama is presented as evolving in his embrace of nature because he unites with an army of monkeys to rescue Sita from Ravana's demon army. Only through the aid of his animal partners is Rama able to discover that Sita is alive on the island of Lanka. Rama then appeals, as Sita did so many times before throughout the text, to Varuna, the early Vedic god of water and the underworld realm. Varuna was once the leader of the Vedic pantheon but later was ideologically replaced by the triad divinities of Brahma, Vishnu, and Shiva. In the *Ramayana,* Rama, by fasting and meditating for three days, asks Varuna to remain calm, so that he and the animals can build a bridge to safely cross over the sea and rescue Sita. However, Varuna does not answer Rama's plea. Rama becomes furious and starts assaulting the ocean and its creatures by setting the waters on fire and shooting the creatures of the sea with divine arrows. Rama, growing more enraged, threatens to use a celestial weapon so powerful that it jeopardizes all creation. The monkey army and Lakshmana grow terrified. Finally, though, Varuna rises out of his oceanic home and confronts Rama, apologizing for ignoring him. Varuna states that he can no longer control the calmness of the ocean as it is full of demonic creatures that are out of his realm of domination, so Rama directs his weapon at the demons and destroys them all, making the waters peaceful, so that he and his army may pass. Most interpretations point to this scene as a representation of Rama, as Vishnu, displaying his dominance over the older Vedic ideology of Varuna; however, there appears to be more to this scene. Vishnu, in Hindu ideology, is presented as the preserver of life; it is telling that Vishnu, in human form as Rama, becomes so emotionally upset that he threatens to destroy all creation. His disregard for the natural environment of the ocean and its creatures, only for his own personal gain to try and obtain his wife back, seems contrary to Hindu ideology that speaks towards the importance of letting go of individual desire and autonomy. This contradiction between Rama's momentary lapse in emotionality may point towards him, in human form, having more to learn about nature and its cycles upon his botanical heroic quest.

As a captive, the text makes it clear that Sita avoids being raped by Ravana. Her purity is essential to her role of ideal wife within the myth's intended message, but in accordance to a plot connected to nature, Sita's purity speaks towards her natural representation of seasonal cycles. Sita is birthed from the soil, marries Rama, follows him into the wilderness, and then is presented as being threatened from accomplishing her symbolic and natural role of mother, which is to propagate in order to assure a future generation. Because her role as mother becomes jeopardized through her abduction, then the cycles of nature are in jeopardy of also being stunted. Rama does eventually rescue Sita though, but he questions her purity, as he is concerned that she may have been raped by Ravana. Offended, but complacent, Sita in her role as wife, as dictated by the laws of dharma, tells Rama that she was able to fend off any advances made by Ravana, and that she is indeed still pure, according to Rama's societal definition of purity. To prove to Rama that she remains unmolested, Sita steps willingly into fire. Though Sita walks into fire, she is completely unharmed by the flames, thus proving her purity to Rama and the onlookers, so that she can return with Rama when he eventually claims his rightful throne. This scene, though, suggests more than Sita proving that she was able to escape being raped by Ravana.

Viewing Sita as a representation of nature might reveal meaning behind the repeated questioning of her purity in the epic. Rama's questioning if Sita has remained pure certainly points to societal concerns attached to the era in which the epic was written. For Sita to be displayed as the ideal wife, so that she may serve as instructor to educate audiences of this role, she must remain sexually bound to only Rama. However, as Sita emerged directly from the soil, a discussion of fertility in accordance to Rama's right to be king is soon realized. Wessing discusses the concept of kingly rule in accordance to Hindu ideology within the *Ramayana*, stating that the ruler was believed to not only be the center of the state but also of the cosmos; in addition the ruler should be married, so as to unite both male and female aspects into the kingdom as an expression of "the ruler's own vitality, centrality, and oneness" (246). Therefore, Rama and Sita, according to Hinduism, may be viewed as two parts of the same being, as again, in Hindu philosophy, all beings are interconnected as one. Rama may be able to finally become the rightful ruler of his kingdom because in symbolic terms he has united with his other half, Sita, though arguably the text suggests that Rama does not fully unite with Sita, and this also might signal the inability of Rama to attain botanical apotheosis. However, in rescuing Sita from the clutches of Ravana, Rama has displayed claim over the land, just as he did by killing the demons that caused havoc in Varuna's ocean waters. Sita's ability to prove her purity may serve to symbolically prove Rama's ability to harness the fertility of the land for his subjects; "When the ruler was an appropriate one ... prosperity would ensue. Fields would be fertile, harvests plentiful, and commerce profitable" (Wessing 247). Symbolically Sita, by proving her purity, secures the throne for Rama, as she, being a representative of nature, proves to Rama's subjects that he is ready to be a fertile and productive king. It is also significant that Rama is finally viewed as ready to rule after having spent fourteen years within the forest because it suggests that he has learned lessons imbued within the natural environment during his exile.

If Sita is a representation of nature, her display of walking unharmed through fire also shows the lasting quality of nature that many world myths discuss. Sita demonstrates to Rama, and the audience of the myth, that in nature, there is no death, similar to how the moose mother in the myth of Manabozho did not die from her wounds but immediately grew her mutilated flesh back to its original form. In Hindu ideology, death is viewed as a transient state, as the cycle of nature perpetuates reincarnation—creation, preservation, destruction, and re-creation are all viewed as necessary and constant aspects of existence. With Sita's display, she fully encapsulates this philosophical view, but does so by using her role as nature representative. Like the forest that does not fully die by wildfire but only gains the necessary revitalizing nutrients that fire brings to initiate new growth, so too does Sita display that humans, as part of nature, must follow the same pattern. It appears that Rama in seeking out Sita could not embrace the necessity of accepting life as transient, portrayed through the loss of Sita, as he was willing to destroy all nature to win her back, but Sita appears to teach Rama that by letting go of selfhood, nothing is truly lost in natural terms.

If Rama and Sita are to be viewed as two parts of one whole, then their unification within the epic would signal the self-actualization of Rama that is needed to complete his heroic quest. However, the legend does not end with Rama and Sita happily living out their human years in peace. Instead, once pronounced queen, Sita becomes pregnant with twin sons, but the people come to question if the sons are Rama's. Rama knows that they are his children, but the text presents it as his duty as king, again according to the concept of dharma, to unquestionably obey the decisions of his subjects. Rama begrudgingly accuses Sita once more of having been raped when in the captivity of Ravana. Sita, understandably saddened by this accusation, leaves her life of opulence once more to live in secluded hermitage. The text shows Rama as again harboring human emotion at his decision, which again suggests that his choice to shun Sita at the demand of his people may not be the right decision for his self-actualization as a botanical hero:

> Pardon, if the voice of rumour drove me to a deed of shame....
> In the dark and dreary forest was my Sita left to mourn,
> In the lone and gloomy jungle were my royal children born, Help me, Gods, to
>   wipe this error and this deed of sinful pride [Valmiki 12].

Again Rama's human emotion whenever he loses Sita is significant to the text. Rama, like his people, must live in accordance to the laws of dharma, but it is revealing that he struggles, as part of a divine being, to adhere to this plan. Perhaps this struggle speaks to audiences of their own hardships in acting in accordance to dharma. The text reveals that Rama lives out his days without the love of his life, and he is clearly saddened by this, but arguably the text does this to send a greater message that speaks towards Hindu philosophy, as well as botanical heroism—that life must be repeated through myriad reincarnations until the soul finds liberation. The soul is liberated from samsara by allowing the desire for identity to be shed. Rama, in wanting to hold onto Sita, displays the human desire to hold fast to the elements of selfhood, but Sita, again as a representation of nature, shows Rama that this is only an element of illusion meant to tie human beings to samsara.

Years later, Rama invites Sita and his sons to come home if Sita will again prove her purity by walking through fire once more, but she has decided that she has had enough of life; Srinivasa Iyengar describes Sita's final act as her "self-transcendence and return to her Mother-Earth" (xiii). Sita is depicted within the text as returning to her Earth Mother, when she lets out a mournful cry, and the earth opens up to receive her. Here Sita clearly shows her identification of adhering to the natural processes of life, as out of the soil she came, and once more she returned to her natural abode having enough of the affairs of the kingdom and of life itself. But, importantly, Sita is depicted not as dying, but simply returning to the natural environment from whence she came:

> Mother Earth I relieve thy Sita from the burden of this life!
> Then the earth was rent and parted....
> And the Mother in embraces held her spotless sinless Child [Valamiki 12.5].

Srinivasa Iyengar states that this scene is indicative of Sita's divinity; "while in other countries it is apparently natural to center divinity in a male image, in India, Godhead is equally—and even more plausibly and frequently—identified with the splendour of the Eternal Feminine in Her infinite variety of form and function" (xiv). In addition, McGrath discusses the idea in traditional Indian society that a hero must be tied to the theme of fertility (18). Both Sita's birth and natural demise are indicative of her role as a nature divinity and as a symbol of the fertility of nature, as Sita's life cycle shows audiences that life comes from death, as again Sita upon her birth was found in a field at the tip of a plow and after her earthly experience, she returned back into the soil. Therefore, Sita reveals that the fertility of nature, just as the lives of human beings, depends upon this cycle.

Luthra discusses how perceptions of Rama and Sita vary in India; many revere Rama, but some condemn his actions towards Sita (141). According to Luthra, Sita remains a figure who refuses to compromise to patriarchal systems (141); Luthra also points to Mallika Sengupta's interpretation of Sita as gaining an "evolved consciousness and great inner strength" throughout the course of the *Ramayana* (143). Luthra states that these readings in terms of the strength of Sita may stem from contemporary society, yet readers of this ancient text cannot ignore the natural references of Sita that allow her to remain distanced from the daily affairs of human life. Even Mahatma Gandhi pointed towards Sita's final act of resistance as heroic, when he stated "'Sita was the incarnate *satyagrahi*'" (qtd. in Luthra 154). Therefore, it appears that Sita, and not Rama, may be the botanical hero within the text.

The text also makes it appear that Rama did not come to a level of spiritual understanding needed to be identified as a botanical hero because he still harbored attachment to his identity-driven life and could not fully internalize that letting go of his selfhood would reveal the greater laws on nature. Sita makes it clear before being enveloped by the earth that life is a "burden" as she states, showing the Hindu philosophy that enlightenment comes in shedding the desires connected with selfhood, so that one may unite with the oneness of all creation. This lesson that Sita reveals in the *Ramayana,* which is in essence botanical apotheosis for the botanical hero, is in accordance to the laws of the environment which are embraced by many nature-dependent cultures.

Nature in nature-dependent communities is often viewed as sacred because it holds a process that encapsulates all life; it calls for the demise of all living beings, but it also assures the rebirth, in various forms, of all matter it claims. Therefore, it appears that this aspect of letting go of selfhood to reach moksha, liberation from samsara, is connected to the same teachings of many nature-dependent cultures, which also instruct the importance of acknowledging the necessary loss of life to initiate regeneration within the environment. Illusions of selfhood can be shed then, with a gained understanding that the loss of life and selfhood in nature initiates a pattern of incessant regeneration that assures on some level that nothing is lost in death or when the self is let go; instead, all is united under one natural order that has no conception of separateness. The concept of moksha, like the adage of a singular wave always being part of the greater sea, is nature's cyclical promise. Just as an individual wave appears to hold its own autonomy as it rolls on top of the ocean, when it finally crashes upon the shore, it becomes evident that it has returned back into its vast source, having lost all of its former definition. Similarly, the single life of an individual can be conceived of this way when viewed in natural terms. While one is living, autonomous identity seems crucial, but wisdom comes in learning that the individual human is similar to the single wave.

Sita, then, serves to teach audiences that letting go of selfhood connects one to the greater laws of nature. Just as she willingly walked into the flames but did not burn, she teaches that in nature, nothing is truly destroyed, and therefore, again, it is Sita who appears as the botanical hero of the epic, though it is significant that the tale does not depict her rising from her earth abode after succumbing to it, as many myths of the botanical heroic quest complete the cycle of nature by showing the hero, in some form, rise again from death. However, the *Ramayana* depends upon the background knowledge of the audience in understanding that Rama, Sita, Lakshmana, etc., are all parts of a unifying whole under the structure of Hindu ideology. Rama may appear to not have learned the lessons of moksha, and thus not be a good example of a botanical hero, but again, Rama is the incarnation of Vishnu, who fully knows the workings of the natural universe within Hinduism ideology. The physical death of Rama, therefore, will not be death but a unification back to his divine self, which audiences of the epic would have known given their foreknowledge of Hindu philosophy. Vishnu, as Rama, unites with his other half, Lakshmi, as Sita, within the *Ramayana* to teach audiences the necessity of striving for moksha, which indeed makes both Rama and Sita, when viewed from the perspective of Hindu philosophy, in adherence to botanical heroism within this epic.

Jason as Male Consort and Medea as Earth Goddess

The myths of the Greek hero Jason and his journey to obtain the Golden Fleece with the Argonauts is told in many versions from as early, and perhaps earlier, as the eighth century BCE. The most famous versions come from Pindar, Apollonius, and Ovid and showcase another quest of the mythic hero; therefore, this text will point towards various versions of the myth in its discussion of the epic. The myth of "Jason and the Golden Fleece" is supposed to represent approximately the thirteenth century BCE, which was a time of religious and political turmoil when the "original vestiges of earth worship continued" (Barnes 119). Barnes states that this tale, in its many renditions, shows decided dramatic techniques meant to replace values found in more traditional earth-based belief systems, like that of the Minoans (113). The hero, Jason, also possesses qualities that tie his legend to a tale that represents a botanical message. Jason's quest begins as an infant when his uncle, Pelias, kills his father, the Greek king of Iolkos, and takes over the throne. His mother, fearing for Jason's life, sends him to live in the wilderness to be raised by a representation of the wild, the centaur Chiron. This natural upbringing is central to defining Jason as a botanical hero; like the Ojibwe Manabozho, Jason, at the onset of his myth reveals that his heroism comes from a deep connection to nature.

When Jason reaches adulthood, the myth declares that he is ready to set off on the archetypal hero's journey, leaving the comforts of his forest home behind to reclaim his rightful throne. Along the way, he encounters what appears to be an old woman who needs his help to cross a fast-moving river; what he does not know is that the woman is Hera disguised to test him. Jason, in accordance to his heroic status, readily offers to carry her across. This mythic element could reveal that he is simply an upstanding hero, but this divine test reveals more when it is understood for its natural connection. Hera has often been represented as maintaining, even into the Archaic, Classical, and Hellenistic periods, attributes that connect her to Neolithic beliefs in a Mother Earth Goddess. The mythic element of Jason needing to carry Hera upon his back through the fast-moving water serves to initially imply that Jason will only succeed upon his quest with the help of more traditional belief systems that acknowledge the importance of nature. Jason loses a sandal while carrying Hera across the river, which will be the signal to Pelias that his adversary to the throne has arrived, but again, this symbol connects Jason to the land. Walking partially barefoot over the land until he reaches his homeland also suggests that the only way he will achieve the throne will be to remember his close tie to the environment.

Jason, arriving at Pelias' palace, is told to partake on a quest that would kill most—securing the Golden Fleece that is kept in Colchis, thus firmly setting in motion common heroic archetypes. Jason is determined to accomplish Pelias' task. The task is no light matter however, and its achievement will test Jason's understanding of the natural cycle. The Golden Fleece, which came from a ram that mythically was said to have taken Phrixus to Colchis on its back and then sacrificed itself, hangs on a tree in a sacred grove that is guarded by again a quintessential mythic element, an enormous serpent. This imagery connects the myth to more ancient components. First, it is important to note that the ram was mythically represented as conscious of making the decision to sacrifice itself so that its golden fleece could hang from the sacred grove; its fleece is said to possess life-giving powers, which seem connected to its decision of self-sacrifice, as many myths from nature-dependent communities promote the message that from death, new life is assured. The grove in which the Golden Fleece is held is also sacred, and its serpent guardian is tied to the Neolithic Earth Goddess. The image of the serpent in relation to an Earth Goddess appears in archeological evidence throughout myriad Neolithic sites and would have been quite well known to audiences of this myth. Serpents, therefore, often serve later as mythic representations meant to demote the power of the represented Neolithic Earth Goddesses; "If the old mind was to be refashioned to fit the new system's requirements, the serpent would either have to be appropriated as one of the emblems of the new ruling classes or, alternatively, defeated, distorted, and discredited" (Eisler 87). Repeatedly myths in the Greek Classical era showcase male heroes who must overcome Neolithic female representatives in order to be deemed heroic by a new generation of storytellers as civilizations moved out of the Neolithic period. In order for Jason to be a hero in his era, he must overpower feminine authority by stealing the sacred Fleece. But Jason has been reared in nature, and thus far in the myth, he is only successful when he remembers his natural ties, and this tenet will remain throughout his tale.

Jason prepares for his quest composing a team of the best heroes Greece has to offer, including Herakles and Orpheus, and assures the creation, aided by Athena, of his mighty ship, the Argo. It is mythically significant that this expedition contains the greatest male heroes of the era, again suggesting shifting social and political ideologies. The Argo also is portrayed as having natural significance, as its mast was created by a consecrated, prophetic oak tree from Zeus' grove in Dodona, or as some sources contend from the grove in Dodona of an earlier nature goddess, Dione, a Titan whose name is the female version of Zeus (Dios) ("Theoi Greek Mythology").

The Argonauts take sail to the end of the known world to find Colchis, which ties Jason to the mythic archetype of the otherworld. First the Argonauts sail to the island of Lemnos, which happens to only be inhabited by women. The legend states that the women offended Aphrodite, so she made them emit a foul stench that made their husbands take Thracian mistresses. The women of Lemnos then rebelled and killed their husbands while they slept. Here the myth focuses on female authority. The women of Lemnos are doing just fine on their own, as they govern themselves; Barnes suggests that they may have been representative of a "matrilineal island" as it may be "at the beginning or even before the Dark Age, perhaps before the Trojan War" (118). This type of scene is common in Greek mythology; for example, Herakles, upon his twelve labors, visits the Amazons, warrior women who also have no need for men and govern themselves. These scenes, though, often serve to confound the male Greek hero upon his journey, thus connecting these scenes to the mythic otherworld, as the otherworld in myth serves to often confuse the hero past preconceived ideas. In this myth, the Argonauts do not kill or overpower the women of Lemnos; instead, they have sex with them, allowing the women to produce the next generation of inhabitants on the island. The Argonauts continue their journey, encountering again many mythic ties to the feminine, such as giants of the Earth Goddess Rhea, sirens who mercilessly sneak food, an island of the moon goddess Mariandyne, a town where Sinope lives, who was said to resist the rape of Zeus by tricking him into giving her perpetual virginity, and then an island of isolated wilderness that only is inhabited by nymphs. On one such island, the famed Herakles is left behind from the expedition, as he is distraught over his companion's disappearance as a result of being lured away by water nymphs. Barnes states that these islands that hold so many female characters represent a purposeful mythic device to shift societal power from matriarchal to patriarchal lines; "One after the next, at the dawn of Greek consciousness, the Argonauts are encountering and then passing by women who ... are caricatures of the old values" (120–1).

Next the Argonauts come to cliffs that no mortals are meant to pass through, as they periodically crash together, crushing anything trying to navigate them. Euphemus sends a dove through the apparently impossible natural structure; it is following after the natural example of a bird that reveals the only way through this explicit representation of nature's authority, and the men survive. One episode related in Apollonius' *Argonautica* shows an Argonaut, Mopsos, receiving a message from a bird, as Mopsos was known for being able to communicate with birds, which told him they must pay homage to the goddess Rhea. The Argonauts heed this message and climb Mount Dindymon to take part in rites for Rhea; the rites produce "miraculous signs indicating the goddess' acceptance of the ritual: the vegetation blooms, wild animals leave their lairs and rub up tamely against the Argonauts, and a fountain suddenly appears in a place that up to that moment was dry" (Clauss 169). Clauss states that religious cults on Mount Dindymon practiced rituals in ancient times that enacted the natural stages of death and rebirth (174). Because Jason and the Argonauts took part in these rituals for the appeasement of Rhea, this shows again the connection of the text to more traditional nature-based belief systems, as Rhea was long associated as a Mother Earth Goddess in Greece.

The Argonauts arrive in Colchis, where they meet King Aeëtes and his daughter, Medea. Because of Hera and Aphrodite, Medea falls in love with Jason. It is only through Medea's mystical knowledge and aid that Jason can be successful on the three tasks that King Aeëtes demands of him. First, Jason is commanded to plow a field with fire-breathing bulls that he must yoke, and it is Medea who gives him a potion that will protect him from the bulls' flames. Then, Jason must plant the teeth of a dragon into a field. The teeth will sprout into an army of warriors, and again it is Medea who tells Jason how to defeat these earth-born warriors, with the simplest of methods—throwing a rock into their crowd, so that they will be unable to discover where the rock came from, and the army will attack each other. Finally, Jason has to recover the coveted Golden Fleece from the enormous serpent of the sacred grove, and once again, it is Medea who gives Jason a potion that makes the serpent fall asleep, so he easily sneaks in and takes the Golden Fleece.

It is important to acknowledge that Medea plays a central role within this myth. Jason is depicted as not being capable of achieving any of his goals without her instruction. Medea's mystical knowledge of the processes of nature might also tie her to Neolithic Earth Goddess figures, as Medea "possessed the charms or enchantments that the Greeks feared in the old religions" (Barnes 122). Lusnhnig concurs that Medea's "origins are divine and she may have started her circuitous story as a goddess. She may even have been originally Greek" (viii). Medea is portrayed within the myth as a priestess of the underworld goddess Hecate, so it is certain that Medea holds wisdom of the workings of nature:

> She is wise far beyond her years.... She can call forth blazing fires. She can quiet rushing rivers. And in the heavens, she can make Silver-horned Selene drive her silver-yoked chariot next to the gold-yoked chariot of gold-helmeted Helios. She can make spring flowers bloom in summer. She can make the grain grow ripe for harvesting in winter ["Jason" 183].

In some versions of the myth Medea performs a remarkable task that further identifies her as a representation of a Neolithic Earth Goddess. Before Jason attempts to complete his heroic tasks, Medea is said to perform a ritual on him that enables his success. Medea makes Jason fall asleep; then she dismembers his body with a knife and places the pieces of his corpse within a cauldron filled with a concoction that only she knows. Jason's body is then miraculously reassembled, and he emerges from Medea's cauldron reborn and ready to fulfill his heroic accomplishments:

> She picked up her wood-chopping blade and chopped the stranger's body into pieces and dropped them into her boiling brew.... And indeed, it came to pass that, swift as the wind, just as Medea's brew had restored the olive branch to life and youth, so the stranger's body now became restored and renewed as it cooked in boiling broth. And so the maiden now lifted him from the broth and laid him, once again upon Mother Gaea ... and so Jason awoke from his death-like sleep ["Jason" 191].

This mythic event is assuredly tied to Neolithic Earth Goddess myths where the Goddess, as a representation of nature, holds the power to take life, but also to resurrect life. Often in Neolithic myths of the Earth Goddess and the male consort, the male consort, after having sexual relations with the Earth Goddess, or her representative, offers his life to her in order to assure the vitality of the harvest. His sexual act as well as his death fertilize the earth. Often these myths portray Earth Goddesses as holding the power to resurrect the male consorts after their deaths; many civilizations enacted the resurrection of the male consort on an annual basis, showing that like the agricultural cycle, death, portrayed through the example of the male consort, was not final, but would initiate new growth. The Neolithic Earth Goddess, then, embodied the conception of the earth itself; the male consort died for her, but because death is only a temporary stage in nature, the Earth Goddess would always produce new life from sacrificed death. Therefore, Medea directly serves this role for Jason, securing in the myth, not only her portrayal as a remnant of a Neolithic Earth Goddess, but also Jason's role as a male consort, which sheds an interesting light on the true message of the myth where Medea serves to teach Jason about heroism in botanical terms.

In addition, the natural symbolism of the three tasks Jason must complete to secure the Golden Fleece is undeniable. So far in his journey, Jason has had to remain ever cognizant of the processes of nature, so it is expected that the crux of his quest includes similar natural elements. His three tasks also are reminiscent of Neolithic myth. Jason performing such agricultural tasks as plowing a field and sowing seeds into the earth, reveals him as playing the quintessential role of the Neolithic male consort. Jason is also tied to the Neolithic male consort because he must face death repeatedly in these agricultural tasks, as surely the fire-breathing bulls, the mythic warriors that rise out of the soil, or the serpent guardian of the Fleece could all quickly spell doom for Jason. The imagery of allowing humans to resurrect out of the earth along with the harvest also connects the myth to the Neolithic period.

To develop a sense of the myth's layered, and perhaps intended meaning, it is important that this scene, that was supposed to be the culmination of Jason's quest, is represented as anticlimactic; Jason simply walks in, takes the coveted Fleece, and sneaks away, as the guardian serpent unassumingly slumbers. This anticlimactic aspect of the hero's accomplishment of the perceived goal is part of many Greek myths that involve male heroes. The ease of which these tasks are accomplished seems not to deliver a conclusive definition of the male hero as all that heroic; instead, the message of myths like this seems to be politically charged, showing male heroes eradicating more traditional, perhaps Neolithic, belief systems by killing off representatives of those belief systems. However, if the myth wanted to impart a message about the need to eradicate representations of matriarchal power and present Jason as heroic, then Jason seemingly would have accomplished the impossible tasks of Colchis without the help of Medea. But Medea's aid is vital to the myth.

Jason encounters many strange creatures and locales upon his voyage that serve to instruct him in lessons that may seem contrary to expected definitions of heroism. The women and other natural representations presented in the myth serve to not heighten Jason's ego, but instead take him down a peg. Therefore, the myth of Jason unexpectedly shifts the focus away from Jason as the hero of the myth and places it upon Medea, or perhaps more broadly, upon nature itself. It appears that the myth is trying to show that for Jason to be heroic, he must not simply overcome myriad challenges he is presented with; instead, he must internalize the lessons of the challenges, most of which arguably involve nature. To be a botanical hero, then, Jason must learn from his experiences with mysterious women and natural elements in order to psychologically transform as a result of the wisdom he receives.

As discussed, Jason's success since the start of his journey depends upon his tie to the elements of nature. He is successful at the first part of the quest because he is guided by mythical characters or elements that represent the laws of the natural world; however, it is upon his homeward journey, as well as his homecoming, where Jason, and many of the other Argonauts, appear to lessen their internalization of the lessons of nature. Apollonius' *Argonautika* points to instances of the important role nature plays within the Argonaut's return expedition, but Jason's grasp of the importance of nature becomes nebulous. On his way to Colchis, Jason appears cognizant that he is at the mercy of nature and its mythic representations, but upon his return expedition, he continuously is portrayed as encountering more and more natural lessons, but this internalization of the instruction seems lost upon him. Jason's inability to fully embrace his experiences upon his journey, perhaps prepares audiences to ultimately view Jason as having failed his botanical heroic journey.

Upon their return, the *Argonautika* relates that Medea's brother is killed to divert Medea's father, King Aeëtes, from capturing the Argo. The sacred wood that makes up the Argo's prow admonishes this deed and tells the Argonauts that the only way they will now be able to return home is if they seek absolution from Circe, the divine enchantress known for her mystical mastery of natural elements. The Argo takes the Argonauts to the river Eridanos where Helios' son, Phaethon, crashed the sun god's chariot into the earth after he lost control of this most powerful of natural elements. Apollonius is undoubtedly making a connection here with Jason needing to learn the power of nature. The body of Phaethon, in a state of perpetual decay, causes the river to emit a powerful stench that permeates the place in remembrance of death; birds that fly over this region still die if they come into contact with the atmosphere. Also the mourning sisters of Phaethon, once they saw his damaged corpse, immediately turned themselves into trees that surround this spot, still guarding the place when the Argonauts enter. It is crucial that the Argonauts must face this stage for the quest to fit archetypal patterns, as it appears now that instead of only a successful heroic journey where Jason easily accomplishes his quest through the aid of Medea, Jason is now immersed in the heroic archetype of the mythic underworld, though here this symbolic underworld is portrayed as overtly natural. The stench and atmosphere of death in this natural underworld is vital to Jason's opportunity for growth. And again, Apollonius connects these natural elements that remind the living of the factuality of death with mystical female characters in the botanical representations of Phaethon's sisters.

In Apollonius' version of the myth, the Argonauts' symbolic underworld journey continues as they advance to Circe's island, and once there, they witness humans who have been transformed into wild animals that tamely surround Circe. Circe herself feels no pity for Jason and admonishes Medea, her niece, for following this stranger that defied her father. Circe demands they leave, and in doing so, the Argonauts meet with elements like Scylla and Charybdis and the cattle of Helios; these encounters serve to remind the Argonauts of the immense power of nature as well as the factuality of mortality. Finally, the Argo brings the men to the desert of Libya, which appears to the Argonauts as nature in a state of death where nothing can apparently survive. It is here, in this again symbolically natural underworld, where Jason meets local goddesses who are once more associated with nature. Buxton states the encounter between Jason and the Libyan goddesses occurs when they are in a "state of helpless indecision ... mourning for their own deaths" (121). In this scene, Jason receives a message from the goddesses of the desert; they uncover the mourning cloak that Jason wears about his head and remind him that as a hero he can only go home once he grasps the lessons of nature. The goddesses state that the "Argonauts' safe return depends on their making fair recompense to their mother" (Buxton 121), and arguably this reference of "mother" alludes to the earth being the mother of all. Jason's former disregard for life, shown by his murder of Medea's brother, is an abomination of nature. To become a botanical hero, Jason must accept death as a necessity, but equally he must also remember the importance of life. Death is a natural part of nature, and most often the heroic journey serves to force its heroes to accept this, but in this epic, the symbolic, natural underworld Jason encounters teaches him the opposite, that death is necessary as a natural event, but if the death is unnatural, then it is a desecration of nature's patterns. Therefore, Jason must learn the value of life to fully become a botanical hero, but arguably, Jason does not do this in any version of his myths.

The Argonauts must carry their vessel, the Argo, upon their backs in order to bring it out of the desert. Finally, almost dying of thirst, the Argonauts reach a place that serves as another symbolic, natural representation of the underworld. Usually within Greek myth the Garden of the Hesperides is described as overtly lush where another massive serpent, Ladon, guards the golden apples of the Hesperides, but when the Argonauts arrive, again described in a state where they are seriously contemplating the possibility of their deaths, this oasis is said to have mysteriously dried up only the day before; "the scene is now one of putrid desolation ... for the serpent has been killed by the former Argonaut, Herakles, and flies lie shriveling on the carcass" (Buxton 122). Again, Jason and the Argonauts are forced to see the effects of a disregard for life. With Ladon killed, the creatures within the Garden of the Hesperides and the Garden itself also begin to die. This disruption of nature by killing the sacred serpent sends a message to the Argonauts that if nature is disrespected, then the repercussions affect the whole eco-system.

The goddesses here, the Hesperides, in a scene remarkably demonstrative of mankind's effect on nature, transform from human form into dust before the eyes of the Argonauts. The death of the serpent, again often associated with the Neolithic Earth Goddess, causing the collapse of the eco-system, sends a message to Jason that nature in its myriad manifestations, Hera, Medea, Circe, the goddesses of the Libyan Desert, and now the Hesperides, must be respected. Orpheus, one of the Argonauts, also reveals the same message so many others have tried to impart to Jason and the other Argonauts.

Orpheus plays his mystical lyre and is able, before the eyes of the Argonauts, to show the results of respecting nature. Nature responds to Orpheus' song as the Hesperides resurrect from ashes into sprouts that come up through the soil and grow into trees. This symbolic process is representative of the cycles of nature, but again, the Hesperides' lessons continue to not be grasped by Jason. The Argonauts resume their journey through the desert, until one of their members, Mopsos, is bitten by a serpent and dies; his corpse decays incredibly fast because the snake which bit him was born from the blood of Medusa's severed head when Perseus flew over Libya after having slayed her. In this scene with Mopsos, death again must be acknowledged as a loss by the Argonauts, as again Apollonius connects this death as being a punishment for the unnatural death of Medea's brother.

One event that Apollonius relates before the Argonauts can reach home reveals that some of the Argonauts may be coming to an understanding of nature and its cycles. One Argonaut, Euphemus, dreams that he is given a clod of dirt from the desert of Libya that he holds to his breast, and miraculously, his body produces milk, which nourishes the dirt. Suddenly, within the dream, a woman grows from the clod, and Euphemus has sex with her. Upon waking Euphemus asks Jason what he thinks the dream meant, and Jason states that his dream was a prophetic vision of the place where Euphemus' descendants will one day be able to go. This dream, and subsequent physical realization of the dream when the island is actually created by these same methods, suggests that at least Euphemus may have begun to realize the interconnectivity of all nature, including mankind's place within the greater eco-system. The archetypes of nature-dependent myths are numerous upon the journey of the Argonauts; they could have served to teach Jason and the other Argonauts important lessons that would have allowed them, or at least some of them, to become botanical heroes as a result of their quest, but the treatment of Medea by Jason in this and later mythic representations portrays him as far from a botanical hero.

Most versions of the myth recount the Argonauts finally arriving back to Pelias' kingdom with the Golden Fleece, but the myths do not end there, as few heroic quests end successfully because, again, the lesson of many heroic myths is to diminish the individual importance of the hero, and at this point of the myth, Jason has not been diminished. Medea sees to it though that he is. Upon returning, Jason finds that his parents were killed by King Pelias, who thought that the Argonauts did not survive their journey. Medea offers to bring vengeance to King Pelias by tricking him with the enticement of restoring him to youth. She convinces King Pelias' daughters to dismember their father's body; Medea then places the pieces of the king's corpse within her cauldron, but now it only boils the remains of King Pelias. The regenerative practices of the Neolithic Earth Goddess, which Medea benevolently used upon Jason in some versions of the myth before his quest to secure the Golden Fleece, are now only presented as destructive. Barnes states that this scene is "brazen patriarchal propaganda. Medea is portrayed as a foreign witch who makes an offer of immortality that she does not ever intend to keep. The story is designed to say to men in the Dark Age, see, these backwoods women promise immortality but do not deliver. The myth therefore intentionally slanders Medea" (130), and proves that "a woman's promise of immortality will kill a man" (Barnes 130). R. Armstrong points out that there are at least two portrayals of Medea presented in mythology; either she is mythically presented as the "young sorceress met by Jason and the Argonauts on their quest for the Golden Fleece, or the terrifying and vindictive jilted lover of later years" (41). The portrayal of Medea as retellings of the myth progressed throughout the ages might point again to the shift of divine female authority to that of divine male authority in Greece.

Euripides' 5th century BCE version of the myth of Jason and Medea, entitled *Medea*, presents Medea mostly as an infamous villain, but Jason is equally presented as non-heroic. Euripides starts his play marking Medea in a new role as a distrustful witch instead of her former portrayal as a remnant of an Earth Goddess. In this later version of the myth, Jason gains political favor, but he eventually falls in love with another woman, Glauce, the princess of Corinth. Outraged, Medea confronts Jason, reminding him that she is responsible for all he currently has; he retorts that it is actually Aphrodite, and not Medea, who made his quest possible, because Aphrodite was responsible for making Medea fall in love with him. Medea, enraged, seeks revenge and easily kills Glauce by giving her a bridal dress with a potion on it that burns Glauce alive when she puts it on. Glauce's father, the King of Corinth, Creon, seeing his daughter suffer, embraces her and also dies by the poison on the dress. Medea flees to Athens, and many versions of the myth depict Hera as becoming disappointed with Jason for not respecting Medea, so Jason, having lost the favor of Medea and the goddess Hera, is depicted in different myths as lonely and unhappy, wandering from city to city without a home. Jason's myths most often end with Jason as an older man going aboard the rotting Argo, contemplating suicide (Graves 624), when the prow falls on him and kills him instantly, which reminds audiences of the power of the sacred and prophetic tree from Dodona that was used to construct the Argo.

Euripides' play *Medea* tells a version of the myth where Medea killed her two boys who she bore to Jason, fearing that they would be murdered as a result of her actions of killing Glauce and Creon, but in most other mythic versions, this never happened. Luschnig concurs that Medea's murder of her children was an "invention on Euripides' part. In other versions the children were killed by Creon's kin, by the people of Corinth … or by Medea accidently. Although the priority of Euripides in making Medea the murderer is in dispute, it could explain both the ancient scholion that tells us the Corinthians bribed Euripides to remove the stain of this legendary murder from them" (xi). Graves contends that Medea was the mother of seven boys and seven girls, and that Medea having thwarted the advances of Zeus, was granted the gift of immortality for her children by Hera if she took them to Hera's altar, and there the Corinthians are supposed to have intervened and murdered the children (621–2); this version portrays Medea in a role more sacred than sinister. Still, Euripides does depict Medea's final scene in the play as representative of her divine role, as he shows her escaping Corinth on the backs of two winged dragons, a method of transportation reserved for the divine.

Clauss states that Jason appears as a passive hero; "he does not make things happen but waits for the dust to settle before taking advantage of the opportunities that others—mortal and divine—have provided.... [His] qualities are not the qualities one normally associates with the best of the Greek heroes" (211). As discussed, the many renditions of this myth serve continuously to tie Jason to natural messages, but Jason fails to internalize these natural lessons, and thus fails at becoming a botanical hero. He is not depicted as rising again out of death, like the warriors that emerge out of the soil in Colchis. Jason only dies lonely and sad at the decree of the tree that brought him so close to learning the lessons of nature that could have brought him mythic wisdom. Instead, Medea is the botanical hero of the myth because in the numerous representations of this myth, Medea clearly grasps the wisdom of the botanical environment. She attempts to teach Jason this wisdom, but throughout the myth he is unwilling to grasp her terrifying and regenerative lessons—the lessons of nature.

Beowulf Battles Nature

The Anglo-Saxon poem of *Beowulf*, written probably between the 7th and 8th centuries CE, but maybe as late as the 11th century CE, was written by an anonymous author. It most likely was compiled from earlier Germanic history and myth, as Crossley-Holland states, "almost every stage of the story has its parallel elsewhere in early medieval Germanic literature" (28). The poem also reveals mythic archetypes that connect the hero, Beowulf, to the botanical aspects of nature. Though this text was written in Christian times, Beowulf appears to represent a Germanic pagan hero (Goldsmith 147); as with many similar texts writing about pagan beliefs in the Christian era, conflicted views of both faiths emerge, as Beowulf, according to critics like Gwara, appears not to be a fully pagan or a fully Christian hero (373). Crossley-Holland states, "Anglo-Saxon England of the seventh and eighth centuries was by no means wholly Christian" (14). In addition:

> The sheer inconsistency of the Christian element in *Beowulf* seems consistent with what we know of Anglo-Saxon England at the time of its composition. It is true that Grendel and his mother are said to be descendants of Cain, and that Beowulf is Christian, but the Danes are portrayed both as heathen and Christian, and Beowulf is also shown to be at the hands of inexorable fate.... It should be remembered that Scandinavia was heathen from top to toe. The *Beowulf*-poet ... has portrayed a society in which worship of the old gods and the new god ... live in tandem. In this ... he has in fact truthfully portrayed his own society [Crossley-Holland 14].

It will never be known to what extent *Beowulf* accurately portrays the pagan or Christian ideology of its time, but the many natural references within the poem can be addressed to attempt to identify Beowulf's character as a botanical hero.

The epic introduces Beowulf leaving behind the comforts of his home in Geatland and seeking adventure away from his known community, and true to the archetypal journey of the hero this places him in the, to him, unknown environment of Denmark. King Hrothgar and the Danes are experiencing a challenge with the presence of a monstrous beast named Grendel; this aspect of the myth quickly forces Beowulf to face an encounter with both the horrific and the mystical, as often the archetypal hero must do upon his or her heroic journey. However, it soon becomes evident that Grendel holds qualities that indicate that he may be a representation of the natural environment, making Beowulf's upcoming battle with Grendel symbolic of him wrestling with nature.

Beowulf himself is portrayed as having many qualities that tie him to nature as well, which might signal him as being a botanical hero. For instance, his name, Beowulf, immediately connects him with a predatory animal—the wolf; Beowulf's "real force is inscribed in his name.... Whatever etymological interpretation of the name Beowulf given by scholars ... the reference to the root for 'wolf' remains a constant. Beowulf thus carries in himself the strength and spirit of an animal" (Asaka & Alias 2). Furthermore, Beowulf's helmet is adorned with the image of a boar; the boar was believed to be sacred to pagan Germanic people (Goldsmith 87), and therefore this may signal Beowulf as holding beliefs connected to the natural world and its powers.

The Danes, at the time of Beowulf's arrival, are in what might appear an odd state. They are depicted as renowned warriors, able to contend with a variety of aggressive onslaughts from neighboring invaders, as many successful kingdoms of the era had to do, but Hrothgar's kingdom is rendered utterly helpless for twelve years because of the presence of one strange creature, Grendel, who comes stealthily out of his wilderness home and attacks the Danes in the night (Asaka & Alias 2). Grendel, who resides in the deep, unfamiliar woods can be identified, as stated, as a representation of nature itself, perhaps nature in its harshest and most unpredictable aspects, as he indiscriminately kills the Danes as they sleep and then devours their corpses in animalistic fashion:

> Grendel swung open the hall's mouth ...
> ... he hungrily seized
> a sleeping warrior, greedily wrenched him,
> bit into his body, drank the blood
> from his veins, devoured huge pieces;
> until, in no time, he had devoured the whole man,
> even his feet and hands [*Beowulf* 67].

The Danes are portrayed in great need of Beowulf's help when he arrives, and it is precisely the presentation of Beowulf as one holding connections to nature that might make him capable of contending with the Danes' problem of Grendel. If Grendel represents nature, and he is the only element that can render the mighty Danes incompetent, then Beowulf must be analyzed for his attributes that make him the right person to help the Danes. If Beowulf is also presented as a natural representation, even animalistic, then the message of the epic has a focus connected to nature.

Even before his journey to Denmark the text states that Beowulf earned his reputation by contending with the environment when he had to swim for seven days battling sea creatures with his sword; therefore, he has proven himself as someone who is capable of dealing with the harsh aspects of nature, and thus the text makes it clear that he is the right man to kill Grendel. However, when looking at what little is conclusively known of Germanic religious belief, it appears odd that the message of *Beowulf* would only be one where its hero must show dominance over the natural environment, when the Germanic people revered nature as sacred. Furthermore, if Beowulf is the one needed hero to contend with the nature representatives that seem to have gotten out of control—Grendel, Grendel's mother, and later the dragon that will terrorize Beowulf's own kingdom—why present Beowulf as a representation of nature himself as his name suggests? Perhaps, then, the text presents a message that shows that nature must not be defeated but embraced.

What is known of Germanic paganism comes from mostly archeological findings, the recorded writings of Roman and later Germanic peoples, Germanic folklore, and Norse religion. Germanic people, and later the Anglo-Saxons to a lesser extent especially after the introduction of Christianity, worshipped the earth as holy through myriad divine nature representatives; Tacitus states in his *Germania* that "The Germans do not think it in keeping with the divine majesty to confine gods within walls or to portray them in the likeness of any human countenance. Their holy places are woods and groves" (109). Mystical creatures that lived deep within the wildernesses, like elves and dragons, were an accepted part of Germanic mythology. Often Germanic heroes validated their heroism by their ability to contend with these mythic beings that were connected with nature. However, as with other world mythologies, mystical creatures within myth, however terrifying, are not always meant to be portrayed as evil; they are instead often mythological elements meant to test the hero, and quite often their symbolic function represents aspects of the natural world that must be embraced instead of destroyed. Greek mythology, for instance, is full of references to horrific mystical creatures that torment brave heroes, but often, these creatures teach the hero that they cannot ever be fully overcome. For instance, Herakles in his final labor captures Cerberus, the three-headed dog that guards the entrance of the underworld, instead of killing him, because Cerberus most likely represents the factuality of mortality and serves to teach Herakles that death is natural and cannot be eradicated. Therefore, battling creatures that appear evil, like perhaps Grendel, his mother, and the dragon, may instead symbolize the hero's need to embrace natural elements respected by the belief systems of nature-dependent cultures. Battling with nature, or overcoming the onslaught nature brings, does not necessarily send a message that one must overpower nature, especially for a people who revere nature; instead, it only proves that the hero is identified as such for being capable of contending with nature in its sometimes harsh and formidable aspects. To identify a hero as such for contending not with warring bands of human invaders, but for opposing natural representatives as the most mighty of opponents, places respect upon the natural environment as being the most terrifying and thus important of obstacles. It is also important to look at the way such heroes contend with nature. Again, the Greek Herakles upon a different labor must kill the massive Nemean Lion that is attacking neighboring villages with his bare hands, as no weapon will penetrate the lion's hide, and Beowulf too will learn that he cannot defeat his adversary, Grendel, with the aid of manmade materials, as he also must only use his natural strength.

Pagan Anglo-Saxons still revered nature much like their Germanic ancestors, but when Christianity came into the picture, sometimes the open worship of nature, including trees, streams, sacred groves, etc., was banned. Though most scholars feel that many pagan practices and methods of worship were incorporated slowly into a new faith that incorporated Christian doctrine, many elements of traditional, pagan worship either were eliminated or were transformed, thus the text of *Beowulf* might show how the reverence of nature as divine was transformed ideologically. Certainly some of the views of nature holding sacred properties might have been transformed regarding the natural world by the time the Anglo-Saxon author of *Beowulf* recorded the epic, which might explain elements that are at odds with one another regarding the natural world and the characterization of Beowulf, as well as the natural representatives he battles. For instance, Grendel is portrayed within the epic as having been ostracized from civilization because he was an evil descendent of the Old Testament character of Cain, and as the text says, in Cain:

> all evil-doers find their origin,
> monsters and elves and spriteful spirits of the dead,
> also the giants who grappled with God
> for a long while [*Beowulf* 49].

This labeling of Grendel in Old Testament terms reveals a measure of cultural conflict at the time of the poem's composition, as the reference to "monsters," "elves," "spirits of the dead," and "giants" are all representative of more traditional Germanic beliefs, so the incorporation of pagan beliefs into Christian definition muddies the symbolic meaning of contending with such elements. Traditional heroes from nature-dependent civilizations, perhaps like the early Germanic tribes, valued heroes who learned not to control nature but to use its resources and wisdom for the good of all. But, if the poet of *Beowulf* labels the agents serving as representatives of unharnessed nature as evil in a Christian context, then the text sends an odd message that is representative of a conflicted ideological time. If Grendel, his mother, and the dragon are evil in Christian terms instead of natural, then killing them is necessary to save innocent and righteous people. However, if more traditional Germanic concepts viewed similar mythological contenders, like Grendel, as natural agents, who were not evil, then killing them off sends a message that humanity, in controlling these aspects, becomes superior to nature, and this would be at odds with Germanic spiritual concepts. In addition, the wilderness in later medieval European literature became identified as a place of foreboding, as Christianity spread and civilizations moved further away from a demonstrable dependency on agriculture as a means of survival. Unchartered forest environments often became identified in European medieval literature as separate from concepts associated with civilization and righteousness; thus unfettered natural environments became places that harbored pagans, who began to be defined in literary terms as uncivilized, untrustworthy, and sometimes evil. Thus, in the Christian era, the wilderness, and those who reside in it and worship it, began to be portrayed mythically with fear and distrust. For instance, at the start of the poem, before Beowulf's arrival, King Hrothgar and the Danes are portrayed as practicing pagan rites to try and dissolve their torment of Grendel:

> At times they offered sacrifices to the idols
> In their pagan tabernacles, and prayed aloud
> to the soul-slayer that he would assist them
> in their dire distress [*Beowulf* 50].

The poet states that the Danes prayed to their pagan "idols" because they "did not know how to praise the Protector of Heaven," and that because they did not pray to the Christian God, the poet continues by saying:

> Woe to the man, who
> in his wickedness, commits his soul to the fire's embrace;
> he must expect neither comfort nor change. He will be damned
> forever [*Beowulf* 51].

Yet, the one person the Danes need is Beowulf, and as stated, he wears "two suits of clothing," as he is portrayed at times as Christian, but at other times as pagan (Crossley-Holland 33). In addition, in the entire text of *Beowulf*, "there are very few specifically Christian references ... and not a single mention of Christ or one of the great Christian dogmas" (Crossley-Holland 33). Therefore, to understand Beowulf's heroism, one must view him as a cultural hero displayed in a time of cultural flux; he is both pagan and Christian, which will make him at times appear as a botanical hero, but also at times appear contrary to the lessons of botanical heroism.

Beowulf, demonstrating the heroic quest, partakes upon his task to kill Grendel with overt confidence; he feels that he immediately can defeat Grendel and forever save the Danes. And, initially the myth states that Beowulf is apparently successful. Grendel is presented as a force that is decimating the residents of King Hrothgar's kingdom; like a natural disaster, Grendel provides no warning when he will reveal his wrath. As discussed, Beowulf tries to over-power Grendel using artificially made weapons, but as Grendel is a representation of nature, the only successful means to combat him is through his natural strength. Again, this is significant because it references Beowulf in terms of his natural abilities and sends a message that to defeat a natural adversary one must take on properties of the adversary, recognizing one's own animalistic tendencies. As discussed earlier, if Beowulf is connected to animalistic traits, as his name suggests, it is important that Beowulf mortally wounds Grendel in wolf-like fashion by tearing his arm off, which presents Beowulf in a similar light to that of Grendel, as they both kill their prey in animalistic fashions.

Grendel ends up retreating back into the wilderness from which he came to die. The death of Grendel is significant in its connection to natural representations, as his death touches upon mythic archetypes found in nature-dependent communities. Grendel's mutilated body allows his blood to soak into a lake, which responds by boiling in apparent rage. Grendel then dies in an underwater lair within the earth that is also the home of his formidable mother, which may showcase that his body is being accepted back into a womb-like reference of nature; as discussed in the introduction, many nature-dependent mythologies present chambers within the earth in womb-like imagery. This scene of sacrifice within water might also reflect back to Germanic practices that required sacrifice to Earth Goddesses. The description of Grendel's mother and her abode suggest that she may be a rendition of a pagan Earth Goddess figure residing within the earth; "Tacitus states that the eastern Germanic tribes worshipped ... an Earth Mother figure that other sources called Nerthus.... The little we can tell about this worship suggests that its center was probably in the land of the Ingwines (the Danes)" (Johnston Staver 151).

Tacitus relates a ceremony for Nerthus that involved slaves being ceremoniously drowned in a sacred lake associated with Nerthus (135). Johnston Staver states that "Human sacrifices were almost certainly a feature of earth worship. The bodies recovered from Danish bogs, having been ritually killed by strangulation, could have been offered to the Earth Mother in a place where they knew the earth would draw the body down ... as ... 'Nerthus' took her offering" (151). Egeler also discusses that the worship of Earth Goddesses was quite acute in Germanic faith; "the cult of these female goddesses ... is richly attested in over 1100 dedication stones and votive altars from the 1st to the 3rd centuries [CE]" (31). Furthermore, during Christian Anglo-Saxon times, "there were rituals to heal a 'sick field' that called on the 'Earth Mother.' All through the Middle Ages, there were country customs of Harvest Queens and May Queens.... These customs are almost certainly festivals based on the old pagan festivals of earth worship.... It is likely, too, that in the minds of the everyday Anglo-Saxons, the customs honoring the Harvest Queen, or Nerthus/Freya, were more important than those honoring Woden or Thor" (Johnston Staver 151–2).

Yet, in *Beowulf*, Grendel's mother is described as "a monster of a woman" who mourns "her fate" as she has to live in a cave beneath the same lake Grendel retreated to, because she too, the text describes, is a descendent of Cain. Grendel's mother awakens after Grendel's death, and she is furious; she also goes to King Horthgar's kingdom:

> The terror she caused,
> compared to her son, equaled the terror
> an Amazon inspires as opposed to a man,
> when the ornamented sword...
> shears through the boar-crested helmets of the enemy [*Beowulf* 83].

Grendel's mother's portrayal as similar to an Amazon warrior may also be important as it connects her with a culture, the Greeks, who have demonstrable ties with more traditional female figures of Earth Goddess worship.

Regardless of her portrayal as an earlier remnant of a Germanic Earth Goddess that must now be destroyed in this later era or simply a Christianized evil descendent of Cain, as it can never be known in which light she was meant to be portrayed, the myth portrays the mother of Grendel as the true force to be reckoned with. Grendel's mother lives:

> in a little-known country, wolf-slopes, windswept
>   headlands ... the lake stands
> There, night after night, a fearful wonder might be seen—
> fire on the water; no man alive
> is so wise to know the nature of its depths [*Beowulf* 86].

Her underwater lair is beneath a lake that is full of terrifying, mystical creatures, and it is significant that it is into this realm that Beowulf must descend, as it again ties him to the archetype of the heroic, as well as the shamanic, quest, as this lair is deep in the recesses of the earth and harbors a terrifying female who can easily kill most opponents, thus signaling that Beowulf is descending into the mythic underworld when he transgresses Grendel's mother's lair.

Beowulf bravely leaps into the primordial lake, witnessing the most horrific mythic monsters the poet could create, and descends further down into the realm of Grendel's mother:

> the seething water
> received the warrior. A full day elapsed
> before he could discern the bottom of the lake.
>   She who had guarded its length and breadth
> for fifty years ...
> grasped him, clutched the Geat
> in her ghastly claws [*Beowulf* 90].

And after a challenging fight using a weapon that he finds within her realm, an ancient sword, he is able to defeat Grendel's mother. This mythic element of killing Grendel's mother, as a possible pagan symbol of an Earth Goddess, or even a Christian symbol of evil, might suggest that Beowulf, as a medieval hero, was successful in eradicating traditional pagan views associated with unharnessed nature, similar to the Babylonian Marduk slaying the primordial Tiamet in her watery abode to declare his dominance in a new pantheon. However, the myth of Beowulf does not end with this apparently significant event, so it suggests that there is more to this myth than solely eradicating traditional views of nature and its representatives.

Beowulf fights Grendel and Grendel's mother in ways that are reminiscent of myths coming out of hunter-gatherer societies. With Grendel, he had to fight him as an equal, using his natural strength. With Grendel's mother, he had to come to fight her in her domain. Like the practice of hunting, Beowulf had to embrace his natural self in order to be successful; he had to fully become the wolf. Myths of hunter-gatherer societies portray a dependence upon the hunt; the people of these communities must kill living beings in order to survive, and their heroes are often the men who are successful in this task. However, myths of the hunt do not showcase the natural adversary as evil, or the hunter as superior to the prey; instead, such myths show respect for the hunted, and also reveal an intimate tie between the hunter and his prey, which shows that the hunter must acknowledge that for the eco-system to continue, he too will one day submit to the same cycle. There are arguably components of this type of respect displayed by hunter-gatherer societies in Beowulf's killing of

Grendel and his mother, just as there are Christian traits of Beowulf eradicating evil for the maintenance of the Danes. The continuation of the poem will solidify if Beowulf kills fearsome monsters that appear to represent nature for ideological purposes, or if he kills them to meet his role in a natural cycle that will call for him to fall prey to the same fate as Grendel and his mother.

Beowulf is depicted as returning to the people of Denmark who are overjoyed that he has rid them of their adversaries; they invite him to stay among them, but Beowulf journeys back to his own home in Geatland, where years later after the deaths of King Hygelac and his son, he gains the kingship for fifty years. The epic proceeds to show how a giant dragon threatens Beowulf's own community because a slave disrupted the slumber of the dragon by stealing gold from its chamber within the earth:

> Thus the huge serpent who harassed men
> Guarded that great stronghold under the earth
> For three hundred winters [*Beowulf* 112].

Again, the portrayal of this primordial monster residing within the earth is representative of Germanic belief systems, as many Germanic legends recount similar tales:

> In choosing a dragon to be Beowulf's last and greatest adversary, the poet was in step with the northern European tradition that the ... great serpent so often represented ... the most savage of all opponents and so in a sense the most worthy test of a man's moral and physical courage. Germanic literature is, indeed, strewn with dragons in myth, legend, heroic poem, saga, and folk-tale [Crossley-Holland 27–8].

The fact that *Beowulf* presents a world in which monsters repeatedly come after humans, shows that even if they are slayed, they can never truly be eliminated, which arguably connects them as representations of the power of nature. Beowulf must learn this truth of the formidable and ever-lasting power of nature to become a botanical hero.

As an old king, he battles the dragon and succeeds in mortally wounding it, but it also succeeds in countering his attack by giving him his own mortal wound. In Beowulf killing the dragon, and the dragon killing Beowulf, the text provides a far different message than the Babylonian Marduk's success at slaying Tiamet. If the epic would have ended with the successful Beowulf killing Grendel's mother, it would have been merely a tale of man's ability to overpower nature, as well as overcome traditional belief systems, but the mythic ending of this epic reveals deeper, nature-oriented meaning. Beowulf's success at killing the dragon must be at the cost of his own life, thus representing the timeless mythic symbolism of nature's never-ending cycles. The dragon represents death for Beowulf, and he fully knows this when he seeks a fight with the dragon.

Crossley-Holland states that the poem closes with an examination of the requirement of the pagan hero to be resolved to die a heroic death against the most formidable of opponents (Crossley-Holland 35). Pagan belief systems revere death in battle as the requirement for a noble hero, bringing a lasting legacy for the warrior. Beowulf fights the dragon to die honorably according to pagan custom; as in Germanic tradition, showcasing bravery at the time of battle allows the warrior to live on in fame among his people. Beowulf's final act makes him a pagan hero, but a botanical hero steps into death, either physical or symbolic, by letting go of his or her desire for individual identity and merely becomes a part of nature. Though the end of Beowulf references most certainly a pagan hero, as opposed to a Christian hero, as the scenes that follow Beowulf's death depict pagan practices not appropriate in Christian ideology, perhaps Beowulf's death is not only about solidifying a lasting legacy for his singular achievements. Germanic mythology often displays a belief in fate, Wyrd, as a concept that dictates the events, and time of death, for each individual. Wyrd cannot be altered or escaped, and Germanic heroes know that to resist Wyrd is to resist the natural workings of the universe. In many ways adhering to a belief that the lives of humans must eventually succumb to the same guiding force that all living beings must succumb to, places importance not on the individual human being, but on a greater system that can be tied to natural law. Therefore, in Beowulf seeking out a final battle with an opponent that comes from the deep recesses of the earth, he has accepted that this death is his fate. Beowulf steps into the battle, which he knows is his death, bravely, and this steadfastness to face death instead of flee the dragon might define him as a botanical hero. Lenders states that "To be a real hero, you have to lose …. In fact, most of the Germanic heroes eventually faced a situation where they could not win. Rather than giving up, they resolved their impossible dilemmas by losing with all the strength and willpower they could muster, and in this way achieved heroic status."

Beowulf fought Grendel and Grendel's mother by harnessing the natural abilities of his name, and it is significant that his demise, that he readily accepts, is in a death so like the ones he initiated. Like a wolf in the hunt, he killed Grendel and his mother, but now as an old man, he must succumb to the same fate for the cycle of nature to be preserved; this acknowledgement of the basic laws of nature strips fame from Beowulf and identifies him as no different than any other living being. Death is as inevitable for him as it was for Grendel, Grendel's mother, and the dragon. Just before Beowulf entered into Grendel's mother's lair, he showed that he fully understood this natural fact:

> The days on earth for every one of us
> are numbered; he who may should win renown

> before his death; that is a warrior's
> best memorial when he has departed from the world [*Beowulf* 87].

Therefore, in seeking out his death by a natural opponent, and then requesting a burial within the earth, a barrow similar to the same abode the dragon lived in, signifies Beowulf's gained knowledge at the end of his life that he is equal to all elements that come from the natural environment.

As Beowulf is dying from the dragon's venom, he slumps down and looks at the lair of the dragon, the barrow within the earth:

> he gazed at the work of the giants,
> saw how the ancient earthwork contained
> stone arches supported by columns [*Beowulf* 126].

This visual into a past time ties Beowulf to his pagan roots moments before his death. The treasure was placed within the barrow by "ancient chiefs" who were the last of their people. Beowulf states that he wants Wiglaf, the warrior who aided Beowulf in battling the dragon, to show him the treasure hoard before he dies. Wiglaf enters the chamber and finds again remnants of a forgotten pagan civilization. Wiglaf carries some of the treasure to Beowulf, who is now quite near death, and Beowulf tells Wiglaf:

> I will not long be with you.
> Command the battle-warriors, after the funeral fire,
> to build a fine barrow overlooking the sea…
> as a reminder to my people….
> You are the last survivor of our family,
> … fate has swept
> all my kinsmen…
> to their doom. I must follow them [*Beowulf* 128].

It is significant that Beowulf's last words tie him so directly to his imaginings of the chiefs who hid the hoard within the earth, and it shows that he accepts the fact that no one remembers the name of the chiefs who buried the hoard, just as one day no one will remember his own name. It appears to some that Beowulf kills the dragon to secure the hoard of gold for his people; some scholars view this as anti–Christian, even anti-heroic, as it seems to present greed as the cause of his demise. But the hoard of gold reveals the legacy of a people who disappeared, as Wiglaf saw "wondrous wall-hangings … and the stoups and vessels of a people long dead" (*Beowulf* 128). Therefore, by Beowulf revealing the items of the hoard to his people, he shows them that the boon he secured for his people is the knowledge that artificial riches, life, and even a lasting legacy are all fleeting. The fact that the people bury the gold instead of keep it for themselves show that they have fully understood this message:

> They bequeathed the gleaming gold,
>   treasure of men,
> to the earth, and there it still remains
> as useless as it was before [*Beowulf* 139].

The treasure only contains man-made items, like the sword that would not work against Grendel; therefore, by burying the gold with Beowulf it solidifies the natural message of the botanical heroic quest—that life is cyclical. Beowulf, though his ashes are buried in an impressive barrow that will overlook the sea, will still one day become like the forgotten chiefs who were presumably interred in a similar barrow as was pagan custom, but the barrow will remain, serving as a natural reminder that all living beings must die. The barrow reminds Beowulf and the Geats that the earth claims the dead, along with what they thought was so important, the artificial hoard. The earth also symbolically birthed a dragon out of this same barrow, a dragon that represented the inevitability of natural death for Beowulf. The dragon emerging from the symbolic womb-like barrow to claim another king that will hold another hoard within another barrow suggests that the same process will be repeated throughout time, and that this cycle is natural and necessary.

The people of Beowulf's kingdom shove the corpse of the dragon off the edge of the cliff into the deep sea below. They then construct Beowulf's pyre and watch as nature reclaims the body of their king:

> the darkwood-smoke
> soared over the fire, the roaring flames
> mingled with weeping—the winds' tumult subsided—
> until the body became ash, consumed even
> to its core [*Beowulf* 138].

Beowulf represents a hero who teaches audiences the importance of embracing nature, and thus in many ways he is a botanical hero. He kills the natural representations of Grendel and Grendel's mother by embracing his own animalistic nature, and in seeking out the dragon at the end of his own life, he shows that he too must readily succumb to the same fate he subjected Grendel and his mother to. He shows audiences that the concept of Wyrd is as natural as the changing of the seasons—that by embracing Wyrd, one accepts the fact that all living beings must die. However, this text falls short of fully representing Beowulf in terms of a botanical hero because it only presents the end of his singular life as a lesson in accepting death. There appears little promise of natural rebirth after destruction, as similar myths of Germanic background show destruction as necessary for all living beings, even divine beings, so that regeneration can occur, as with the Norse myth of Ragnarok. The text ends showing Beowulf as brave and wise for accepting the fact that he must die, but his death produces nothing regenerative, as Beowulf's people are referenced as being doomed to attacks from their neighbors, and the cycle of heroic barrows seems only one that will be forever repeated, sending a message that is more fatalistic than renewing. This fatalism, that stunts Beowulf from fully becoming a botanical hero, might reflect the time and the culture in which the epic was produced. The Anglo-Saxon author of *Beowulf* presumably wrote it in a time of cultural flux where his immediate ancestors were most likely exiles in an environment vastly different than that of their heritage, and when Christianity was calling into question beliefs held for centuries. Because of the nature of the conflicted times in which this epic was composed, perhaps it is enough to state that Beowulf in some ways represents a botanical hero who understands the importance of adhering to nature's laws, but in other ways, contradicts his classification as a botanical hero, serving more as a Germanic hero who seeks a lasting legacy, or a Christian hero who declares dominance over perceived evil in the name of professed righteousness.

Sigurd and Brynhild—Leaves Upon the Wind

The 13th century Icelandic epic *The Saga of the Volsungs*, or the *Volsunga Saga*, presents again a quintessential hero in the character of Sigurd. The myth also provides many connections that tie the text to the importance of the natural environment, as the Norse also worshipped nature as sacred. At the start of the work King Volsung is given a divine wish-maiden by the central Norse god, Odin, and his wife, Frigg. The wish-maiden is sent with an apple, that upon eating it, King Volsung and his wife, the queen, then conceive their child who will one day become king.

King Volsung then has twins, a girl named Signy and a boy named Sigmund. At Signy's wedding feast, the myth presents Odin arriving, disguised as an old man, stating that whoever is capable of lifting a mystical sword that has been set in a sacred Barnstock tree will be the next rightful king. This element that indicates the king's right to rule using nature imagery is similar to the tales of King Arthur pulling the sword from the stone and signifies the approval of nature in the rightful kingship of whoever may retrieve the sword; this approval on the part of nature ties to traditional Norse belief systems where the king must be able to secure fertility throughout the land, which is similar to Indian belief as shown with Rama in the *Ramayana*.

Signy, as is often the case with female characters in Norse mythology, is attributed with mystical wisdom and prophetic powers. Her marriage has been a forced one, even though she tried to tell her father that it will produce the downfall of their people. Still King Volsung insists, and sure enough her brother Sigmund and her other nine brothers are captured by Signy's husband, Siggeir, King of the Goths, and sentenced to death. Signy arranges it so that the brothers are held in stocks instead of being immediately killed, under the guise that they will be humiliated before dying, but she does this to try and gain time that will allow some of them to live. Each night, though, a natural element, an enormous old she-wolf, comes out of the forest and consumes each of the nine brothers as they remain bound within their stocks, and Signy, not capable of saving them, can only watch. Eventually though, she places honey on the face of Sigmund, her twin and last remaining brother, and when the wolf comes, instead of eating Sigmund, it simply licks the honey off of his face. Again, this natural connection serves to reveal Sigmund as having been chosen by natural elements.

Signy then helps Sigmund to escape and hide in the forest, as everyone in the kingdom assumes he was consumed by the wolf. Depicting Sigmund as having this other female half as his twin sister also mythically ties him to nature, as Signy soon reveals that she holds powers again mythically attributed to a representation of an Earth Goddess. The Norse, coming in part from traditional Germanic belief systems, held goddesses in high regard; they believed, as discussed with the Germanic beliefs in *Beowulf*, in the importance of goddesses as representations of the natural world. Ellis Davidson points out that Snorri Sturluson's *Prose Edda* lists sixteen goddesses important to Norse religion, but also states that the direct role of these goddesses has mostly been lost to history, as they often do not appear in the surviving Norse myths we recognize today (10). It is documented, though, that the Norse believed in a divine order known as the Vanir, who were thought to be older than the more well-known divinities of the Aesir; the Vanir were a divine pantheon who were directly associated with nature and fertility but were overcome by the Aesir when the two pantheons entered into battle. After the epic battle, the Vanir still held a position of prominence as a sub-group of the Aesir. It is also believed that the divinities of the Vanir, especially the goddesses, were still worshipped and held in especially high regard by the Norse people. The Vanir goddess Freyja, for example, was often associated as a goddess of natural fertility; she was believed to be of such importance to the Norse that her worship continued widely even into the era in which Snorri Sturluson composed the *Prose Edda*. Freyja, like other Earth Goddesses, was believed to be represented by many names depending upon the region of her worship; Snorri Sturluson contends that Freyja, in her various Earth Goddess identifications, was "the deity who ... survived last of all of the gods" (Ellis Davidson 121). Her portrayal in Norse mythology shows her as associated with other traits given to Earth Goddesses in various cultures, such as metamorphosing between animal and human form, mysticism involving the natural elements, and other traits associated with the fertility of nature. In addition, the societal role of women in Norse communities was high when compared to other cultures of the time; this is reflected in their belief systems as well, as many women were regarded as holding shamanic and prophetic abilities. Understanding the Norse belief in Earth Goddesses and the role of prophetic women within the culture, may shed light on the female mythic characters within this epic, most specifically Signy's interaction with Sigmund and later Brynhild's relationship with Sigurd, as both Signy and Brynhild help to secure elements of botanical heroism upon their male counterparts.

Like the Greek Jason at the mercy of countless women along his voyage, while Sigmund hides within the forest, he must completely rely upon Signy in order to stay alive. Signy, in traditional Earth Goddess symbolism sends two of her own sons, born of her evil husband King Siggeir, to live in the woods with Sigmund, but each proves unworthy, as deemed by her and Sigmund, so Signy instructs Sigmund to kill each of them. Then Signy switches bodies with a passing sorceress, so that Signy, disguised now as this beautiful sorceress, can seduce her brother Sigmund and produce a suitable heir to her family name. Arguably these scenes within the *Saga of the Volsungs* identifies Signy in the role of a nature goddess, as she clearly portrays a mastery of mysticism in relation to the natural environment, much like the Greek Medea. In order for her offspring, Sinfjötli, to become truly heroic, he must maintain his connection to both the feminine and the natural. Later myths reveal that Sinfjötli seeing that his father Sigmund has been tricked into almost consuming a glass of poisoned wine, takes the glass from his father and consumes it himself, dying before his time. Sigmund takes the body of his son to the fjords, where Odin disguised as a ferryman takes the body of Sinfjötli, signaling him, and his actions in life, as sacred.

In time, Sigmund becomes king of Hunland and serves nobly, but as an old man, an invading army forces him to once again enter battle, and though he fights admirably, his time for death arrives. Again Odin, disguised as an old man, comes and fights Sigmund causing his sword, bestowed to him by Odin himself, to smash to pieces. Once his mystical sword breaks, Sigmund dies asking his wife to preserve the pieces of the sword for his unborn son. Already within the saga a pattern of conceding to death when fate decrees it becomes central to the text, as shown with Sinfjötli and now Sigmund; this pattern will be further repeated with the saga's protagonist Sigurd, Sigmund's unborn son. This acceptance of death is displayed throughout the epic as largely without resistance on the part of the mythic characters, as it was with Beowulf, signaling again a message within the myth that death should not be resisted, as it is natural. Sigmund's queen is then taken captive to now become the king of Denmark's queen; though she is pregnant with Sigmund's child, the king of Denmark treats her and her child, Sigurd, as his own. As the years pass, Sigurd is treated with respect, but eventually Sigurd's tutor, Regin, convinces Sigurd to kill the dragon Fafnir that keeps watch over an enormous hoard of treasure. Regin reveals his own family history to Sigurd stating that the dragon is really his own brother Fafnir who killed their father Hreidmar to obtain the treasure that their father received from the god Loki for the payment of his dead son Otter.

Shape-shifting and mysticism play an enormous role in this tale, as both brothers, Otter and Fafnir, are experts as changing their shapes. Shape-shifting was also a common part of Norse belief; this ability to metamorphose into an animal form signaled a close connection to nature, and will also impart the lessons of nature onto the mythic characters who come into contact with the shapeshifters. Both Norse and Germanic belief systems incorporated animalistic transformation as part of a belief in Totemism. Many Germanic and Norse societies often adopted totem animals, such as the wolf or bear, in an attempt to internalize attributes of the animal; initiation into these totem communities often required the initiate to spend solitary time alone in nature "in imitation of the group's totem beast. As his training progressed, imitation gave way to identification. The warrior achieved a state of spiritual unification with the bear or the wolf" (McCoy). Often association with the totem animal led to a belief that some could achieve the ability to shapeshift at whim into the form of the animal; "The sagas contain numerous accounts of elite warriors shapeshifting" (McCoy). The famed Viking berserkers would often enter into battle naked except for their "animal mask and pelts, howling, roaring, and running amok" (McCoy), and often they would bite or discard their shields, asserting as Neil Price states, a "reminder that their ultimate identity is no longer their social persona, but rather their 'unity with the animal world' that they have achieved through 'self-dehumanization'" (qtd. in McCoy).

In correlation to the Norse belief in animalistic metamorphosis, the character of Otter in *Saga of the Volsungs* is described as loving to swim all day in nature, choosing to appear as an otter over any other creature. While he is in his otter form, the gods Odin, Loki, and Hoenir accidently kill him for a meal. This event causes Hreidmar to demand payment for the death of his son, mandating that the divinities fill the otter skin, the corpse of his son, with gold. Loki obtains the gold from the dwarf Andvari, who has also changed form to that of a fish in the deep sea because the Norns decreed he should guard the treasure hidden in a sea cave in this natural form. Andvari states that whoever holds the treasure, and an accompanying gold ring, will be forever cursed to lose everything, as the gold must remain hidden within nature's recesses. Still, to save his life, Loki takes the payment of gold to Hreidmar for the death of Otter. The corpse of the shape-shifted son Otter is demeaned by being filled entirely within and without with gold, as requested as payment by Hreidmar. Many myths provide audiences a chance to come to terms with the reality of nature's most primary lessons, and here the corpse serves as the reality of death. It is significant that the harsh and natural reality of death is attempted to be covered up with the artifice of wealth, as the myth continues to perpetuate a message that manufactured materials, as portrayed through the hoard of gold, will never be able to outweigh the realities of nature. Loki cautions Hreidmar about taking the treasure, which he states should truly remain at the bottom of the deep sea, thus showing respect for nature as opposed to man-made materials, but Hreidmar disregards this warning and takes the payment.

The myth continues to prove that the sea is the only proper place for the gold as it meets its prophesized destructive aim, with Hreidmar being killed by his son Fafnir, who takes the hoard and forces Regin to flee for his life. Regin, as tutor to Sigurd, under dubious terms convinces him to kill Fafnir and take the cursed treasure. Sigurd accomplishes the task with instruction from Odin again. Upon killing Fafnir, Sigurd is then entirely coated in his blood, which will protect him from ever being injured, except nature intervenes when a small leaf falls from a tree and lands upon Sigurd's shoulder. The leaf leaves behind one area on Sigurd's body that is susceptible to harm as this portion of his body was not soaked in the dragon's blood of immortality. After Sigurd kills Fafnir, he eats a portion of his heart and from this obtains the knowledge of the once powerful Fafnir; this is a common mythic element, as consuming the body of another creature or natural element often is portrayed as providing one with wisdom, like the Celtic tale of Fionn mac Cumhaill eating the body of the Salmon of Knowledge, or the Christian Eve consuming the apple from the Tree of Knowledge. After Sigurd consumes a portion of the dragon's heart, he is able to understand the language of the birds, and they proceed to instruct him that his tutor Regin intends him harm, so Sigurd then murders Regin.

Sigurd's slaying of the shapeshifting Fafnir serves to initiate him in a mythic cycle that will force him to accept his own mortality. As discussed with *Beowulf*, many Germanic and Norse texts define heroes by their ability to kill the most formidable of opponents—the dragon, but as with *Beowulf*, the dragon signifies not only a fearsome opponent, but death itself. Beowulf finally achieved, in part, botanical heroism because he faced his own death by freely entering into battle with the dragon. However, Sigurd's killing of Fafnir occurs at the start of his quest, so unlike Beowulf, he leaves the battle feeling invigorated. Many mythic heroes start their journeys with overt confidence, and again this stage is natural, as the state of youth and vitality, much like the seasonal state of summer, is as natural as death, but in most heroic quests, this stage cannot last, as in nature perpetual summer is an impossibility. Therefore, Sigurd must arrive at the acceptance of his own demise to be identified as heroic, and he must understand his demise as natural to become a botanical hero.

When Sigurd kills Fafnir, in dragon form, he is being mythically instructed on the natural cycle of life and death. Fafnir appears in the text as possessing shamanic abilities, as he can transform into the most feared of creatures; therefore, Fafnir propels Sigurd towards his own heroic journey that will lead him to accept his loss of self-hood, and again this is a requirement of the botanical heroic quest. It is also significant that this scene foreshadows the one element that will undo Sigurd, which is again the imprint the leaf left upon his back, suggesting already at the start of his quest the one thing that will end his quest. In addition, Fafnir as symbolic shaman serves to show Sigurd that transformation between forms readily occurs in nature, as mythic metamorphosis often sends a message to audiences that humans and representations of the natural world are inextricably intertwined. Mythic metamorphosis also often imparts a message that death, when viewed in natural terms, is transitory, as when one thing dies in nature, it returns in different form, as matter never entirely disappears. Therefore, Sigurd's early destruction of Fafnir thrusts him upon a quest to fully submerge himself into the designs of the natural environment.

Knowing that the treasure is cursed, and truly belongs at the bottom of the sea, Sigurd still takes it, along with the ring. He meets his fate, another foreshadowed element of his own demise, by finding the sleeping Valkyrie Brynhild. Brynhild's role within the myth is also tied to death and the cycles of nature, and will also help bring Sigurd to the culmination of his heroic quest. Brynhild was cursed by Odin for disobeying him when she, in her role as a Valkyrie, decided to let an old man die in battle instead of a young man, when Odin decreed that the older man should live. Brynhild's decision provides insight into the lessons of this myth.

Brynhild, as a former Valkyrie, is supposed to be a harbinger of death, but she chooses to defy Odin in order to let what seems to be the most natural option take its course—letting the young outlast the old. But, she is punished by Odin for maintaining the natural order; Brynhild holds the role that has been seen in many myths thus far of the female serving as a representation of the natural order for the male hero of the epic. Brynhild represents both life and death in her portrayal as a Valkyrie; therefore, she also represents the inevitable laws of nature. Odin punished Brynhild to live a life of a mortal instead of an immortal Valkyrie, so he places her, by the means of a sleep thorn, within a deep sleep until Sigurd arrives to marry her. Brynhild's defiance and subsequent punishment of mortality speaks of her important role. She, when paired with Sigurd, will spell the inevitability of death in the natural order of life—one that cannot be masked with treasure or evaded with mystical blood. Vital to the myth is that Sigurd openly knows that by taking the cursed treasure and finding Brynhild, he is meeting with his own fate to die. Sigurd does none of this unknowingly, as before it all happened his uncle warned him of his fate. Brynhild, as a former Valkyrie and now mortal, could not be a clearer representation of inevitable death that must come to all, and still Sigurd seeks her out without fear, and this also marks him as holding at least some qualities of a botanical hero.

Sigurd and Brynhild fall in love, but remain apart, as Brynhild tells him again about their fate—Brynhild will continue her role as a maiden of battle, and Sigurd will marry Princess Gudrun. Again, it is significant that they both know their undesirable fate and willingly take part in their roles, as it suggests the requirement of the botanical heroic quest to shed one's illusion of self-importance in the face of a greater nature.

Because Sigurd has been given a secret potion by Gudrun's mother, Queen Grimhild, Sigurd forgets Brynhild and indeed does marry Gudrun. Queen Grimhild arranges for her son Gunnar to marry Brynhild; this only happens because Sigurd changes his shape to that of Gunnar and tricks Brynhild into accepting the marriage. Once Brynhild and Gunnar are married, Sigurd remembers his love for Brynhild but maintains his duty to Gudrun. Brynhild, though, eventually finds out about Sigurd's trickery and the deceit of Queen Grimhild, and she embraces her role as a maiden of death. She threatens to kill her husband Gunnar if he doesn't kill Sigurd, and though Sigurd comes to her and reveals that he has always loved her and would rather lose everything to be with her and keep her alive, she is still convinced that both Sigurd and she must die.

When Sigurd is out hunting, Byrnhild's husband Gunnar planned for his youngest brother Guttorm to kill Sigurd by stabbing him in his one susceptible spot, his shoulder. Unbeknownst to her, Sigurd's wife Gudrun pleaded to Guttorm to protect Sigurd on this hunt and sewed a leaf on his jacket to alert Guttorm to the one spot he must protect, but instead, her care served as Sigurd's demise, as the deceitful Guttorm now knew the one place to attack. Symbolically, again, the quite literal symbol of nature, the leaf sewn on Sigurd's jacket, serves to remind audiences of the ultimate role that nature always plays in the lives of mortals. Though Sigurd is a hero, and more noble than most, he cannot be immortal, as even Odin, the leader of the Norse Aesir, is not immortal.

Sigurd's death scene is described in abundantly natural terms to remind one of his inescapable tie to nature; "blood gushed from Sigurd's back and chest. The stream waters ran red, and the ground was drenched with blood. Furiously, like an enraged, wounded boar, Sigurd tried to kill his murderer— but his weapons lay by the tree, and he was too weak to reach them. Thus, the greatest of heroes fell with his death wound among the wildflowers.... Sigurd sank back upon the blood-drenched flowers. Death quickly stole upon him, for he had no weapon and no strength to keep it at bay" ("Sigurd" 268). Sigurd becomes the one who is hunted, and just like the hunted boar he sought upon his afternoon hunt, and Fafnir in dragon form who he killed upon the start of his quest, he must now succumb to the laws of the natural world. The myth reminded audiences of this inevitable fact all along, and when Sigurd finally dies, the myth concludes by again showing the futility of holding on too closely to the sagas of human beings.

Sigurd then comes close to being a botanical hero, as he throughout the myth meets some of the components found within the botanical heroic quest; for example, he openly accepts the futility of believing his life to be overtly important, as he consistently knows that a greater force dominates his fate, but Sigurd, like Beowulf, fails to fully become a botanical hero because he mostly serves as a fatalistic hero, never reaching a state of spiritual apotheosis that will allow him to be symbolically resurrected. Still, nature is given the last word in this myth, as the cursed gold and the ring must eventually return, through death and misfortune, to its rightful home at the bottom of the sea, just as the hoard in *Beowulf* had to be buried in acknowledgment that man-made materials, just like the lives of human beings, will never outlast the laws of nature.

Arthurian Legends—Regenerative Nature and the Holy Grail

The many myths involving King Arthur also portray aspects of botanical heroism. King Arthur is based on "a legendary king of Britain who may have been based on a real 5th or 6th century chieftain, although the evidence is scanty" (Wilkerson 71). Chrétien de Troyes, Sir Thomas Malory, and Geoffrey of Monmouth captured the first Arthurian legends, only to be followed by many others who portrayed Arthur as the first Christian king to unite the warring pagan bands of Britain.

Arthur's father, King Uther Pendragon, is told by the mystical Merlin to have Sir Eckland raise the young Arthur, as Pendragon will soon die, and Arthur is destined to be the king of all Britain. Arthur proves his divine right to be king by famously pulling a sword out of a stone in a nearby churchyard. Again, as was the case with Sigurd's father, Sigmund, nature plays a role in revealing

Arthur as a hero. Nature also further solidifies Arthur as heroic when he obtains his rightful sword, Excalibur, and its magical sheath from the Lady of Lake. Matthews contributes the natural imagery connected to Arthur's swords to the Celtic belief that the Goddess of the Land or the Goddess of Sovereignty is bestowing her empowerment to the rightful king as an ambassador of the land (35). These mystical and decidedly natural elements define Arthur in his role of king, but they also show that the myths of King Arthur will closely align with natural elements in order to reveal their mythic messages towards botanical heroism.

Though the literary legends surrounding King Arthur were composed in Christian times, many scholars, like Matthews, contend that some of the themes in Arthurian legends may have come from an attempt to portray older Celtic traditions. Therefore, Arthurian legends blend often imagined Celtic tradition with Christian belief, though some aspects resonant with actual Celtic tenets more than others. As Loomis states "there are scholars who deny altogether that Arthurian romance is constructed out of the ruins of a pagan Pantheon" (4), but he states that there are far more who acknowledge some connection to paganism in Arthurian legend (4). For instance, "the Grail heroes, Gawain, Lancelot, Boors, Perceval, and Galaad, all may … have descended into Arthurian romance from the realms of Celtic mythology" (Loomis 156). Loomis argues that the women in Arthurian legend also repeatedly serve to test the heroes, as they often do in Celtic myth, to aid many Arthurian heroes in attaining botanical heroism.

Nature in Arthurian legends also serves to bring some Arthurian heroes close to botanical heroism. The legend of *Sir Gawain and the Green Knight* undoubtedly points to the importance of nature, and in doing this, the myth might again be purposely attempting to recount Celtic principles in regard to nature, but more significantly, the role of nature within this myth serves to instruct Gawain on elements needed to attain botanical heroism. In this myth an enormous green knight appears during King Arthur's New Year's festivities in Camelot and challenges The Knights of the Round Table to chop off his head; the catch is that in one year's time, the person who does the deed must be ready to also lose his head by the hand of the Green Knight. None of the knights take up the Green Knight's offer, so King Arthur is forced to accept the gruesome challenge. This causes Gawain to stand and remark that he will indeed accept the challenge on the behalf of King Arthur. Gawain lifts the Green Knight's axe and decapitates him, but the Green Knight merely bends over, picks up his head, and tells Gawain he will see him in one year's time.

Already the myth presents important botanical aspects, as the appearance of the Green Knight suggests natural references:

> Then into the hall comes a frightening figure,
> He must have been taller than anyone in the world....
> But more than anything
> His color amazed them....
> The whole of him bright green....
> In his hand he held a branch of holly
> That is greenest of all when the groves are bare,
> And an axe in the other hand, huge and monstrous [*Sir Gawain* 15–7].

The Green Knight's color suggests that he is tied to vegetation, as does the fact that the Green Knight's head, once severed, can continue to speak, suggesting that he is tied to the regenerative, botanical aspects of nature. In addition, the heralding of one year where Gawain will lose his head ties the myth to the cycles of the seasons.

Gawain must leave Camelot and transgress into a dark and, to him, foreboding forest, where he must contend with wild and unharnessed nature, and true to the archetypal heroic journey, this environment, that he must enter into alone, is quite different from his realm of experience, and thus represents to him the mythic otherworld:

> Many nights he spends by himself, with no one...
> [He] rides ... into the wilderness of Wirral, where there were few living....
> The knight followed strange roads
> Across many a wild hill....
> So many marvels the man met on those mountains....
> Sometimes he fights with dragons, and with wolves....
> And at other times with bulls and bears and wild boars....
> Thus in peril and hardship and the risk of his life
> This knight rides through that region until Christmas Eve, alone [*Sir Gawain* 51–3].

Gawain chooses to take with him a significant artifact that also might add meaning to the myth—his shield that portrays a pentacle on one side, a symbol that some connect with both Celtic belief and Christianity, and a picture of the Virgin Mary on the other, an overtly Christian reference. This shield might mark, at least in part, a message within the myth that points to Gawain wrestling between two faiths, an older Celtic religion and the new religion of Christianity.

Eventually Gawain makes his way to a castle where Lady and Lord Bertilak reside; this castle is also located in "the depths of the forest so wild he marveled at it" (*Sir Gawain* 53). Invited to stay as a guest before he finds the Green Knight's chapel, Gawain enters into a situation with Lady Bertilak that will test his Christian faith. Lord Bertilak asks Gawain to partake in a wager where the two men trade whatever spoils they get each night Gawain stays at the castle, and Sir Gawain agrees. Lord Bertilak is gone three consecutive nights hunting, and each morning when he returns, he gives Gawain the game he killed on the hunt. Sir Gawain spent each of the three knights with Lady Bertilak who tried her best to seduce Gawain each night, but still each morning, Gawain had to return what spoils he received in the night, so each morning Gawain must kiss Lord Bertilak as Lady Bertilak kissed him. Gawain passes this test, but fails the most important challenge. On the third night, Lady Bertilak kissed Gawain three times but also gave him a magic girdle that enables him to remain free from harm. Knowing that he will have to soon face the Green Knight's challenge, Gawain decides to keep the spoil of the girdle for himself, only kissing Lord Bertilak three times, and thus breaks his promise to Lord Bertilak.

Gawain leaves the Bertilaks' castle and finds the chapel of the Green Knight, which is presented as simply a mound covered by foliage within the forest:

> He looked around him and saw it was a wild place
> With no signs of a shelter to be seen anywhere....
> Then off in an open glade he saw what might be a mound...
> It had a hole at the end and on either side,
> And thick matted grass had grown all over it.
> And inside it was all hollow, only an old cave [*Sir Gawain* 149].

And here at this immensely wild abode, Gawain finds the Green Knight standing outside his home sharpening his axe. Gawain walks up to the Green Knight and offers his head. The Green Knight swings his axe two times, but each time just rests the axe upon Gawain's neck, but the third swing, the Green Knight brings the axe down hard enough upon Gawain's neck that it cuts his skin just enough to leave a mark. The Green Knight then stands before Gawain and remarks that he knows Gawain is wearing a magic girdle, and because of this Gawain has broken his solemn vow to the Green Knight and to Lord Bertilak. Knights of the Round Table pride themselves on being honest as well as brave, and so Gawain knows that in lying, he has failed himself and Arthur. However, this failure is not the most significant part of the myth. Gawain's failure, according to a Christian interpretation of the myth, comes in him choosing to wear the girdle that makes it clear that he fears death. This point of the myth suggests that Gawain, instead of adhering fully to the Christian faith that promises that righteous behavior in life will lead to an afterlife of bliss, falters and maintains a connection with Celtic religion. The Celts believed that the soul resided within the head of a person. Though this text was written by a Christian author hundreds of years after Christianity became the dominant faith over Celtic religion, the text and its use of Celtic symbols, most distinctly the focus on beheading, suggests that the author had at least some limited knowledge of Celtic faith. When Gawain chooses the magic girdle and deception over dying a noble death in order to save his head, it suggests that he values an older, more traditional faith, which shows him failing in Christian terms, but perhaps succeeding in Celtic or botanical terms. The Celts believed that a close tie with the natural world was essential, and this myth still holds remnants that point towards a respect of Celtic belief systems, but more succinctly, towards nature.

The experience with the Green Knight is revealed to be set up by Arthur's half-sister Morgan Le Faye, another apparently Celtic representation (Loomis 5), who the text describes as:

> Morgan the Goddess...
> There is no power one can possess
> That she cannot tame [*Sir Gawain* 167].

Loomis states that Morgan Le Faye is referred to as a "Goddess" in *Sir Gawain and the Green Knight,* which points to her role as a Celtic nature representative (192). In many Arthurian legends Morgan Le Faye also holds the ability to heal Arthur of various wounds, which is another trait given to many Celtic Earth Goddesses. Loomis also connects Morgan Le Faye to the Lady of the Lake as "originally the same person" (193). Morgan Le Faye's mastery over the lesson both Gawain and the other Knights learn within this legend signals again a female, perhaps Earth Goddess representative, who instructs mythic heroes on the teachings of the natural environment.

Gawain, after his encounter with the Green Knight, always wears his green magic girdle in order to remind him of the lesson he learned from the Green Knight. In addition, Arthur and all of the other Knights of the Round Table also wear green girdles forevermore. Again, the symbolism of the Green Knight is overtly connected with that of nature. His color, his chapel as a hill within the recesses of nature, his ability to die and be resurrected, and of course his connection to Morgan Le Faye's mysticism all serve as reminders to Gawain and King Arthur's court of the importance of respecting nature, allowing Gawain to internalize the tenets of botanical heroism.

The otherworld, a common tenet in Celtic mythology and Arthurian legend, also allows some Arthurian heroes to become botanical heroes. A famous tale of Arthur and the otherworld is captured in the Welsh *Mabinogion,* entitled "The Lady of the Well." This myth shows the character of Owain finding the otherworld through a series of natural representations. Owain seeks out this mystical place after hearing of the failure of another knight who tried the journey. Owain finds that first he must traverse extreme wilderness before he can find his goal, again a common theme for Arthurian legends. Owain seeks a knight who guards a sacred well, and again the concept of a sacred well makes this legend reminiscent of Celtic mythology. Owain finds the well and the knight, and throws water over a slab of rock that protects the well and finds that a great storm is produced with enormous hail that almost kills him. Owain survives this natural obstacle and goes on to fight the knight, killing him. This act initiates Owain's immersion into the otherworld.

Owain goes to a mysterious castle and marries the widowed queen, the Lady of the Well, widow of the very same knight he killed. Her household has quintessential aspects of the otherworld, as food is always abundant there for example. Owain upon marrying the Lady of the Well becomes himself the defender of the well, taking over the duties of the man he killed. Owain defends the well for three years when Arthur comes looking for Owain, and Owain, unbeknownst to both parties battles one of the Knights of the Round Table in order to defend the well. When the two realize their identities, Owain goes with Arthur back to Camelot, promising that he will return to his wife in three months, but again, as with stories of the otherworld, immersion back into one's former life proves difficult once one leaves. Owain, in Camelot, finds that he completely forgets his former existence and stays with Arthur for three years, until a maiden comes to Arthur's court and scolds Owain for his deception to the Lady of the Well. Suddenly, Owain remembers what he left behind.

Owain again partakes on a journey away from the known existence of Camelot to embrace a life that is full of uncertainty, and again, clear representations of nature dominate the scenes. Owain, enters into a life as a wild man immersed within the deep wilderness of the mountains; "he wandered about like this until all his clothes disintegrated and his body all but gave out and long hair grew all over him; and he would keep company with wild animals and feed with them until they were used to him" (*Mabinogion* 131). This motif of the myth suggests the element of the botanical heroic journey where the botanical hero must lose his or her identity in an embrace of the importance of nature.

Slowly Owain adopts a new identity, which serves as a symbolic rebirth for him. His immersion and connection to the wild transformed him, so that the myth closes with him preferring to remain in the remote wilderness; "Owain wanted nothing except to travel the remote and uninhabited regions of the world" (*Mabinogion* 133). He soon encounters a lion that befriends him, and from this point on, any conquest Owain faces can only be accomplished with the help of this lion, which serves as another representation of Owain's new identity that is at one with nature. When Owain accepts the lion as an essential part of himself, he fully enters his new identity and is permitted to be reunited with the Lady of the Well, staying with her forever, and becoming a true botanical hero.

It is the tales of the Arthurian Knights' quest for the Holy Grail that are among the most popular of the Arthurian legends. The Holy Grail was said to be the container used by Jesus Christ at the Last Supper when he and his disciples met before Christ's crucifixion. Mythically Joseph of Arimathea was said to have saved the cup, caught Christ's blood within the Grail at the crucifixion, and taken it with him to France or England. Because it contained the blood of Christ, the Holy Grail was said to hold healing properties, thus becoming an icon to initiate the quests of many of the Knights of the Round Table. Loomis states that the Grail legends may also have connections to Celtic practices and "are a mystifying compound of mythological tests" (269). Again, central to the importance of the Grail legends, is that the Grail serves as a representation of "the vitality of nature" (Loomis 269). The Arthurian Holy Grail is portrayed as quite similar to the Celtic belief in sacred wells, or cauldrons, such as the "'Cauldron of Rebirth,' which restored the dead to life" (Wood 37). Mystical cauldrons are a common element in Celtic myth, often portraying, as MacLeod states "healing," "transformation," or "wisdom" (143). The Welsh *Mabinogion* presents the myth of Bran being defeated in battle by an opponent, King Matholwch of Ireland, because he possesses a mystical cauldron that holds the power to bring back to life any deceased person who is placed inside it, and so he revives each of his deceased warriors so that they may fight again. Therefore, tales of the Holy Grail, when connected to Celtic conceptions of death and renewal, help to identify the heroes of Arthurian Grail myths as potentially learning the crux of botanical heroism—the natural lesson of life, death, and rebirth.

Loomis also connects the Grail encounters to scenes reminiscent of the Celtic otherworld (158). For example, Perceval's story of discovering the Grail relies heavily upon images found in many versions of the Celtic otherworld. First of all, Perceval finds the Grail in a castle that is hidden away within a vast wilderness while he was looking for his mother who was raised in the deep wilderness of Wales. True to Celtic myths of the otherworld, Perceval only is able to find the castle when he stops looking for it. Perceval, thought to be only a "pure fool," finds that it is the Fisher King who lives within the castle and protects the Grail. The castle, though, is full of mystery. Instead of being in a place that Perceval expected, perhaps a place ordained as holy, it seems ominous. The Fisher King himself is suffering from an old wound that will not heal. At dinner that evening a procession appears where a young man holds a bleeding lance, supposedly the spear that pierced Christ at his crucifixion; two men carry branched candlesticks, and finally a young woman enters holding the Grail. Perceval, finally attaining his goal, finds that he is immersed within an otherworld environment. Instead of being forthright and asking what the items are, even though it appears part of him knows they are the holy relics, he merely sits there speechless. This is important because it shows that the quest is not about attaining the Grail. The Grail, again a possible connection to the Celtic concept of the Cauldron of Rebirth as discussed in the Welsh myth of Bran, holds mystical properties of restoring youth to the old and health to the sick. As an element of rebirth and rejuvenation, the Grail becomes a representation of the processes of nature to continually restore all that it has taken in death. Perceval being rendered speechless shows his reverence of nature. Perceval, though he sometimes gets attributed as being a "pure fool," perhaps is able to see the Grail precisely because he could not speak in its presence, which might reveal his knowledge that he is insignificant in the scope of nature. As Barnes states, "after years of journeys ... of all the Knights of the Round Table ... the secret of life and death was ... seen ... by a simpleton" (216); therefore, the meaning of the Grail "was the transformation that comes from heading into the cauldron, the fires of life," so that the "Grail would always be here and there and everywhere" as a symbol of rebirth for the everyman (Barnes 218).

The next morning Perceval wakes up and finds that he is alone at the castle, and that his mother has died. Arthur instructs Perceval to return to Camelot, but once there a mysterious elderly woman appears and admonishes Perceval for his reluctance to ask what the significance of the items were; she claims that his inability to speak did not heal the wounded Fisher King. The myth centers on life and death. Perceval left his mother's lifestyle within nature to enter into Arthur's Camelot, and it is significant that in order to find his mother once more, he enters the deep wilderness, and it is there that he learns this important lesson of regeneration. Though he failed to ask about the items when faced with them, the myth suggests that this does not matter. By not asking about the sacred items, he only forfeited his chance to see the regenerative properties of the Grail. Not asking about the Grail might suggest Perceval's acknowledgment of the necessity of death, signaling him as a possible botanical hero because he shows an understanding of nature's necessary processes of life and death. The night he did not speak was the same night his mother presumably died, and these events are intricately tied within the myth, suggesting that Perceval has learned that the Grail is capable of regeneration, but that death is a requirement for this natural process.

Other Arthurian legends show Lancelot, who helped to cause the downfall of Arthur's kingdom by his love of Guinevere, as being reared by the Lady of Lake, revealing that again the mystical female, as a representation of nature is responsible for giving Arthur his power, but also in taking it away, which might also point to Arthur himself as being a botanical hero. The Lady of Lake made Arthur promise that upon taking her sword and sheath that he would one day give her a favor—the favor turned out to be that her adoptive son, Lancelot, should become a Knight of the Round Table, though of course he would be in large part responsible for the demise of Arthur and Camelot. After Arthur, and his trusted knight Gawain seek out Lancelot after he saved Guinevere from burning for her infidelity with Lancelot, a fate Arthur hesitatingly approved of for his disloyal wife, he finds that his son, who he thinks is his nephew, Mordred, has taken over his kingdom. Upon rushing back to retrieve his throne, Arthur finds himself in a ferocious battle that ends with almost all of his knights dead, him killing Mordred, and Mordred mortally wounding him. Arthur instructs Sir Bedivere, his sole remaining knight, to throw Excalibur back into the lake, as a possible symbolic representation of the botanical hero acknowledging the superior role nature plays in the lives of all heroes, similar to the gold hoards of both Beowulf and Sigurd being rightfully placed back into natural environments. Arthur received the means for him to be king from the gift of the natural representation of the Lady of the Lake, and at his death, it is to her that he must return the sword and sheath. Arthur is then taken back to the Lady of the Lake where she and three other women take him in a boat and row away. As Allan and Phillips state of the Lady of the Lake, her Celtic origins are clear; "she preserved the memory of the healing water spirits of earlier times" (48), and so therefore, Arthur's return to her as a nature representative could signal him as a botanical hero. In addition, Arthur is believed upon death to enter the mythical otherworld of Avalon, and again Avalon, though a late edition to Arthurian legend, still "echoes of much earlier beliefs about.... Islands of the Blessed" from Celtic mythology (Allan & Phillips, *World*, 114), that also connect him to botanical heroism, as this mythic locale foreshadows Arthur's resurrection and speaks towards the regenerating promises of nature, just as the Grail myths did.

The Arthurian legends' connection to Celtic myth reveals a great deal of importance on the role that nature places within the legends, but the lasting legacy of the myths of Arthur and their tie with nature may simply come from the fact that nature always holds an important connection to the lives of humans, and thus it is used as a mythic tool to understand the cycle of human lives. Mythically, it is believed that Arthur will be healed in Avalon and will come back to his empire when he is needed. King Arthur himself may not be entirely a botanical hero because he arguably remains tied to aspects that define his selfhood as overtly important. This portrayal of death and promised resurrection of Arthur certainly points to archetypes of the processes of botanical nature, but the identification of Arthur as superior to his subjects seems to define him with too much singular importance to be recognized as reaching a state of spiritual apotheosis. Moreover, it is often Arthur's knights, and not himself, who mostly embark on heroic quests within Arthurian legend, so they, and not Arthur, may be portrayed as coming closer than their king to representations of true botanical heroes.

More than the heroes presented in this chapter, many myths of the botanical hero put additional focus on the necessity of the hero facing the underworld as a means to contend with his or her own insignificance and mortality in order to come to a full understanding of botanical wisdom. This aspect of the mythic underworld within the botanical heroic journey will be the focus of the next chapter.

CHAPTER 2

Caves and the Underworld

"The cave you fear to enter holds the treasure you seek."—Joseph Campbell

"I only went out for a walk, and finally concluded to stay out till sundown, for going out, I found, was really going in."—John Muir

The chthonic realm of the underworld often is portrayed within myth as the place that houses the deceased according to many cultural belief systems. What is significant is that in almost all versions of the ancient underworld, it was not conceived of as a place of evil, but rather a natural realm where the dead return. The underworld is often identified as a region within the recesses of the earth, such as a cave, as in Eleusis in Greece, where Persephone was said to be dragged into the underworld by Hades and where initiates enacted sacred rituals meant to instruct them about the factuality of their own mortality. Sometimes, the entrance of the underworld was imagined as a body of water, like Lake Avernus near Campania in Italy, where Romans long believed one could reach the underworld beneath the water. The natural location of the realm of death signals an important aspect of the underworld's meaning within mythology. As discussed in the introduction, the underworld locale within the earth connects it to many myths from nature-dependent cultures that portray the realm of death in natural terms with womb-like references, where life emerges but also must return upon death. The creation of human beings often was mythically depicted in many nature-dependent societies using birth imagery out of the earth itself, as many of the first beings in world myth emerged from directly out of the ground, like the American Indian Navajo creation myth displays; therefore, in many myths birth and death are portrayed as interconnected within the underworld in an endless cycle of regeneration. Thus, the underworld, when viewed in natural terms, depicts the inevitable progression of nature's cycles.

Also, as discussed in the introduction, many rituals were conducted in underground caves or man-made stone structures to instruct initiates on views

70

related to the temporality of death for all beings within nature. Many locales, such as the Ness of Brodgard in the Orkney Islands of Scotland, were thought to be part of ritual landscapes designed to link the living with the dead through ritualistic processions meant to give initiates a representation of nature's promise of annual renewal upon death that applied equally to crops, animals, and humans alike. In Greece, the Eleusinian Mysteries were meant to also provide initiates an experience thought to be related to death and rebirth. By partaking in the rituals at Eleusis, it is believed that initiates "had entered into the mystery of life, death, and *the return* .... The profound gift of the goddess Demeter was the promise of life beyond the grave, a rebirth" (Barnes 197).

The underworld is often mythically portrayed as a place in which one can journey into and out of its depths. Shamans in many nature-dependent communities often are described as journeying to the underworld in order to help an individual community member or the tribe as a whole. There are also many myths of divine transgressors into the underworld; these myths show that even divine beings must concede their own illusions of self-importance and accept the laws of nature. The Greek Demeter, for example, demands the return of her daughter Persephone from the clutches of Hades, but Demeter must relinquish her divine power to accept the natural cycle, as mythically portrayed by her daughter Persephone annually dying, but also resurrecting each year. Therefore, the mythic underworld motif, whether it be told through the representation of a shaman, divine being, or mythic hero, often signifies a transformation of the protagonist in accordance to the cycles of nature.

One crucial component of the underworld experience is fear. The mythic underworld can be defined as such if it induces terror in the hero, so quite often the underworld is portrayed as holding elements, such as ferocious monsters, the spirits of the dead, dreamscapes of personal loss, visions of defeat, or most integral, visions of the death of the hero. The underworld serves to transform the botanical heroic journey into a spiritual quest because its terrifying elements force the hero to ultimately let go of his or her autonomous identity. The underworld often teaches the botanical hero that no matter what, his or her identity will be wiped away forever upon his or her inevitable death. However, in correlation with nature-dependent belief systems, those who journey into the underworld within myth often show that the underworld also serves as a place that is necessary for producing renewed life.

Stepping into the Cave—Perseus and Medusa

The Greek myth of Perseus and Medusa is believed to date further back than Homer and Hesiod. The many versions of this myth present an underworld experience for the hero Perseus that is extremely terrifying. The appearance of the gorgon, and more specifically Medusa, is historically complex in ancient Greece. Some Greek sources identify gorgons as giants birthed by Gaia and defeated by the Olympians. Athena also wears the face, and in some renditions the skin, of the gorgon Medusa in her myriad representations. The portrayal of the snake is shown quite often in Greek art from the Minoan, Mycenaean, Archaic, and Hellenic periods as a symbolic representation of the chthonic, as snakes can be venomous, causing almost instantaneous death. Snakes also slither close to the ground, inhabit caves, and can go within the earth during winter and come out again in spring, which understandably makes them symbols of the chthonic in their ability to seemingly transgress into and out of the underworld. Snakes as chthonic figures are also symbols of death, so they are often depicted within myths as terrifying, just as the myth of Perseus shows Medusa to be. However, the snake was also a symbol of natural regeneration presumably because of its ability to go dormant in winter and then "resurrect" each spring, as well as its ability to periodically shed its skin and symbolically regenerate a new self, representing the cycles of nature that dominate myth—birth, death, and rebirth. It is this regenerative quality of the snake that adds more to the classic telling of the myth of Perseus and Medusa.

In addition, as previously discussed, Barnes contends that snakes often referred to Pre-Olympian belief systems; she states that serpents were "vestigial symbols, carryovers from an earlier age when the women in Crete and perhaps Thebes had serpents coiled around their heads" (163); therefore, they were used symbolically by Greek bards to refer back to matriarchal belief systems (Barnes 163). The symbol of the serpent, as discussed with the myth of Jason and Medea, was well known to the ancient Greeks as a sacred symbol in connection to the Neolithic Mother/Earth Goddess, so transforming her symbol was often a vital task within mythology meant to reeducate audiences. The symbol of the serpent either had to be eradicated and replaced by new male-oriented divine authority, or the symbol had to be incorporated into the ownership of the new authority.

The account of the Perseus myth is outlined most completely in versions by Apollodorus and later Ovid. The Perseus myth presents the Greek hero Perseus as the son of Zeus and a mortal woman, Danaë. Zeus was said to copulate with Danaë as a shower of gold; this natural reference connected to Perseus' birth signals his role as holding some of the components of a botanical hero. Perseus is the rightful heir to the throne of Argos, but because of an oracle that decreed that Perseus would one day kill the current king, Acrisius, his own grandfather, he is exiled with his mother in a wooden chest that is set afloat in the Aegean Sea for both of them to die. Here again, there is evidence of the early importance of nature upon the character of Perseus, as even as an infant he must depend on the natural domain of the sea in order to survive. Perseus and Danaë are found by a fisherman on the island of Serifos, who takes them to the island's king, Polydectes. Years later King Polydectes falls in love with Danaë, though Perseus feels that he is unworthy of his mother. Because of Perseus' disdain, King Polydectes plots to send Perseus far away from his kingdom by convincing Perseus to seek the head of the gorgon Medusa.

Therefore, Perseus leaves behind his known community to venture upon his heroic quest. Upon his journey he encounters a valuable helper, again a common mythic archetype, Athena, who instructs him that he must seek out the far recesses of the known world, the sacred Garden of the Hesperides, where the triad goddesses live amongst the trees that harbor the fruit of Hera. Mythically, as discussed in the myth of Jason and the Argonauts, Hera also left the serpent Ladon there to guard her precious apples. It is significant that Perseus must venture to this faraway place that clearly demonstrates unfettered natural imagery. The symbols of the Garden of the Hesperides are numerous. First because it is mythically described at the edge of the known world, the Garden for Perseus becomes the mythic archetype of the otherworld. Fitting to its role of the otherworld, it is teeming with verdant nature, quite unlike its depleted depiction in the *Argonautica* because in the myth of Perseus, Ladon is still alive. The myth states that Perseus must enter the otherworld of the Garden of the Hesperides in order to obtain the weapons needed to defeat Medusa. He is said to successfully make it to the Garden because of the information he received from the three Graeae, and once there, he obtains a sack to contain Medusa's powerful severed head, a sword from Zeus, and the helm of darkness from Hades that will allow him to remain invisible when needed. Again, the myth suggests that in first needing to go to this natural otherworld environment to obtain the tools required to be successful, he is gaining more than physical artifacts to help him kill Medusa; instead, Perseus in gaining wisdom that is connected to nature's laws.

The mythic tie to perhaps earlier Neolithic belief systems in Earth Goddesses, as here seemingly presented as Hera who values her sacred apples so much that she leaves the massive serpent Ladon in charge of guarding them, is significant to Perseus' role within the myth. As discussed since Minoan times, the symbols of snakes have often been connected to the conception of a Mother Earth Goddess. In having the snake Ladon, a symbol that is often associated with death and the underworld, protect the sacred apples, mythic symbolism suggests that when Perseus enters into this sacred garden he will gain the wisdom needed to finish his quest as a botanical hero precisely because the knowledge that he obtains from the Garden of the Hesperides will be tied to both nature and its laws of death.

Once Perseus receives his lesson in the Garden of the Hesperides, he is ready to venture into the next stage of his quest—the symbolic underworld, and here it meets all requirements of terror. Perseus enters the lair of Medusa and her gorgon sisters alone, as most heroes must be solitary when they enter the realm of death. The gorgon's lair, again with its many snakes, presents clear underworld imagery, as Perseus is depicted as venturing within the earth to face what could easily be his imminent death. According to the myth, the gorgon's lair is a place that no mortal has survived, and Perseus must contend with seeing the stony remains of the men who came before him to try and defeat Medusa presented around every corner. Perseus, in viewing only death within the inner realms of the earth, is fully learning the laws of nature. In his terrifying experience within his respective underworld of Medusa's lair, he sees that he will one day assuredly die as all those before him have died because of their contact with the gorgons.

The myth of Perseus details that he enters the gorgons' lair, and using a mirror, or some versions state his polished shield, he is able to see that Medusa is sleeping, so he easily cuts off her head without a fight at all. From Medusa's severed head, Pegasus, the winged horse, and Chrysaor, a warrior of the gilded sword, emerge, said to be the offspring of the god Poseidon. The noise of the situation awakens Medusa's two gorgon sisters who try to seek out the murderer but cannot see Perseus as he wears the cap of invisibility from Hades, so Perseus is able, again easily, to escape their wrath. Wilk points out that though Perseus is revered, he does not seem to embody the qualities expected of a hero; "Perseus—armed to the teeth with miraculous aids from a plethora of supernatural entities, slaying the monster as she sleeps, and then escaping by donning a cap of invisibility—doesn't seem terribly heroic" (90). In addition, the ease of Perseus' task of killing Medusa, and his subsequent success of saving the princess Andromeda, who was chained to a rock and offered to a giant sea monster to offset Poseidon's wrathful decree that he would cause a great flood for being dishonored, also signals to audiences that Perseus may not be a true hero, and certainly not a botanical hero.

Most Greek heroes must face struggle, not only success, in order to hold the status of hero, and to an extent this strife often aids some Greek heroes in attaining botanical heroism. Perseus does experience hardship within his later mythic life, as Perseus accidently kills his grandfather, King Acrisius, by throwing a discus that kills him at athletic games that he was partaking in, thus fulfilling the prophecy Acrisius feared. Perseus, having accidently killed Acrisius, does not want to be the king of Argos, so he trades kingdoms with his cousin Megapenthes and rules Tiryns for many years, but according to Greek custom, even an accidental death must be avenged, so Megapenthes ends up murdering

Perseus. Though the end of Perseus' mythic life shows him as experiencing hardship, his myths still do not present him as a true botanical hero. Perseus is said, upon his death, to have been commemorated by the Olympians by being transformed into a constellation, and though this projection of him does serve to connect him to natural elements, the myth of Perseus does not offer information that suggests that he was spiritually transformed as a result of his heroic journey, which may signal other messages found within the myth.

The gorgons, of which there are usually three depicted, were said to be immortal, except for Medusa, who could be killed; they were most often mythically portrayed as having "scaly heads, boar's tusks, brazen hands, and wings. They had protruding tongues, glaring eyes, and serpents wrapped around their waists as belts" (Wilk 87). The gorgons, most specifically Medusa, must be horrific to view, so terrifying that those who view them turn to stone, because they serve as a representation of the fear of death. Some depictions of the myth of Medusa depict her as once angering Athena, so she was turned from a beautiful mortal woman into her monstrous form, but this appears a revised version of a much more ancient mythic being. Frothingham contends that archeological evidence supports that Medusa may have been originally worshipped as an Earth Goddess. Frothingham points to a depiction of her at Corfu that shows her among many animals, most notable are lions that stand subdued next to her; "Medusa is conceived here as the Great Mother. As both a serpent goddess and a mistress of beasts" (357). Frothingham continues to state that this depiction in Corfu suggests that Medusa played a vital role in the battle between the Olympic pantheon and the primordial giants; "One fact is certain, Medusa occupies the centre as a great goddess … she was the equivalent of the Cybele, Artemis or Great Mother, who is accompanied by or holds lions or birds" (357). Frothingham also connects evidence of Medusa as a remnant of Earth Goddess worship in Crete. In Crete a temple was found dating from the sixth century BCE that depicts two antefixes that portray gorgons; the first shows typical gorgon features as horrific, but the second, possibly from an earlier period, shows a beautiful gorgon:

> She is represented on the antefix to below the waist, and there are four snakes; two she holds in her hands and two spring from behind her shoulders. There are no snakes connected with the hair…. The mouth is open and the tongue protrudes, but no teeth are indicated…. In the Crete of that time it would seem, therefore, as if Medusa … was … the same as the old mother snake goddess of the Minoans [Frothingham 364].

Therefore, Frothingham states that "Medusa was not an evil demon … but primarily a nature goddess … a procreative and fertilizing energy … an embodiment of the productive and destructive forces of [nature]. After dominating in pre–Hellenic times, she was given in later times a subordinate part in the

Olympian system" (349). Campbell concurs by stating that "the legend of Perseus beheading Medusa means, specifically, that the Hellenes overran the Earth Goddesses' chief shrines and stripped their priestesses of their Gorgon masks, the latter being apotropaic faces worn to frighten away the profane. That is to say, there occurred in the early thirteenth century BC[E] an actual historic rupture, a sort of sociological trauma, which has been registered in this myth" (*Occidental*, 152–3). Barnes declares that the belief systems of the Minoans were "unintentionally ... carried forward by the very myths that were intended to dispose of them" (10). Many Greek legends recount tales where male protagonists defeat serpents meant to be associated with traditional belief systems of Goddess worship; for example, Apollo kills the serpent Python and Herakles kills the serpent Ladon. However, Wilk does not concur with Frothingham, Campbell, Barnes, and Eisler, arguing that there is not enough research to declare the gorgon as a representation of Earth Goddess worship, but Wilk does insist that the artistic depiction of the face of the gorgon is meant to demonstrate the face of death; it is "the decaying head of someone dead for a period ranging from a few days to one or two weeks" showing "bulging eyes, which look like a parody of a stare; grossly protruding tongue ... revealing the rictus grin" (Wilk 225–6). Whether the Medusa is a symbolic mythic element to remind audiences of traditional Earth Goddess worship is not of primary importance and does not lessen the message of the myth in its relation to the cycles of nature. Medusa as a representative of the laws of nature is the true element that Perseus must contend with.

Perseus does not seem very heroic when put into botanical terms, which suggests, like in the myth of Jason, that there are other messages presented within this myth. Jason's myth displays most vividly the character of Medea, who arguably steals the show. Medea is the botanical hero of Jason's myth because she knows well the lessons of the natural world and attempts to teach them to Jason, but Jason fails his own botanical heroic quest because he is unwilling to heed her knowledge of nature and its necessary cycles. Similarly, Perseus arguably fails his botanical heroic quest, even though he obtains intimate knowledge of the underworld, because he fails to internalize the true immensity of Medusa and her lair. The myth of Perseus seems to be only a social construction created to eradicate the ideology of nature worship. Therefore, it becomes clear that Perseus, like Jason, does not embrace the necessary lessons of nature's cycles; instead, Perseus attempts to simply ignore them, by quickly killing the sleeping Medusa before he could stare into the horror of her being.

Like the terrifying face of the Indian Kirtimukha that hangs above many temples in India to remind onlookers that life encapsulates both horror and bliss, the myth of Perseus suggests that if he would have looked at Medusa, he would have witnessed the laws of nature, most specifically his own death, but because he does not look into her eyes and merely cuts off her head and places it into his sack, he misses the transformative power the underworld provides and does not become a botanical hero.

The Only Way Out Is Through the Labyrinth— Theseus and Ariadne

Similarly the Greek myth of Theseus and the Minotaur, recorded by Plutarch and other Greek and Roman authors, such as Catullus and Ovid, showcases the necessity of a horrific underworld to the journey of the hero, but again, this myth presents only a partially realized botanical hero. Young Theseus of Athens volunteers to save his city, so that twelve Athenian youths can be spared from their destiny of being shipped to Crete to be sacrificed to the Minotaur, a creature who is half bull and half man.

The labyrinth is a symbolic underworld for Theseus as it represents death and becomes Theseus' time to face his own mortality. From the moment that Theseus walks into the labyrinth, he is appropriately filled with terror. The labyrinth is completely dark; it smells of death, and as the giant doors close locking Theseus within, he knows there is no way for him to escape this terrible task.

Theseus' heroic journey provides a good example of the quintessential psychological journey of the hero into his or her own unconscious. One imagines that Theseus is initially confused as to where to go within the labyrinth, much like the challenge of facing the unconscious. The myth suggests that the Minotaur, waiting in the dark recesses of the unknown, is something all people may have within themselves, and this signals that Theseus may be symbolically battling with elements of his own identity rather than a real monster, and therefore, could be a good candidate for botanical heroism. Because the Minotaur may be a representation of the wild or animalistic nature within all human beings, his labyrinthine existence might suggest more of a psychological process for the transgressor, in this case, Theseus, than an event made to rid the world of an evil adversary, and many renditions of the myth supports this as they make it hard to view the Minotaur as evil. Once Theseus finds and gruesomely slays the Minotaur, some versions present the creature as looking momentarily more like a man than a monster after he has died. R. Armstrong states that the Roman Catullus portrays the death of the Minotaur in sympathetic terms as he "resembles a great tree falling.... The Minotaur's heroism and humanity are [therefore] delicately asserted" (89). The whole scenario is mystifying and confusing, and this is what adds depth to the message of the myth. Theseus seems heroic because he is portrayed as brave enough to face the dreaded Minotaur, but the nebulous portrayal of the real savagery of the Minotaur forces audiences to question if Theseus is really a hero for brutally killing the Minotaur. R. Armstrong states that, "the real cruelty in Catullus ... is perpetrated by Theseus and not by the Minotaur, who comes to be identified ... as one of the victims of the hero's sense of his own glory" (90). R. Armstrong also asserts that "what is usually left understated, an undercurrent of sympathy for the monster and disapproval of the behavior of men, can sometimes rush to the surface, leaving us with a world reversed, where the heroic, civilizing forces struggle to retain their accustomed praises and position in the right" (92). Furthermore, the background associated with this myth brings in elements that will continue to test Theseus' botanical heroism.

This myth presents a long history of intrigue connected to the Minotaur and the island of Crete. The fact that the Minotaur was born half bull and half human, after his mother Pasiphaë, wife of King Minos, and daughter of Helios, the sun, could not overcome her lust for a prized bull, points to a mythic representation of the animalistic nature in humanity, as well as to the cultural history upon the island of Crete. The myth states that King Minos fails to sacrifice a pure white bull Poseidon sends to him, preferring to keep it for himself, so he sacrifices a lesser bull. Enraged, Poseidon demands retribution, which comes when Pasiphaë, with the help of Eros, falls in love with the bull meant for Poseidon, so she disguises herself as a cow in a costume made by Daedalus, designer of the labyrinth, has sex with the bull and is then impregnated by the bull, eventually giving birth to the Minotaur.

As Barnes states, "for millennia Minos and Pasiphaë have been stand-ins for all that was bad in Crete and that the Athenians and the Greeks were meant to replace" (101). In reference to this, many scholars believe that the myth of the Minotaur at least in part discusses the Minoan culture from Crete being reduced mythically to a demoted position, as the representation of the bull in Crete, as well as in places like Çatal Hüyük, is often portrayed alongside Mother Goddess representations (Eisler 22). Conway supports this view with his statement that "The Minotaur (which translated means bull of Minos) could be a literary demonization of Minoan political authority. The defeat of the Minotaur ... signals a reversal of power with the fall of the Minoans and the rise of the Mycenaean Greeks." Indeed there are many symbolic attributes within this myth that appear to be in part political propaganda against traditional belief systems. First of all, Europa, King Minos' mother, was originally a Phoenician princess who may have been connected to Astarte, the Phoenician moon goddess, but in the back story that leads to this myth, Europa is mythically related as a mortal woman who was drawn to a beautiful white bull, which was Zeus in disguise. The bull/Zeus was said to have carried Europa off into the sea and brought her to Crete, after raping and impregnating her, which resulted in the birth of King Minos.

In addition, Pasiphaë, who becomes wife of King Minos, was the daughter of the sun god Helios, and was also originally worshipped as a moon goddess on Crete, which suggests that her role within this myth may have been transformed to suit shifting political purposes. Pasiphaë was said to come from Colchis, also Medea's homeland, and like Medea, Pasiphaë was skilled in the knowledge of how to use the resources of nature for mystical purposes. When once discovering that her husband, King Minos, was unfaithful to her, she cast a spell upon him that made him ejaculate hideous creatures while in the throngs of his affairs that would destroy the mistresses, showing her power in connection to mystical agents. She was also said to have "wandered over the isolated and decidedly wild mountains in pursuit of her beloved bull"; she was "likened [by Ovid] to one of the followers of Bacchus" (R. Armstrong 98), suggesting a spiritual element to Pasiphaë's attraction to an animal, as followers of Dionysus/Bacchus, otherwise known as maenads, often are mythically described as entering into a transformative spiritual state because of their ability to release their inhibitions and embrace their wild, animalistic selves through such behavior as frenzied dancing, intoxication, orgies, etc. In some representations of the myth, Pasiphaë was described as having sex, not with a bull sent by Poseidon, but with the god Poseidon in the form of a bull, which also suggests that Pasiphaë's sexual act may at one time have held sacred meaning, as it involved a union with a divine being in animal form. Over time the myth became distorted, projecting King Minos' mother, Europa, as mating in a divine act with Zeus in bull form to produce King Minos, but then showing Pasiphaë as wrongly mating in a lascivious act with an actual bull in order to punish King Minos. In addition, bull worship has been well documented in Crete, and the symbolic exemplification of Pasiphaë's offspring, in monstrous bull form, wishing to devour the harmless youths of Athens, might also point to strife between Crete and Athens and reflect a memory of the cultural displacement of Minoan culture. Therefore, this myth should be analyzed with at least a consideration that remnants of themes associated with traditional, nature-dependent belief systems might exist within the myth, which can allow one to reexamine the characters in the myth to see if any of them appear as botanical heroes.

Theseus, is the character who would seem to be the best contender for the botanical hero of the myth, but Theseus, upon the completion of his mission, seems not to transform, which is a requirement of the botanical, and archetypal, hero after having experienced the mythic underworld. Theseus, like Perseus, goes into the symbolic underworld of the labyrinth, easily achieves his task, and again without much of a climax, as with Perseus' myth, comes out of his respective underworld mostly unchanged. Also like Perseus, Theseus only slays the one who inhabits this underworld, the Minotaur, because he accepts the societal label of the Minotaur as a monster, like Perseus only accepted Medusa's identification as a monster, but both the Minotaur and Medusa have mythic ambiguities that might suggest more importance to their characters, and these ambiguities, as discussed with Medusa, might point towards representations of traditional cultures that embraced nature as sacred, where human beings played a less dominant role within the eco-system.

As discussed, the mythic underworld is supposed to be a place where the botanical hero, through often symbolic representations, confronts the factuality of his or her own demise. The confrontation of mortality is essential in teaching the botanical hero the realistic workings of nature, thus allowing the botanical hero to self-actualize because he or she has redefined selfhood according to less important terms, as simply one part of nature, rather than by illusions of grandiosity. Like Perseus, though, Theseus seems not to grasp this vital component of the mythic underworld because he is not portrayed as fully contending with his own death when facing the Minotaur. Perseus did not look into the face of the Medusa, because if he had, he would have witnessed the full immensity of death; instead he used mystical agents that guided him swiftly through his mission without being transformed; similarly, Theseus fails to understand within the myth that the "monster" with the labyrinth may in fact represent parts of himself.

By easily slaying the Minotaur, he simply kills off, without embracing essential parts of his own selfhood, parts that are dark, animalistic, and maybe taboo, thus failing to achieve spiritual transformation because of his unification with all aspects of natural existence. If the Minotaur, at least partially, is mythically supposed to represent remnants of bull worship by Minoan culture, then Theseus, in only murdering the Minotaur and then fleeing the scene lauded by the Athenians as a hero, fails to grasp the intentional lessons of the nature-dependent Minoans.

As stated, there is evidence that the Minoans most likely worshipped Earth Goddesses and that the myriad representations of bulls in artifacts found throughout Crete, similar to those of other Neolithic communities like that of Çatal Hüyük, may represent male consorts who, at least symbolically or mythically, would die and be reborn annually. If the Minoans' veneration of the bull was linked to other Neolithic practices that depict Earth Goddesses and their respective male consorts, then the annual death of the bull, in at least symbolic or mythic sacrifice, since the only documented depiction of actual bull sacrifice in Minoan culture is displayed on the Hagia Triada sarcophagus that is dated after Minoan culture was under Mycenaean rule, would most likely be viewed as a conciliation of life in accordance with the greater scheme of the harvest. Often in such rituals of sacrifice in many Neolithic communities, the notion of death had to be internalized by participants or onlookers of the sacrificial scene. Central to the theme of sacrifice within many nature-dependent communities, which will be a concept discussed in more detail in the next chapter, is the vital understanding that the act is done in the context of natural regeneration, so that death is viewed as essential in order to continue the success of crop production for instance, but also death becomes viewed as only one momentary part of a continuous cycle, which explains in Neolithic myth why many male consorts often are depicted as resurrecting or being reborn. Although, there can be no certainty about the details of or the meaning behind the Minoan practice of sacrifice, or if the death of the Minotaur in this myth is reminiscent of sacrifice, still, the message behind Theseus' brutal killing of the Minotaur displays that he does not respect, internalize, or even understand any of the significance of the bull to the cultures that existed in Crete. Even as a mythical product of another era and culture, Theseus, arguably, still has the prime opportunity to embrace a concept of sacrifice and death that carries with it an understanding of the severity of his task in taking a life, but by easily killing the bull representative as nothing more than a monster and then fleeing as a perceived hero, Theseus internalizes nothing of the intent of the underworld within journeys of botanical heroism. Instead, like Jason and Perseus, Theseus again seems to merely represent a male hero who defines the requirements of a new ideology that calls for the eradication of concepts associated with the worship of nature and its representatives. Therefore, again, looking towards other characters portrayed within the myth, who might represent a connection to a, perhaps bygone, value of nature, can arguably reveal candidates for botanical heroism.

Theseus is portrayed as being successful upon his mission because of help he receives from another mythic woman, in this case Ariadne, King Minos' and Pasiphaë's daughter, the princess of Crete, also the half-sister of the Minotaur. Ariadne, like her mother and grandmother, may also represent an older connection to the Minoan Earth Goddesses worshipped at Crete, as "originally Ariadne was a vegetation goddess in Crete…. Sometimes Ariadne was associated with the surname 'Very Holy Maid,' because her name is a variant of Ariadne from the Greek word *àgni*, which means 'the most holy'" (Trckova-Flamee). The worship of Ariadne "spread from Crete over the islands of Naxos, Delos, Cyprus, Chios, Lemnos to Athens and the Peloponnese, especially

Argos. Due to her influence over the islands she was sometimes named 'the sea woman.' The cult of Ariadne consisted of a ceremonial dance, orgiastic rites and some lamentations" (Trckova-Flamee). In the myth of Theseus and the Minotaur, Ariadne is essential to aiding Theseus in accomplishing his task, just as Medea was evidenced as doing in the myth of "Jason and the Golden Fleece," which might signal that Ariadne, like Medea, is the true botanical hero of the myth because she may represent tenets that perpetuate the lessons of nature as opposed to a male-oriented political ideology. Ariadne, like Medea, is portrayed within the myth as possessing the needed knowledge for Theseus to slay the Minotaur, who is her half-brother; she gives him a sword and assures Theseus' successful return out of the labyrinth by providing him a clue of thread to unravel as he walks into the labyrinth, so he can simply follow it back out again upon the completion of his mission. Her intimate knowledge of the skills and tools needed to accomplish the task might point towards her representation of one associated with the activities surrounding sacred sacrifice. However, within this myth, like Medea, Ariadne in helping Theseus, forsakes her father and homeland, and gives up what possibly was a more powerful and sacred role for her in Crete.

The myth continues, upon their escape from Crete, to show Ariadne and Theseus harbor on the island of Naxos, where they presumably have sex, and for conflicting reasons depending on the version of the myth being told, Ariadne awakens to see that Theseus has abandoned her there. This mythic episode is obscure. Theseus is often mythically portrayed, again much like Jason, as arrogant and wrong in this act against Ariadne. R. Armstrong states that in the Roman Ovid's version of this myth, Theseus appears "more savage than an animal to Ariadne" (79). Like Medea, Ariadne betrayed her father and homeland and played a role in causing the death of her half-brother in order to help Theseus achieve his heroic quest, and it seems that in Theseus accomplishing his mission and then taking Ariadne's virginity and leaving her alone, she has been punished. But, perhaps Ariadne represents again more within the myth, as she appears by the conclusion on the myth as not punished, but rewarded for her behavior.

The myth holds a mysterious element that might serve to represent Ariadne as a botanical hero, rather than Theseus. After Ariadne is left by Theseus, Dionysus/Bacchus, the god of the grape harvest, wine, and fertility, sweeps into the scene and instantaneously marries Ariadne. In Ovid's description of the myth when Dionysus/Bacchus appears to her, "it was the wildness of the god, his tendency to appear in (complete or partial) animal form, which rendered him so very attractive to Ariadne" (R. Armstrong, 79). This mythic element connects Ariadne to both Europa's attraction to Zeus in bull form and

Pasiphaë's attraction to the bull of Poseidon. This generational mythic linkage of women sexually coupling with gods in wild or animalistic forms might also point to traditional, nature-worshipping belief systems placing significance on goddesses in relation to nature. Audiences of the myth cannot help but ask why Dionysus/Bacchus appears to Ariadne wishing to marry her, and then remains wholly chaste to her, his wife, forever. R. Armstrong states that a theme of wildness versus civilized society permeates most versions of this myth. Dionysus/Bacchus clearly brings wildness back to Ariadne, which she may have always had as displayed in her mythological connections to Cretan women, Europa and Pasiphaë, who preferred the wild over the civilized. After Theseus leaves Ariadne, Catullus describes the island of Naxos as being incredibly wild and isolated; in fact, Ariadne initially thinks that she is in danger of being ravaged by wild animals, but at this telling moment, Dionysus/Bacchus appears to her. He comes to her accompanied by his frenzied maenads; Catullus states the maenads "wreathed themselves with twisting serpents, some celebrated the secret rites ... others beat the drums with hands lifted high, or raised thin chimes on polished bronze cymbals" (64). This behavior associated here with the maenads is in line with practices long held for Earth Goddess worship, as found with the Phrygian worship of Cybele, another Mother/Earth Goddess whose similar worship was practiced all over Asia Minor and was carried into Greece in about the fifth or sixth century BCE. The rites of Cybele were similar to rites associated with Dionysus, as his worship was also depicted in Greek myth as coming into Greece from the east and was also connected to belief systems that practiced the worship of nature. The arrival of Dionysus into the myth articulates a message that Ariadne represents belief systems that better align with those of the followers of Dionysus, rather than the ones associated with Theseus and Athens. Ariadne's and Dionysus' mythic unification through marriage suggests that Ariadne's role in assisting Theseus in his murder of her half-brother may symbolize ideology connected to practices within nature-dependent communities, and may in fact be reminiscent of Neolithic practice. Considering Ariadne's former role as a Minoan vegetation goddess, maybe Ariadne's role within the myth is similar to Dionysus' role as a god of the grape harvest in showing death as connected to the cycles of nature, similar to how other Neolithic myths portray the rituals associated with their respective Earth Goddesses and the sacrifice of their male consorts. Viewing Ariadne at least partially in Neolithic terms might address the odd mythic events of Ariadne aiding in the death of a male bull representation, and then copulating with another male figure, Theseus, before marrying a divinity, who is clearly linked to nature. In this Neolithic context, Ariadne may be better understood as copulating with Theseus and then casting him aside upon the island of Naxos, instead of him abandoning her, just as she, and some of her Neolithic Earth Goddess counterparts, aided in sacrifice after copulation in order to initiate successful harvests. Perhaps, then, Ariadne's mythic role is to show Theseus that he and the Minotaur are one and the same, providing him the opportunity, that he arguably fails, to see that by killing the Minotaur, he is forced to contend with the inevitability of his own demise.

After Theseus leaves Ariadne, he returns home to Athens, but suspiciously forgets to raise a white flag to replace the black flag on his ship, which signals to his father, King Aegeus of Athens, that he failed his mission and has been killed by the Minotaur. King Aegeus, in grief for his lost son, jumps off a cliff to his death, which allows Theseus to then become the king of Athens. In later myths Theseus is said to venture into the actual underworld of Hades with his friend Pirithous to try to abduct Persephone. Once there, the underworld proves more than they anticipated as Theseus and Pirithous find that when they sit to rest they cannot get back up because their limbs become immobile, so they are forced to sit and observe the horrors of the underworld, as harpies encircle them displaying to the men their faces of death. The myth portrays Theseus and Pirithous as severely terrified by this experience. One wonders why Theseus was willing to join his friend on such a foolish and audacious act if he fully grasped the horror of the symbolic underworld during his experience in the Cretan labyrinth. His willingness to go to Hades to try to help Pirithous abduct Persephone shows that Theseus still has not learned the lesson of the mythic underworld, which is the full immensity of death. Once forced to sit and symbolically experience his own death frozen in the underworld, Theseus seems to arrive closer to this realization, as he must wait in Hades until Herakles on his twelfth labor saves him, though Herakles is unable to save Pirithous, who must remain in Hades.

When Theseus returns to his kingdom, he finds that his wife Phaedra, another woman from Crete, sister of Ariadne, falsely accuses his son by an Amazon warrior, Hippolytus, of raping her, when in actuality it was Phaedra who longed for the free-spirited and nature-loving Hippolytus, but was shunned by him. Theseus, thinking Hippolytus raped Phaedra, begs Poseidon to kill his son, and later Theseus finds that this is precisely what happens when a tsunami in the form of yet another great bull overpowers Hippolytus' chariot. Once Theseus has lost his son and heir, he learns the brutal truth—that Phaedra invented the lie of rape to protect her own indiscretions. Phaedra then commits suicide, and Theseus is left to face his depleted life without anyone who cares for him. Soon, Theseus loses favor with his people and finds that he later is exiled from Athens. He goes to the kingdom of King Lycomedes, where Lycomedes ends up murdering Theseus in ironically the same way his father died, by throwing Theseus off of a cliff. Theseus had ample opportunities to embrace the lessons that death presented to him in his underworld experiences, but his mythic portrayal does not show a profound transformation of his spiritual wisdom in connection with the processes of nature; therefore, he does not appear to be a botanical hero.

This myth, like many other mythic examples discussed thus far, is replete with mythological remnants of myriad belief systems throughout various historical eras. The many connections to nature-oriented women, Europa, Pasiphaë, and Ariadne, seem reminiscent of at least a discussion of traditional nature-dependent, perhaps matriarchal, belief systems. The reference to the sacrifice of the quintessential Minoan symbol, the bull, also seems explicitly connected to Neolithic meaning; however, this myth, like many others, makes it difficult to say exactly what the intended message of the myth is. It appears as both a myth that demeans the civilization of Crete as well as its traditional belief systems, but it equally appears as conflicted with this portrayal, as it shows sympathy for the Minotaur and especially for Ariadne, as opposed to Theseus. This conflict suggests strife in reconciling between matriarchal and patriarchal conceptions as civilizations changed; therefore, the myth asks audiences to rethink mythological characters such as Europa, Pasiphaë, Ariadne, Dionysus, and the Minotaur for their representation as mythic characters who readily embraced nature. Ariadne's successful unification with the wild Dionysus in marriage, which is often mythically portrayed as making Ariadne immortal, contrasts significantly with the mythic failure of Theseus upon his return to Athens, suggesting a mythic endorsement of Ariadne's role, as a representation of nature, as opposed to Theseus' role as fleeting hero. Furthermore, Ariadne and Dionysus live on together, not affected by the assault of Crete and the Minotaur; this shows that Ariadne and Dionysus possess qualities that cannot be sundered by any newly created mythology, which is fitting if they are meant to be representations of the cycles of nature. Ariadne's mythic marriage to Dionysus sends the message to audiences that embracing one's own wild nature, with its harsh and bountiful aspects, is necessary and completely natural, and attempting to kill this off, as Theseus rashly killed the Minotaur, only produces fragmentation of the self. Therefore, Ariadne, and not Theseus, is the true botanical hero of the myth.

Unnatural War and Achilles' Underworld

The eighth century BCE Greek text of Homer's *Iliad* presents many characters that have been portrayed as heroic, but the text arguably challenges the definition of heroism and presents the concept of the hero's journey more in botanical terms with its focus on the psychological underworld Achilles creates for himself. The *Iliad's* central character, Achilles, starts his role in the Trojan War already defined by the Achaeans as the greatest warrior of all time. However, in maintaining heroic archetypes Achilles is presented in a time of flux, as he is refusing to fight in the war close to the onset of the epic. Achilles resists fighting because he is offended that Agamemnon has taken Briseis, a woman Achilles obtained in a raid of a neighboring community allied with Troy. Achilles' refusal to fit his defined persona as exemplar warrior indicates that he is intentionally leaving behind his known existence for an unknown experience. Though Achilles is amidst comrades throughout the whole epic, he is repeatedly represented as being removed from them. As Redfield states, "Achilles is himself the explorer, and he explores alone.... The other characters in the poem find him baffling and speak to him in protest and incomprehension ... all say that Achilles is not behaving as human beings behave" (7). Achilles' societal peers desperately want him to join them in battle, as without their best warrior, they are struggling to survive. But, in Achilles' steadfastness to remain separate from his battle comrades, he defines himself as partaking on a heroic journey.

Moreover, Achilles is beginning a journey required of a botanical hero. Achilles starts the essential process required of the botanical hero of stripping away the confines of self-importance by reevaluating his former definitions of self. In the *Iliad*, Achilles' refusal to blindly follow the wishes of his fellow Achaeans, which started before the war when he dressed like a female to evade even going to Troy, signals his disassociation from the perceived importance of the mass cause of warfare. His refusal to fight presents a different option to his comrades and the reader. In refusing to take part in battle, he is choosing to redefine his outlook on a life well lived.

The botanical hero must step away from the average perception of a meaningful and productive life. Many of the Achaeans in the *Iliad* view success in battle, and the fame achieved through an honorable death, as heroic, but Achilles continues to offer sentiments that point towards his understanding of the importance of a natural and simple life:

> I say no wealth is worth my life! Not all they claim
> was stored in the depths of Troy, that city built on riches....
> a man's life breath cannot come back again [Homer, *Iliad*, 265].

In Achilles not desiring fame, he reveals that he does not value what others deem as important. The botanical hero must see that a perception of self-importance is an illusion, and Homer's dialogue signals this:

> Like the generations of leaves, the lives of mortal men.
> Now the wind scatters the old leaves across the earth,
> now the living timber bursts with the new buds
> and spring comes round again. And so with men:
> as one generation comes to life, another dies away [Homer, *Iliad*, 200].

Achilles also shows that he is attempting to break the beliefs of his community that deal with faith in the Olympians and the concept of divine fate. Fate has ordained that Achilles will do great deeds in battle, but he seeks a different path. His desire for a simple life of being happily married to Briseis shows his wish to fulfill the natural cycles of life, instead of meet his ordained destiny of what his community deems a noble life. At this point of the epic, Achilles believes that the prophecy of his "noble" death will stunt this natural process. Throughout much of the *Iliad,* he is a voice for an alternative of a natural life rather than an untimely and unnatural death through battle.

Patroclus, Achilles' closest friend, commiserates with the Achaeans; he longs for Achilles to fight, because he feels only Achilles is capable of providing a win for Greece. Finally, when doom seems imminent for the Achaeans, and Achilles is approached by a group of his respected Achaean comrades, such as Phoenix and Odysseus, Achilles consents to let Patroclus enter battle dressed in his own golden armor:

> But take this command to heart—obey it to the end.
> So you can win great honor, great glory for me….
> Once you have whipped the enemy from the fleet
> You must come back, Patroclus. Even if Zeus
> The thundering lord of Hera lets you seize your glory,
> You must not burn for war against these Trojans,
> …not without *me*
> You will only make *my* glory that much less [Homer, *Iliad*, 415].

This statement appears as a contradiction; it provides evidence that perhaps Achilles does not grasp the value of life quite yet. Achilles has only lived in a fantasy of what life might be like if he could marry Briseus, again a woman he gained possession of as a result of a successful raid against her people, and live far away from the battlefield. Instead of being a figure who stands up against war itself, trying to encourage others to resist as he has resisted, he has only, up until this point, been a character who values the possibility of his own "better" life. Sending someone he clearly is close to, Patroclus, into battle solidifies that Achilles still must learn about the value of life and the cost of death.

Patroclus dons Achilles' golden armor and enters the battle, but not able to fight with Achilles' vigor, Patroclus dies at the hand of Hector, the Trojan prince. Patroclus' death signals to Achilles more than sorrow; in Patroclus wearing the armor meant only for Achilles, and then dying in it, Patroclus teaches

Achilles about death, not the death of those removed from him that he has undoubtedly witnessed often in warfare, but the death of himself. When Patroclus' corpse is brought to Achilles, Achilles begins the quintessential stage of the heroic quest known as the underworld. Van Nortwick supports this assertion by stating that it is the moment when Achilles loses Patroclus that Achilles creates for himself his own dark underworld; "true to the internalized drama of Achilles' spiritual journey, the movement into darkness is symbolized not by an outward trip to the underworld ... but rather by a kind of ... conjuring up of a darkness *that is Achilles himself* ... the Hades that Achilles visits is himself" (*Somewhere*, 66).

In Achilles' own psychological underworld, he enters into a mad frenzy seeking revenge upon Hector. Enraged Achilles begins to kill so many Trojans that their dead bodies choke the waters of the divine River Scamander. The River Scamander begins to wrestle Achilles and tries to drown him. This scene is important because it shows that though Achilles is born of the divine sea nymph Thetis, and thus has a natural connection to water, he is depicted in this scene as resisting this natural element, which might signal to the reader that he is battling with his true, natural self. The Olympians intervene to keep Achilles from meeting his approaching end just yet. As Achilles pursues Hector, Homer describes him in animalistic terms, as a falcon hunting down its prey or a hound seeking the hunt for example. Achilles appears "not as a leader of men but as an isolated destroyer—a kind of natural force, like a fire or flood" (Redfield 107). Within the text, Apollo states that Achilles' thoughts are wild and animalistic, like those of a lion, and Heiden comments of this scene that "lions cannot refuse to be savage, since savagery is their means of sustenance and survival" (195). Achilles, like the Hindu Shiva, can be viewed as a representation of the necessity of death and destruction in the natural world. Like a lion, Achilles stalks Hector and forces him to face death. Achilles can be viewed as losing his burgeoning enlightened state in his choice to become a warrior again, or he can be viewed as merely an agent of nature itself. Van Nortwick also discusses how Achilles in pursuing Hector becomes like an animal, but that perhaps "the animal savagery of Achilles ought not to be set apart from his divinity.... In him, the two extremes coexist in lethal solution" (*Somewhere*, 73). Therefore, it might be possible to view Achilles as connected to a mythic message of death itself, perhaps death as it exists in nature. Yet, the *Iliad* presents Achilles' enraged choice to kill Hector in only futile terms; the epic offers no regenerative value of Achilles' adoption of violence. Therefore, if Achilles is to be a representation of nature's cycles, it seems there needs to be a promise of renewal after the onslaught of destruction, as in myths where destruction is necessary in order to propel a message of nature's vital means towards replenishment through demise, renewal is often assured. For example, in Hinduism and many other world philosophies, when the world is destroyed, it is only one part of a natural cycle that uses the destruction of one world to initiate the birth of a new world.

Before Achilles battles Hector, and then again moments before he kills him, Hector begs Achilles to treat his corpse with respect, so as to allow his family to mourn him and to allow him to properly rest within the underworld. However, Achilles denies this request in an overt fashion. After Achilles slays Hector, he fastens his corpse to the back of his chariot and drags the corpse back over the battlefield to the Achaean encampment. While back at camp, the funeral proceedings for Patroclus begin, lasting many days, and each day, Achilles again drags Hector's corpse behind his chariot, but Hector's corpse will not decay or become decimated by Achilles' violence to it because the gods have protected it. The act of Achilles fastening and then dragging Hector's corpse over the battlefield and around the Achaean encampment while he is mourning Patroclus' death is highly significant. Fastening the corpse to his war chariot connotes agricultural imagery of fastening the plow that will till the earth to ensure a plentiful harvest. Because it is Hector's body that is dragged over the earth, it suggests a scene of sacrifice, similar to the Neolithic myths of the male consort necessarily dying to ensure the fertility of the harvest, thus saving the community. However, Homer in the *Iliad* makes it clear that Hector's corpse does not serve any beneficial, natural purpose. The corpse does not decay, so it cannot enrich the soil. The field in this instance is also not one that will yield a plentiful crop, as it is a battlefield. Homer is using agricultural imagery in a scene of utter barrenness to send a message that war, and most specifically the murder of Hector by Achilles, produces nothing of benefit, and therefore is decidedly unnatural. Instead of being a myth that helps audiences acknowledge the necessity of embracing death as natural; the *Iliad* sends a message that Hector's death, as with most within the text, is unproductive.

It is also significant towards an understanding of Achilles' psychological makeup that he cannot stop dragging Hector's corpse near Patroclus' tomb; it indicates that Achilles has not yet fully faced the factuality of death, as the botanical heroic journey requires within the mythic underworld:

> My dear comrade's dead—
> Patroclus—the man I loved beyond all other comrades,
> Loved as my own life—I've lost him [Homer, *Iliad*, 470].

Achilles' resistance to fight in the war was because he longed for a regular life with a family; more succinctly, he did not want to die. But, when Patroclus dies, he speaks to his comrades utterances that make him appear as if he has accepted his own fate that determines if he kills Hector, he will soon die:

now I'll go and meet the murderer head-on,
That Hector who destroyed the dearest life I know.
For my own death, I'll meet it freely—whenever Zeus
And the other deathless gods would like to bring it on! [Homer, *Iliad*, 471]

However, the text shows evidence that Achilles indeed does not yet fully accept the full meaning of death or the factuality of his own impending demise. As long as Achilles holds onto Hector's corpse, it appears that he is attempting to hold onto his own life, as the text suggests Hector and Achilles are two sides of the same character. Hector represented everything Achilles thought he wanted in life as a family man, as Hector is systematically presented within the *Iliad* as fighting to save his wife and child, his parents, and his people from doom. Therefore, in killing Hector, Achilles has eradicated his former dream of living a similar life, and perhaps his need for a singular identity with a lasting legacy, but the key here, what separates him from self-actualized heroes, is that Achilles symbolically killed his ego-driven self unknowingly. The botanical, self-actualized hero must fully comprehend the necessity of letting go of the self, often through the lesson of mortality, in order to fully realize the value of nature's cycle of incessant life.

Like the Neolithic male consort, the botanical hero steps into death when it is his or her time willingly, with a knowledge that death is natural and necessary to revitalize the earth, and therefore death mythically becomes presented as not an end but a new beginning—it becomes a message full of everlasting life, not a decisive end. It may appear that Achilles has psychologically accepted the fact that his dream of a regular life was futile, and perhaps only connected to concepts of the importance of his singular identity, so he shed it and willingly stepped into death, but in reality, at this point in the text, Achilles is merely a man who acted without thinking. He killed Hector, and then improperly desecrated his corpse not for regenerative purposes; this in itself shows that he does not conceive of the full cost of death. When Hector died, Homer describes it as Hector "leaving his manhood far behind, his young and supple strength" (Homer, *Iliad*, 553); this description reveals Hector's death as clearly unnatural, showing that nothing beneficial will result from it. Achilles only carried out his violent actions towards Hector, and the other Trojans standing in his way, because he was consumed by vengeance; therefore, at this point in the text, Achilles does not possess the psychological wisdom of a self-actualized, botanical hero. Arguably, though, Achilles learns more as he continues his journey through his own psychological underworld.

During Patroclus' funeral, Achilles is described as sitting again isolated from the other Achaeans into the deep hours of the night before Patroclus' corpse is to be properly burned. Achilles believes he sees Patroclus come to him in a dream, chastising him for waiting so long to perform the proper funerary rites. Patroclus also requests that Achilles' bones be buried with his own. This scene is important to the epic because it finally shows Achilles' full acceptance of his own death. When Achilles murdered Hector, he was not cognizant of his actions, but here, seeing Patroclus, and hearing him foreshadow his own death, Achilles begins to understand the magnitude of death. The *Iliad* continues to present Achilles with the factuality of death when Priam, the king of Troy, comes to Achilles to beg for the return of his son Hector's corpse. In this scene Priam teaches Achilles what is lost in death, and with this lesson, Achilles sees perhaps fully now the importance of life. Earlier in the text, Achilles seemingly spoke as an agent who valued life, as all he wanted to do was escape the senseless violence of war and return home, but as he spoke these words, he also initially hoped for many of his Achaean comrades to die in order to show Agamemnon how much he was needed. Achilles also willingly sent his best friend into battle for nebulous reasons that pointed towards him gaining further fame, as discussed. But it is not until Achilles enters his own psychic underworld, becoming a physical embodiment of death as the animalistic agent of death that he was always prophesized to be, that Achilles can now finally psychologically recognize the magnitude of what death means. Priam, sitting at Achilles' feet, begs him for the body of Hector to be returned to him:

> Pity me in my own right...
> I have endured what no one on earth has ever done before—
> I put my lips to the hands of the man who killed my son."
>   Those words stirred within Achilles a deep desire
> To grieve for his own father. Taking the old man's hand
> He gently moved him back. And overpowered by memory
> Both men gave way to grief. Priam wept freely
> For man-killing Hector, throbbing, crouching
> Before Achilles' feet as Achilles wept himself,
> Now for his father, now for Patroclus once again,
> And their sobbing rose and fell throughout the house [Homer, *Iliad,* 605].

Van Nortwick states of this scene, "there is recognition here of the basic fact of human existence that Achilles has been unable to accept: all humans, Hector and himself included, are united by their mortality" (*Somewhere,* 81). Here is the transformative moment for Achilles, as it appears he now fully understands death.

The natural cycle is a continuous pattern, and death is essential to the cycle, but it does not mean that senseless death should be initiated through aggression. If life is unnaturally aborted for senseless reasons like murder or warfare, it stunts the natural cycle of life, as too much death is just as unnatural as no deaths at all. Many myths from nature-dependent cultures instruct audiences that killing too many animals in the hunt is an abomination of nature's laws; the same message resounds in the *Iliad*. Though death is central to this text, and aggression is presented as a natural human state, the text makes it clear through Achilles' journey into his own psychological underworld that death is only one part of a more dominant natural pattern that ceaselessly perpetuates life. The cycle of nature is ultimately about life, not death. Death, when viewed in natural, cyclical terms, is a momentary experience that helps to perpetuate new life; therefore, natural death must be acknowledged as inescapable when the time arrives, but what must be realized is that death is merely an agent to continue life. Life must be firmly embraced as valuable, or else the natural cycle is pointless. Achilles does become a self-actualized hero, as he alone within the text appears to learn the true cost of death, and thus the value of life, but he still does not become a botanical hero, as he does not, even symbolically, resurrect from death, as nature's cycles demand. Vital to understanding the message behind Achilles character within the *Iliad*, one must look to how he is portrayed in Homer's *Odyssey*. Achilles meets the protagonist of the *Odyssey*, Odysseus, as he is in Hades, and Homer makes it clear that Achilles cannot resurrect out of Hades as a botanical hero would be able to do; Achilles is instead stuck in the underworld. Odysseus in Homer's *Odyssey* displays his admiration towards the dead Achilles, for what Odysseus believes was an honorable death, by stating:

> But you, Achilles, there's not a man in the world more blest than you—
> there never has been, never will be one.
> Time was, when you were alive, we Argives honored you as a god,
> and now down here, I see, you lord it over the dead in all your power.
> So grieve no more at dying, great Achilles [265].

But, Achilles' retort to Odysseus shows that Achilles views his own death as folly, as he would give up all of the fame he achieved in warfare only to be able to be alive again, living a simple life:

> No winning words about death to *me*, shining Odysseus!
> By god, I'd rather slave on earth for another man—
> some dirt-poor tenant farmer who scrapes to keep alive—
> than rule down here over all the breathless dead....
> For I no longer stand in the light of day [Homer, *Odyssey*, 26].

Within the *Iliad*, Homer presents the death of Hector, which will inevitably lead to Achilles' death as pointless; in fact, the epic closes with a profound sense of the meaninglessness of the ten year war. Because of Achilles, Hector dies, leaving his family vulnerable; many subsequent myths capture the devastation that followed the taking of Troy, showing Hector's family, and most Trojan families being murdered or enslaved. Achilles also dies an almost impossible death because Paris pierces his one point of weakness with an arrow that was divinely guided. In addition, the myths surrounding Agamemnon, Clytemnestra, Electra, and Orestes also present the destructive aftermath of the Trojan War. Clytemnestra kills Agamemnon upon his journey home in partial vengeance for her belief that he sacrificed their daughter Iphigenia. Electra and Orestes then plot to kill their mother Clytemnestra for the murder of their father, but once Orestes commits the act or murder, the Erinyes haunt Orestes. These myths show audiences that there is no escape from death for anyone, but they also present the possibility that war unnecessarily invites death and destruction, and need not be so readily adopted.

The *Iliad* perhaps offers a glimpse into ancient perceptions about the shift from the bygone culture of the Minoans in the Neolithic period, for instance, who were, at least compared to the Achaeans and Dorians, largely peaceful. Most scholars believe that the Achaeans and Minoans merged belief systems, which may account for the apparent turmoil between traditional and more modern belief systems found within the works of Homer. Homer wrote well after the Achaeans took over domination, as well as after the Dorian invasions against the Achaeans, which largely led to the period known as the Greek Dark Ages. Homer's era was, therefore, in great part defined by male hierarchy proven through warfare. However, the *Iliad* seems to systematically question the values of hierarchal supremacy and warfare, as Achilles throughout most of the work openly counters Agamemnon's rule and the concept of war in general. In addition, women are almost non-existent in the text, which seems odd, since in Homer's next work, the *Odyssey,* women appear to dominant the work. The almost total absence of female perspective in this work, which focuses primarily on death and destruction through warfare, becomes important in a time when Neolithic belief systems were distant but most likely still remembered by audiences. For Achilles, Briseus embodies the life he desires; he imagines love and peace in his future if he could only flee warfare and actualize his idyllic dream. However, Briseus is only identified as a possession in this text that resulted from violence done upon her people, just as the Trojan women will become possessions obtained through war. Perhaps Homer is identifying that Achilles' dream of an idyllic life as a married farmer is a reflection upon the same "golden" age Hesiod, writing about the same time as Homer, discussed in his *Theogony,* a time that seems clearly connected to the bygone days of the Neolithic period where warfare was not as embraced as in the periods that followed. Eisler contends that though Homer's and Hesiod's era was dominated by a patriarchal, violent culture, they still grasped onto a, perhaps idealized, memory of traditional Neolithic culture; for Hesiod war wasn't a part of human nature; Hesiod believed that war, with the god Ares, was brought to Greece in the Bronze Age and then by the Dorians with "their weapons of iron" (Eisler 108). Perhaps evidenced in the *Iliad* is a contrary voice to that of the dominant culture when Homer wrote his epics that embraced warfare over peace. If Neolithic culture, perhaps Minoan culture, with its embrace of peace as the natural state of man, still existed in the minds of Homer's and Hesiod's audience, as J. V. Luce concurs by stating that though "'Minoan culture went dormant for a time, ... [it] sent up fresh new shoots in the shades of Mycenaean citadels'" (qtd. in Eisler 108), then perhaps Homer wrote the *Iliad* envisioning an alternative to the barrenness represented through the war-ridden battlefield of Troy.

Perhaps Homer, through Achilles, was questioning his culture's embrace of war as inevitable and natural, as at the epic's conclusion, one is left with a sense that Achilles did have a choice not to kill Hector. Perhaps his rage at the death of Patroclus did not have to lead to his adoption of violence. Perhaps if Achilles accepted Patroclus' death as societally driven, not natural, then he could have shed the need to become an embodiment of destruction, since his devastation would only propel societal gains on the part of the Achaeans. The *Iliad* suggests that Achilles is heroically right to step outside of the confines of his society that demands he step into his warrior persona and readily accept his own demise. Achilles, throughout most of the *Iliad*, serves as an alternative view for the reader of the epic. His resistance to fight in the Trojan War and his extended dialogue of wanting to go home and live a simple life as a farmer, instead of die a worthless death in a battle justified by Agamemnon and Menelaus, teaches audiences the possibility of a different choice than that of the popular voice, and presents Achilles as coming close to botanical heroism because of his apparent understanding of the value and necessity of all of the life cycles.

In the *Iliad*, Homer reveals that senseless killing in constant warfare serves no regenerative purpose and is thus unnatural; it thwarts the community and stifles the promise of a better future, as it did for the Trojans and many of the Achaeans as they attempted to go home. Therefore, Achilles in questioning the validity of war, with its countless examples of senseless killing, comes close to understanding the magnitude of both life and death within the natural cycle, but he personally fails at becoming a botanical hero, because he is ultimately unable to thwart the power of war even within himself. His choice to kill Hector only perpetuates unnatural destruction, producing a landscape that is unnaturally barren, due directly to the lack of respect the characters within the epic, including Achilles, showed for the laws of nature. Regrowth or renewed life is left out of this myth, sending a message of warning to audiences of the epic. Still, the example of Achilles' psychological struggle gives audiences a chance to carry further the nascent wisdom Achilles gathered for himself, so that humankind may one day reach botanical apotheosis in their embrace of the value of life while naturally permitted to be alive.

Odysseus and the Earth Goddesses

Homer's other epic, the *Odyssey,* also presents the character of Odysseus in heroic terms. It is important to reiterate that like the myths of Jason, Perseus, and Theseus, Homer wrote his epics in a time of political and religious conflict. Barnes states that in many ways the *Odyssey* provides political connotations meant to confirm patriarchal beliefs over matriarchal belief systems (126). Yet Eisler counters this by stating that in the *Odyssey* "some of the most powerful figures are female," suggesting that the dominating influx of the Achaeans and then the Dorians did not fully eradicate traditional goddess-oriented belief systems (109). Though this is difficult to conclusively prove, it does remain clear that female creatures and characters are explicitly tied to messages associated with nature within the *Odyssey.* Odysseus' ten year journey immediately following his decade at the Trojan War presents myriad scenes of the archetypal heroic quest. Odysseus repeatedly must face otherworldly experiences along his journey, as he and his crew reach distant islands inhabited by strange beings, like the Cyclopes, the Lotus-Eaters, and the Sirens. Each of the places that Odysseus and his crew land immediately thrusts them into one otherworld environment after another, and each island presents natural elements often associated with overt nature. For example, early in Odysseus' narrative of his journey that he relates to the Phaeacians, a people who finally help him return home after almost twenty years, he recounts his tale of the island inhabited by many Cyclopes that he visited soon after leaving Troy. The unfettered, natural assets of the island provide all of the resources needed by Odysseus and his famished men, as they break the Greek code of hospitality by gorging themselves on these resources without first gaining permission. The men's unappreciative greed of these resources leads directly to the massive Polyphemus, one of the Cyclopes, trapping Odysseus and some of his men in his cave. Immediately, this scene with Polyphemus serves as a glimpse of the mythic underworld for Odysseus and his men. Polyphemus' cave is within the recesses of the earth, and once inside, it meets the requirements of terror associated with the underworld as Polyphemus begins to consume some of the men. Odysseus, being a man renowned for his quick wit, devises a plan to escape. He introduces himself with the name "Nobody," and then invokes Polyphemus to get drunk. Once Polyphemus is intoxicated, he falls asleep, so Odysseus stabs him in his one eye and then hides while the awakened and enraged Polyphemus tries to find the man who did this to him. Showing the almost implausible genius of Odysseus' plan, the other Cyclopes come to see why Polyphemus is crying out in agony within his cave. When they ask what happened and who mistreated him, Polyphemus names his culprit—"Nobody." This causes the other Cyclopes to confusedly walk away.

Later a suffering Polyphemus opens the entrance of his cave by pushing aside the heavy boulder that blocks the entrance to let out his sheep and goats; Odysseus and his men hide underneath Polyphemus' sheep by holding onto their fleece as they walk out of the cave. Polyphemus feels the animals' backs to make sure the men are not trying to escape, but of course they do because of again Odysseus' cunning. It is true that Odysseus witnesses the terror associated with the underworld in this episode, but it is also apparent that he does not yet grasp the true meaning of the underworld in this scene. Odysseus witnesses terror and death, but having escaped, he marks himself as an unrealized hero, as he holds too closely to his own concept of self-importance, as shown when an enraged Polyphemus, having realized the men escaped, goes to the edge of a cliff in search of the men. Odysseus and his men could have escaped unnoticed, but Odysseus feels the need to loudly declare to Polyphemus that his name is not Nobody, but instead Odysseus. This yelling of his name to Polyphemus enrages the Cyclops who pleads with his father, Poseidon, to avenge him, which causes most of the calamity Odysseus and his men must endure for the rest of their journey. Odysseus' arrogance in this scene shows that Odysseus must concede his tie to the importance of his famed identity as a crucial component to fulfill his botanical heroic quest.

As Odysseus and his men continue to try to get home, they encounter more components that show that their journey is one connected with nature. As stated the symbolic otherworlds that Odysseus encounters are teeming with unfettered representations of nature. Also, many natural events impede the journey of these men, such as an early hurricane that destroys most of Odysseus' fleet. Scylla, a giant six-headed monster who devours six men indiscriminately, and Charybdis, a massive whirlpool that swallows whole ships, also represent natural elements for the men to contend with. In addition, the island that holds the cattle of the Sun God and King Aeolus' bag of wind also present representations of the power of nature, as Odysseus' men learn by their disrespect of these elements. And most evident is Poseidon's role within the epic, as his presentation as the angry sea, traps Odysseus in Poseidon's natural environment until Odysseus has apparently learned the necessary lesson of the might of nature. Therefore, the unceasing presentation of natural elements within this myth repeatedly forces Odysseus to acknowledge the power of nature.

One of the most significant scenes for Odysseus' heroic quest involves his actual journey to the underworld of Hades. Odysseus is told by Circe, the daughter of Helios and the aunt of Medea, who again comes from Colchis, that he must venture into Hades before he will ever be able to return home, so Odysseus voyages to what was considered the edge of the world, makes a sacrifice to the dead, and thus is permitted to enter Hades. Once in the underworld, he must witness its scenes of horror, as he sees all around him the spirits of the dead. He encounters one of his own crew who died at Circe's home by drunkenly falling off of her roof and promises him that he will perform the proper rites upon his corpse when he returns. Odysseus summons the blind and infamous prophet Tiresias and inquiries about the fate of his journey. He also meets his own mother, who unbeknownst to him died while he was gone. He meets his fallen comrades from the Trojan War, most notably Achilles, who as discussed, educates Odysseus on the value of life.

Vitebsky connects Odysseus' immersion into the underworld with the tales of the shamanic journey found within many nature-dependent communities. Vitebsky states that like the shamanic journey, Homer's tale shows Odysseus descending into the depths of the earth to obtain knowledge; "the object of his journey is to rescue himself by reaching his wife and his home. On this voyage, which is one of self-discovery…. Odysseus can be seen as both shaman and patient" (71). Vitebsky continues by saying that "in many cosmologies, the underworld is the land of the dead, and in the shaman's journey there is a kind of death" (72); therefore, in Odysseus descending into the realm of the dead, a necessary tenet to both the shamanic journey and the heroic quest, he should emerge psychologically changed as a result of contending with his own impending mortality, but the text will reveal if Odysseus gains the botanical wisdom that comes with this heroic stage.

It is true that in Hades, Odysseus is presented with the opportunity for meeting the requirements of the underworld in the heroic quest; as Dougherty states "the world of the dead … represents the ultimate expression of the other and the outer limits of Odysseus' travels" (98). Odysseus is indeed described as filled with terror upon viewing the inescapable scenes of death that the underworld presents. He also contends with the fact that those close to him have died, which could introduce to him the realization that his time on earth is limited. He additionally becomes psychologically confused when Achilles disrupts his former conception that a noble life should be lived to seek acclaim. Odysseus, up until his experience within Hades, has proved that he adheres to the societal view that the successful warrior is most revered, and those who die in battle died an honorable death, leaving a legacy that will live forever in their remembrance. However, this perception is not at all the one presented to

Odysseus by Achilles; instead, Odysseus learns from Achilles that life, even a simple life on earth, is invaluable. This lesson would seem to force Odysseus to transform away from a disillusioned man, holding too closely to a false sense of self-importance, into the beginning stages of botanical enlightenment, but the text suggests otherwise. Indeed, it is hard to see a decided transformation within Odysseus after his journey to the underworld. Van Nortwick states that Odysseus does not ever fully accept his own demise of self because of his experience in Hades; so "his arrival in the underworld can effect no permanent change" within Odysseus (*Unknown*, 61). Van Nortwick states that Odysseus' ascent from Hades, which mythically should mark a clear psychological rebirth, "does not seem to result in an inner transformation in Odysseus. His experiences in Hades would certainly lead us to expect some change as a result of his journey into darkness … [yet] we see nothing analogous to [this] … as a result of these encounters" (60–1).

Odysseus upon his quest is systematically asked to learn humility, which at times he seemingly does upon his heroic journey. Odysseus seems to learn that his behavior with Polyphemus was unacceptable and irrationally endangered his men. After seven years on the goddess Calypso's island, the lone Odysseus seems to have lost much of his former egotistical pomp. In fact, when readers first encounter Odysseus in the *Odyssey*, it is after most of the events upon his journey home have already happened, and he is depicted as crying, distraught with the knowledge that he is helpless to go home, which signals a changed Odysseus. Further signaling a transformation within Odysseus, the text states that Calypso offered him immortality if he would only stay with her, but Odysseys refuses this and adamantly chooses to be mortal, wanting only to return home to his family, suggesting perhaps that he understood and valued the words of Achilles when he was in Hades. Furthermore, when Odysseus does finally make it off of Calypso's island, he is depicted as a battered man, a shell of his former self. Again at the hard mercy of Poseidon, Odysseus washes ashore the Phaeacians' island completely naked, signaling his vulnerability. With the Phaeacians, as he hears a bard sing of his own former achievements, Odysseus is said to weep like a woman who has lost her husband in war, and Kenaan states that this "analogy to a weeping woman marks, as is often observed, a turning point in the Homeric narrative. It functions as a trope that sets the stage for the dramatic climax of the hero's self-recognition. Indeed, making a connection between Odysseus and the feminine opens up a whole psychological landscape that will be crucial for his homecoming" (175). Furthermore, when Odysseus arrives home to Ithaca, instead of a grand celebration for his return, he lands on its shores asleep and awakens not knowing where he is. He must also continue on as a beggar in his homeland before he can be reunited with his family. All of these mythic elements signal that Odysseus' journey did transform him, reducing him to a state where he must concede that his identity is only a small part of a larger cycle, which is a necessary conciliation of a botanical hero.

It is true that Odysseus seems to learn humility along his quest, and that the presentations of mythic otherworlds and the underworld of Hades helped him learn this lesson of letting go of his former identity. When he arrives home, it again does seem that he has learned Achilles' lesson about simply enjoying life while one can because death is inevitable. However, the *Odyssey* presents Odysseus's psychic transformation as not entirely lasting, if it was ever there. In order to regain his kingdom, Odysseus feels that he must massacre all of the suitors who are there depleting his resources, coveting his wife Penelope, and seeking the means to kill his son Telemachus. This massacre appears textually strange, as Odysseus wants to test the suitors before he massacres them to see if they are indeed wicked, so Athena is presented as making the suitors act evil by having one suitor throw a stool at Odysseus while he is disguised as an old beggar, which is the proof Odysseus needs to show that they are indeed unworthy of life, so he kills them all. If the test is meant to prove the suitors evil, then Athena's intervention in making their behavior worse than it would normally have been seems unfair. Furthermore, the text shows Odysseus continue his rampage of death by hanging twelve maids because they were said to have had affairs with the suitors. And perhaps most confounding of all for the apparent psychological growth of Odysseus is that the text makes two references to the fact that Odysseus will only remain home for a short time and will once again leave to pursue a land far away from Ithaca where he will die. This odd ending of the *Odyssey* can be interpreted in many ways; it can be said that Odysseus' massacre is a symbolic purging of his former self, so that he is ready to live as a transformed and enlightened hero. But, it can be equally said that Odysseus in causing so many more deaths, beyond those that already occurred in the Trojan War and as a result from perhaps his unsuccessful abilities to be a good leader in bringing his crew safely home, signals that in fact Odysseus has not attained the enlightenment of the botanical hero.

As with the Greek myths of Jason and Perseus, the female characters within the *Odyssey* signal to audiences lessons connected to nature. With the long history of goddess worship being attached to earth worship in Greece, making a connection between the numerous women in the myth to nature seems appropriate. In almost every important scene of this text, women hold powerful roles. For example, Athena assists Odysseus throughout his entire quest; it is clear that without her aid, he would not have successfully arrived home or survived the onslaught of the suitors once in Ithaca.

The role of Circe in the *Odyssey* directly ties her to Earth Goddess representations, as she is presented as surrounded by all forms of wild beasts when Odysseus and his men arrive on her island. Also, Circe can at whim transform men into animals, as she easily does to Odysseus' crewmen, turning them into swine. Her role within the myth is multidimensional. Quite explicitly, the interaction between Circe and Odysseus shows remnants of the Neolithic myths of the Earth Goddess with her male consort. Circe's ability to transform men into animals and then back again into men is symbolic of the natural progression of the cycles of nature. Circe is also the one who instructs Odysseus to venture into Hades, which again shows her in the light of an Earth Goddess because she presents Odysseus with the experience that can teach him the natural necessity of accepting death. Though Odysseus longs to return home to his wife Penelope, the *Odyssey* recounts many instances where he must have sex with divine or semi-divine females, and Circe's sexual scene with Odysseus showcases again scenes reminiscent of traditional Earth Goddesses with their male consorts. Sex in terms of the Earth Goddess was traditionally considered a sacred act, one that ensured the continuation of nature's cycles; therefore, when Circe and Odysseus have sex, the scene is meant to illicit traditional concepts that most likely would have been known to audiences of the time.

But, the myth again shows, like with the myths of Jason and Perseus, an attempt to eradicate the power of the Earth Goddess in favor of the male hero when Odysseus, instructed by Hermes, learns the means to overpower Circe. Hermes tells Odysseus to take a potion that keeps him from being transformed by Circe into an animal, then to draw his sword with the threat of killing her, and finally to have sex with her. This he does, and it immediately works, suggesting that this portion of the myth yet again serves to reveal a political agenda where the male hero has superseded the power of the older Neolithic Earth Goddess. Again, this scene would have been mythically understood by Greek audiences as referencing the "danger a mortal man risks in sleeping with a goddess: death or emasculation" (Van Nortwick 55). However, it is important to note that Odysseus does not just murder Circe and walk away the perceived victor, like Perseus or the Babylonian Marduk does to their female opponents; instead, Odysseus stays with Circe for a year. Presumably, it is in this year with Circe where Odysseus could have had the time needed to learn the lessons of the natural life cycle taught by her, as a possible representation of an Earth Goddess in her natural otherworld, but, as discussed, the epic is ambiguous about if Odysseus has become transformed as a result of his time with Circe and his subsequent journey into the underworld. An argument can be made that Odysseus does not transform upon his heroic journey, because he has long been resistant towards learning the lessons of nature. Instead of succumbing to Circe, like he later does not fully succumb to Calypso, and losing his selfhood to become one with nature in an animalistic transformation, he resists her and overpowers her, perhaps losing the insight the metamorphosis into animal form may have taught him.

The Greek Plutarch, in his *On the Use of Reason by Irrational Animals,*[1] discusses his imaginings of what the conversation between Odysseus and Circe must have been like from the standpoint of one of Odysseus' crewmen, Gryllos, who was turned into a swine by Circe. Plutarch imagines that Odysseus in asking to have his men transformed from swine back into human form, receives an answer from Circe that is quite revealing of Greek perception on the nature of metamorphosis. In Plutarch's version, Circe tells Odysseus that he should ask his men if they indeed want to return to their former human shape; "inverting the *Odyssey's* privileging of the human over the bestial, and showing no deference whatever to his erstwhile leader, Gryllos tells Odysseus that he prefers his current existence to his former life as a man ... as Gryllos depicts it, a pig's life is far from beastly" (Buxton 138). Plutarch's version of this conversation is largely comical, but it also reveals the Greek adoption of animal nature within humans as admirable, when Gryllos says to Odysseus, "'if you think that you are superior in courage to the beasts, why do your poets call the best fighters 'wolf-minded' and 'lion-hearted' and 'like a boar in valour,' though none of them ever calls a lion 'human-hearted'" (qtd. in Buxton 138).

With Circe, it appears that Odysseus comes close to realizing the lessons of nature that Earth Goddesses often reveal, as he enjoys himself within her realm, where ferocious animals thrive relaxed by her side, and momentarily loses his intent to leave, but again the fact that he does leave and shows a conclusive lack of change in identity afterward, exposes the fact that he resisted the influence of the metamorphic transformations he witnessed all around him. Many myths from nature-dependent cultures show the benefit of metamorphosis into animal form; for instance, Manabozho's experience as a wolf taught him essential lessons of nature that allowed him to reach botanical apotheosis. In tales of the shamanic journey, the shaman is often presented as spiritually enlightened because of his or her willingness to lose identity by becoming an animal, so that he or she may learn from the animals. In addition, many Greek myths present humans being transformed into animal or botanical elements, such as Narcissus being turned into a flower or Daphne being transformed into a laurel tree; these metamorphic changes are not necessarily viewed as negative, and instead may signal spiritual enlightenment. Many divine beings in Greek myth easily shapeshift between animal representations, such as Zeus' and Poseidon's multiple disguises, and again this transformation might suggest a necessary unity with nature towards understanding Greek perceptions of divinity. And finally, Greek myths of representatives like Dionysus' maenads show the transformative value that often comes in embracing one's animalistic side. But, the *Odyssey* does not present Odysseus as learning much of anything from the evidence of animalistic metamorphosis all around him. To attain apotheosis, botanical heroes must concede selfhood and unite fully with nature because of their gained knowledge upon their quests that death and a loss of identity in natural terms are not loses at all, but instead, signal a psychological acceptance of the facts of nature's cycles on the part of the botanical hero. Therefore, Odysseus' time with Circe is largely wasted as he fails to grasp the transformative potential she could have offered him. Repeatedly, Odysseus "has been shielded in advance from any vulnerability" (Van Nortwick, *Unknown*, 61); with Circe, and many other instances, he faces opportunities that might have transformed him by protecting "himself with his drawn sword" (Van Nortwick, *Unknown*, 61). His subsequent underworld experience at the suggestion of Circe also, again, confirms his lack of transformation into a botanical hero.

In addition, Calypso represents another Earth Goddess representative, and perhaps his final chance to attain the wisdom nature affords, but again, Odysseus fails to grasp unification with her, and thus fails botanical apotheosis. Calypso holds Odysseus within her grasp, so that he may ponder life for the final seven years of his long journey. Calypso's island should signal to Odyssey the lessons of nature, as it is described as filled with natural beauty and abundant resources. The woods on her island teem with "fragrant" trees, and the meadows are thick with flowers and herbs; four springs sit outside the entrance of her cave surrounded by grape vines bearing ample fruit (Van Nortwick, *Unknown*, 14). Van Nortwick states that "nature here is fecund and at the same time subject to a kind of restraint that seems to emanate from the goddess" (*Unknown*, 14). The portrayal of nature in relation to Calypso points to her being tied to the Greek conception of an Earth Goddess, as does her home within a womb-like cave. Barnes states that the divine ambrosia Calypso is said to have suggests that the audiences of the myth are being "led backwards into some enchanted world of the deep past" (127). Significantly, Calypso is "pre–Olympian," as she "keeps the double-edged axe—the unmistakable symbol of the sacred in the Cretan palace culture…. Homer therefore brings the hero, after a series of narrow escapes with seductive women or women who will eat a man alive, to yet one more woman whose sacred association is Cretan" (127). As stated, Calypso offers Odysseus immortality, but he resists. Calypso's ability to make this promise also recalls her Earth Goddess association; "immortality here ... is the central promise of the ancient Earth Goddess ... suggest[ing] that the cycle of life is endless" (Barnes 128). In addition, Calypso's capability to control the process of time suggests her role as a representation of nature itself. If Calypso is a representation of a traditional Earth Goddess, then her role within the epic should be to educate Odysseus towards self-knowledge, yet Odysseus, like Jason, Perseus, and Theseus, is again portrayed as resisting the message of the Earth Goddess representative. Calypso wanted Odysseus to be her life-long mate, but Odysseus refused her, and thus proves his lack of transformation upon his journey. Campbell maintains that heroic apotheosis is often signaled in myth by the hero uniting fully with the myth's goddess representation. Campbell states that a successful quest "is commonly represented as a mystical marriage of the triumphant hero-soul with the Queen Goddess of the World.... For she is the incarnation of the promise of perfection" (*Hero*, 109–11). For the botanical hero, the union with the mythic Earth Goddess shows the hero's willing unification with the reality of nature's laws. Therefore, instead of resisting Calypso's proposal, like Perseus refused looking upon Medusa's face, it seems in order to fully achieve unification with Calypso, Odysseus should have succumbed to her, thus gaining natural immortality. Calypso's promise of immortality may signal spiritual apotheosis for Odysseus. As stated, the enlightened botanical hero must resolve to let go of his or her former selfhood, and here on Calypso's island, Odysseus is unable to do this, as all he longs for is his return home to reestablish his former life. Odysseus leaves Calypso's island when first presented the chance with a scene that is indicative of his lack of transformation because of his inability to have grasped the natural lessons of Calypso. When Odysseus constructs his raft that will enable him to leave, he reconfigures "the shapes and textures of trees and plants to fashion something artificial, the result of imposing human intelligence and order on nature. The boat is to be a vehicle for Odysseus' return to time and mortality, and its making symbolizes his rejection of Calypso's mysterious cosmos with its inhuman harmony of art and nature" (Van Nortwick, *Unknown*, 19). In leaving behind Circe and then Calypso, many view Odysseus as noble for wanting to return to his regular, mortal life with his own wife and child, yet in mythic terms, Odysseus has not become obliterated psychologically, which is the required goal of the botanical hero's journey. The botanical heroic quest must eradicate the hero's preconceived conception of selfhood, as well as what he or she initially believed to be important in life. The botanical heroic journey, like many archetypal heroic quests, centers upon changing the hero into possessing a more spiritually refined psychology, but Odysseus in only wanting to go home seems to consistently resist the opportunities presented to him that would allow him to glimpse a side of the universe that is spiritually transcendent. In perhaps allowing himself to truly be "Nobody" to Polyphemus by keeping his mouth shut and not proclaiming his perceived importance by yelling out his name, or in perhaps embracing his animalistic side with Circe, or staying forever with Calypso, he would have internalized lessons about the natural world that instead remain remote to him throughout the entirety of the epic. If Odysseus finally did learn that he really is, in natural terms, nobody, then perhaps he would have understand that Calypso's immortality was the immortality that nature itself promises humankind, which is essentially everlasting life if one is willing to forfeit identity.

Penelope is another female character who is integral to the text. One interpretation of her shows Penelope as just the steadfast wife of Odysseus, who remains staunchly faithful to him for twenty years, not ever knowing if he is dead or alive. But, Penelope's resoluteness to reject all the suitors who come to Ithaca reveals more to her character. Penelope has been controlling the kingdom of Ithaca single-handedly since Odysseus' departure, and her refusal of all suitors might suggest that she likes her position of authority. Eisler states that Penelope "is a strong and determined woman" (107), and her refusal to marry the suitors who would take her power from her suggests "that even after the Achaean invasions of Greece, matrilineal succession was still the norm, as well as the prerequisite to any claim of rulership" (107). Odysseus' return, and his odd killing of Penelope's twelve maids suggests, again, components within the myth that strive to merely show a male hero killing the older representation of matriarchal power instead of a botanical hero who has attained spiritual apotheosis. Montiglio supports this view of Odysseus as unheroic by stating that Odysseus became a favored character in Athenian drama of the fifth century to hold in quite contemptible favor, as he was portrayed in negative terms in many of the most renowned plays of this period, such as Euripides *Trojan Women* (2–7). This portrayal of Odysseus in negative terms after Homer's epic narratives undoubtedly has many reasons, but perhaps one of them is that he was viewed as a failure of his heroic quest.

Therefore, when one looks at the *Odyssey* in its entirety, it appears conflicted on the heroic role of Odysseus. At times, Odysseus appears to learn the lessons presented in the Neolithic myths involving the Earth Goddess and the male consort—the botanical lessons that are inextricably connected to nature's ceaseless cycle of life, death, and rebirth. He seems to grow more humble and acknowledge the value of life, as a botanical hero must, but, at other times, the text suggests that Odysseus comes close to reaching a state of botanical apotheosis, but ends up failing to fully realize enlightenment, because he always ends up rejecting the final leap, only resorting again and again to his old persona, much like Achilles did.

Aeneas' Unnatural Sacrifice

The Roman text of Virgil's *Aeneid* presents Aeneas as also coming close to grasping botanical wisdom through his heroic quest and experience in the underworld, but also arguably finally failing to reach apotheosis. The *Aeneid* recounts the fall of Troy and Aeneas' mythic escape to become one of the founders of Rome. Aeneas, like Odysseus, encounters many hardships as he sails from Troy to Rome; they too have their symbolic components, but more so, they serve as a means to connect this Roman text, written to appease Emperor Augustus, to the mythological arrival of Trojan lineage to Italy. However, Virgil does present two scenes in particular within his *Aeneid* that do link this myth to botanical aspects.

First, Aeneas' interaction with Dido reveals again a female character who is ripe with ambiguity. Dido is depicted as the Queen and sole ruler of Carthage, as her husband died, and she is portrayed as doing an excellent job in her role of supreme leader. However, Aeneas' mother Venus intervenes and makes Dido fall in love with Aeneas. The text presents this circumstance as contrary to the desires of Dido, much like the myth of Jason portrays Medea when she holds a dominant position at Colchis as priestess to Hecate being reduced, again presumably against her wishes at the bidding of Hera, to falling in love with Jason, a stranger who has come to destroy her father's hold on his kingdom. Dido, in loving this stranger to Carthage, also subjects the security of her kingdom; therefore, the downfall of these powerful women presented in both myths suggests that they are again products of the eras in which they were written when female authority was often mythically challenged.

At Venus' bidding, Dido falls in love with Aeneas, and they have sex within a cave, which also suggests, along with her powerful role as Queen, that she may be another mythic representation that is at least reminiscent of an Earth Goddess, as caves were often connected to Earth Goddess worship:

> Primal Earth herself and Nuptial Juno
> Opened the ritual, torches of lightning blazed,
> High Heaven became witness to the marriage,
> And nymphs cried out wild hymns from a mountain top [Virgil 101].

Dido believes that they are married because of this scene within the cave that to her is sacred, and also full of practices associated with more traditional earth-based, goddess worship, but as they have not formally gone through a marriage ceremony, and yet live openly as lovers, rumors begin to fly about Dido's continued capability to rule. In addition, Dido, once in love with Aeneas, does indeed falter in her ability to govern:

> Towers, half-built, rose
> No farther; men no longer trained in arms
> Or toiled to make harbors and battlements
> Impregnable. Projects were broken off [Virgil 98].

Aeneas is depicted as loving Dido, but as receiving the message that he must leave her to achieve his fate of helping to found Rome. Though Aeneas feels great pain at leaving Dido, the gods increase his resolve to leave, until he does so. His emotional state as he listens to the lamentations of Dido is captured with natural imagery, which evokes a sense of questioning between the role of nature and mankind:

> God's will blocked the man's once kindly ears.
> And just as when the north winds...
> contend with themselves
> To tear away an oaktree hale with age,
> The wind and tree cry, and the buffeted trunk
> Showers high foliage to earth, but holds
> On bedrock, for the roots go down as far
> Into the underworld as cresting boughs
> Go up in heaven's air: just so this captain,
> ...stood fast; tears fell in vain [Virgil 112].

Aeneas seems to personally want to stay and live a happy life with Dido, but the gods make him resolved to forego his personal desires. This appears to make Aeneas a hero who sacrifices his personal desires for something greater, but the text allows audiences to question just exactly what Aeneas is sacrificing himself for. Aeneas steps into his perceived sense of duty to chase a goal that is decidedly unnatural. Aeneas' depiction as being related to a tree that withstands the force of the winds in denying Dido certainly sends a societal message that male heroes should not succumb to the requests of women, especially women with power, but the natural imagery he is portrayed as connected to makes this message one that can be questioned. The tree, meant to represent Aeneas, has its roots reaching deep into the underworld, presumably to show how steadfast Aeneas is in his resolve to carry on with his mission; however, Aeneas will soon have to journey into that underworld, and there he learns about life through the lessons of the cycles of nature, which adds an important philosophical conversation into the text.

Aeneas, like a tree, may seem to remain devoted to his resolve, but also like a tree, he has the opportunity to symbolically live both on earth and below it when he visits the underworld while fully alive, revealing to him that his mission to found Rome may not matter as much as he thinks it does. Aeneas can be compared to the heroes of Beowulf and Sigurd in his view on the nature of life. All three heroes sacrifice their lives under a view that to die for something greater is ideal. All three heroes view life as transient and mortals as mere subjects to the laws of fate. This viewpoint seems to be aligned with the goal of apotheosis for the botanical hero; however, there is a decided difference in value systems that makes all the difference in the spiritual achievement of the hero. The vital component for the botanical hero to reach enlightenment is not just to die, or not truly live out his or her life in an acceptance of the necessity of sacrifice; instead, botanical heroes must psychologically accept that death is natural, so that they learn to embrace life with more fervor while they are alive. Aeneas' choice to leave Dido seems to spell out the beginnings of his journey into stripping away the components of his persona to reach botanical apotheosis, but instead, it appears as not a choice at all because the gods have dictated it, which suggests that instead of nearing botanical enlightenment, Aeneas may only be a pawn to achieve Virgil's societal and political goals—goals that are out of the realm of nature.

Van Nortwick points out that Dido "is to be a second self for Aeneas, representing parts of himself unrealized, holding out the prospect of a richer, more complete life" (*Somewhere*, 103). Van Nortwick continues "to suggest that a hero reaches a higher level of spiritual development by acknowledging and integrating aspects of himself objectified in a woman" (*Somewhere*, 117); he states that "Virgil is merely pushing further an element of the second-self dynamic already present, if underplayed in ... the *Iliad*.... Patroclus represent[s] in various ways qualities that could be associated, in the cultures out of which the poems emerged, with femininity" (*Somewhere*, 117). Van Nortwick points out, similar to Campbell's scholarship of the heroic quest, that the hero to become fully an archetypal, self-actualized hero, must internalize aspects of both the traditionally masculine and feminine. Van Nortwick also connects concepts of the feminine within heroic myth with the natural world, and this connection is vital to understanding archetypal heroes in botanical terms. However, Aeneas fails to embrace these "feminine" attributes that are often mythically connected to natural systems, thus failing at seeing the importance of life, nature, or anything but founding Rome. Van Nortwick states of Aeneas that Virgil is "at pains to show how Aeneas is unsuited to the role of masculine leader. Perhaps the most striking aspect of this portrait is the reluctance of Aeneas—he did not choose to lead the Trojans, and would rather have died at Troy. Passive, rather than active ... he trudges along" (*Somewhere*, 98). Therefore, Aeneas is not a botanical hero, because there is no real psychological turmoil; he is just following ordained rules, making him at best a societal hero.

Duty bound, not to Dido but to Rome, Aeneas leaves Dido alone in her kingdom with her people who now distrust her intentions. Dido, feeling ruined, orders a pyre to be constructed with Aeneas' belongings, first stating that she is having it constructed to perform magic rites that will either restore Aeneas' love for her or cause her to be free of her emotions for him. Dido states that she has obtained the help of a priestess to perform her needed magical rites:

> A priestess of Massylian stock has come;
> ... custodian
> Of that shrine named for daughters of the west,
> Hesperides; and it is she who fed
> The dragon, guarding well the holy boughs
> With honey dripping slow and drowsy poppy.
> Chanting her spells she undertakes to free
> What hearts she wills, but to inflict on others
> Duress of sad desires; to arrest
> The flow of rivers, make the stars move backward,
> Call up the spirits of deep Night. You'll see
> Earth shift and rumble underfoot and ash trees
> Walk down mountainsides [Virgil 113].

These references to a powerful priestess explicitly points to a traditional view of Earth Goddess worship. Dido climbs atop of the constructed pyre and has the priestess of the Hesperides perform rites that the text clearly aligns with chthonic divinities, such as Hecate and Diana. Instead of fully waiting to see the effect of these sacred rites connected to goddess and earth worship, Dido follows through with her plan. The next morning, she considers sending a fleet to destroy the Trojan ships, but instead prays to the gods to destroy Aeneas before he can found Rome. Dido then climbs atop the pyre once more, and as it burns, she stabs herself with Aeneas' sword, killing herself. It is significant that Dido does not harbor a belief that the sacred rites performed will work; instead, she simply dies. This could suggest that she knows her reign of matriarchal rule has come to an end, or it could mean that she has fully committed to death. As stated, Dido's role within the *Aeneid* is a conflicted one. There are components that show Dido in a position of incredible power that might tie her to remnants of Earth Goddess worship. When Aeneas lands at Carthage, the description of the wildness of her kingdom is significant, as Dido is clearly aligned to this wild description when Virgil connects her appearance to the goddess of the wilderness, Diana. Dido is also wild in her passion. R. Armstrong states that Dido is presented "as something of an honorary Cretan woman" in her appearance as both wild and autonomous (106); the *Aeneid* "clearly ... identifies Dido" with Crete, as she "identifies with nature rather than culture, passion rather than passivity" (R. Armstrong 107). Also, it is important that later in the text, after Dido's death, Cretan women, Pasiphaë and Phaedra, "accompany her in the underworld" (R. Armstrong 107). Van Nortwick concurs that Dido, "not Aeneas, is the true heir to Achilles" (*Somewhere*,

136), but Van Nortwick states that Aeneas is poised as a new type of hero that must sacrifice all for societal gain. Therefore, Dido may appear as the best contender for the botanical hero of the *Aeneid,* as she is portrayed at the beginning of the epic to possess strength similar to other botanical heroes, but Dido falls into a portrayal of weakness, killing herself with the sword of a societal hero. Furthermore, Dido's suicide is described in final terms; therefore, it is not a symbolic gesture of a mythic Earth Goddess or botanical hero showing that life comes from death in nature's cycles. The shade of the dead Dido only meets and shuns Aeneas upon his journey into the underworld, displaying her as not a botanical hero, or a representation of an Earth Goddess. Therefore, for the most part, Dido is depicted as only a character who is overtaken by the male hero, Aeneas, and his fate to found an empire.

Upon Aeneas leaving Dido, "grieving, and in tears" (*Aeneid* 159), he sails finally to Italy where he encounters the Cumaean Sybil who guides him through the underworld. The Cumaean Sybil is often connected to the Roman conception of the Great Mother Goddess, or Magna Mater. In Roman belief, the Cumaean Sybil is also directly connected to nature, as she is said to have read the oak leaves scattered by the wind in order to decipher one's fate. She also, as presented later by Ovid in his *Metamorphosis,* was said to represent all the stages of life, as she once was a beautiful maiden desired by the god Apollo. Apollo promised to give her anything she wished, and so she held up a handful of sand and asked for as many years of life as the grains of sand she held in her hand. Apollo granted her wish, but she still refused to have sex with him, so he did not grant her everlasting youth for all the years she would live. Ovid presents the Sybil as knowing that she will grow so old that her form will become increasingly small, so that one distant day no one will be able to recognize her as human. It is her knowledge of the fleeting nature of life connected with the natural imagery of sand that reveals that she well knows her life and her autonomy will be reduced to the size of each grain of sand she held in her hand. The Sybil's knowledge of the cycles of nature makes her the one who is capable of leading Aeneas through the underworld.

Interestingly, the physical place that inspired Virgil to construct Aeneas' journey to the underworld is said to be the Phlegran fields in the Campania region of southern Italy. The physical location is certainly a place of mystery with its volcanic emissions creating an eerie atmosphere, but what is quite telling is that in this region the Romans believed, and Virgil's text supports this, that there is a lake, Lake Avernus, that is said to be the direct entrance into the underworld. It is this area where Aeneas met with the Sybil in Cumae and entered the underworld through her cave. Interestingly, Lake Avernus, even today, is not at all eerie, as one might imagine the entrance of the underworld to be, but quite the opposite; it is, and presumably was in ancient times, an area of serene beauty surrounded by verdant and thriving nature. What is also interesting is that this region was, and continues to be, agriculturally productive, which suggests a Roman view of the underworld not as a place of horror, but again a natural place symbolic of nature's regenerative processes—suggesting that Aeneas going into the womb of the regenerative earth, will enable him to also emerge out again reborn, like so many botanical heroes have done before him.

Aeneas' journey into the realm of death is sufficiently horrific to meet the requirements of the heroic archetype of the underworld, as he witnesses the spirits of those who died before him, including his beloved father, Anchises. This encounter with death shows Aeneas, like it did for Odysseus, that he will one day cease to live. As stated Aeneas also sees Dido there, who wrathfully refuses to speak to him. The underworld for Aeneas, though, does not seem to psychologically transform him enough to make him a botanical hero, as he leaves there having gained the assuredness that he will help to found the legendary Rome, and thus his descendants will honor his name for years to come. Again, this signal towards honor and fame thwarts the true message of the underworld for the botanical hero, as, again, the realization of the necessity to lose one's identity is crucial for the botanical hero to reach a state of spiritual apotheosis.

Before Aeneas enters the underworld, the Sybil tells him that in order for him to ascend from the land of death, he must look for the golden bough that is sacred to both Juno and Prosperina that:

> When torn away, in place of it a second
> Grows up without fail, all gold as well,
> Flowering with metallic leaves again [Virgil 164].

The use of yet another natural symbol in relation to Aeneas, this time of the golden bough, alludes to Aeneas needing to fully learn the lessons of the underworld, as not only a place of death, but of regeneration, like the referenced bough itself.

Aeneas again views the lessons of natural regeneration when in Elysium, a place of overt and natural beauty, within the underworld, where he finds his father's spirit, Anchises, who tells him that the spirits here drink from the River Lethe, so they forget their former lives and reincarnate:

> When they have turned Time's wheel a thousand years,
> The god calls in a crowd to Lethe stream,
> That there unmemoried they may see again
> The heavens and wish re-entry into bodies [Virgil 185–6].

In this passage, Anchises reveals to Aeneas a view of reincarnation that is quite in accordance to the pattern of cyclical nature, showing that from death, new life is produced. It is also significant that this is revealed to Aeneas within the underworld, as again many myths from nature-dependent communities discuss death in the natural terms of returning into the earth only to remerge in rebirth. Aeneas has been given the key to the wisdom of nature that must be embraced for a hero to become a botanical hero.

However, Aeneas' ascension from his journey into the underworld proves that he does not fully understand or embrace the wisdom he obtained while within the earth. Just as he never really grasped the significance of Dido; he does not fully understand the significance of the underworld with its feminine and natural references of the golden bough, Proserpina, or the Sybil.

Aeneas fails his botanical heroic quest because he solely follows an ordinance to found Rome under pretenses of violence to the people already living there. Aeneas' "trend toward diminished self-knowledge seems to continue—unquestioning acceptance and loyalty are the hallmarks of Aeneas' new disposition" (Van Nortwick, *Somewhere*, 150). Aeneas therefore has learned nothing from the useless devastation he witnessed on his homeland of Troy, and so never learns the value of life, even after journeying into and out of the underworld; therefore, the *Aeneid* presents Aeneas as ultimately failing to become a botanical hero.

Rather, the Cumaean Sybil perhaps serves as the botanical hero of the text, as she lives between life and death, transgressing into and out of the underworld, reading the wind-swept oak leaves to interpret the events in the fleeting lives of mortals. The Cumaean Sybil heroically accepts that she is no different than a grain of sand, as a botanical hero must.

The Underworld Is Within—Ershkigal, Ishtar and Nergal

The botanical hero often must come to a point where he or she realizes that the underworld is in fact within his or her own psyche. In an Akkadian myth involving the Queen of the Underworld, Ershkigal, she is portrayed as revealing yet another side of death.[2] The myth opens with the gods holding a feast, but as they are unable to invite Ershkigal, because death is not permitted to leave the underworld, they invite her to send her messenger, Namtar, whose name means Fate, to collect some items from the feast and bring them back to Ershkigal. Once Namtar enters the feast, he finds that the gods all bow down to him in honor of Ershkigal, all except one god named Nergal, who refuses.

When Ershkigal heard from Namtar that Nergal refused to bow in reverence of death, she sends her demand to the gods that Nergal must die. The gods, upon hearing this message agree and send Nergal to the underworld. The honor that the gods show Ershkigal is central to this myth, as it shows a deep respect for Ershkigal, and more importantly, for the concept of death even by the divine beings within the myth.

The myth of the Sumerian and later Akkadian/Babylonian Inanna/Ishtar also shows Inanna/Ishtar as having to learn to respect death by meeting her sister Ershkigal in the underworld. This myth shows Inanna/Ishtar, as the Queen of Heaven, knocking, full of conceit, upon the doors of the underworld, demanding to be let in. The doors open, but when Inanna/Ishtar enters the underworld, she soon finds that the underworld will not permit her or anyone to hold onto conceit. Instead, immediately upon entering the underworld, Inanna/Ishtar finds that everything that ties her to her identity is stripped away from her, as one by one, she loses all items that connect her to privilege and power, until she stands before her sister naked. Ershkigal then makes Inanna/Ishtar feel the full ramifications of what mortals must endure by giving her the most debilitating diseases she can think of, in order to dispel Inanna's/Ishtar's belief that she is invincible. Finally, Ershkigal hangs the body of Inanna/Ishtar, which now has been so desecrated that it resembles a corpse, from a hook and begins to speak to her. Ershkigal tells Inanna/Ishtar that as ruler of the underworld, she has had to contend with the harsh facts of death every day. She has had to feel what it is like to have lovers cry to her about having died before their wedding day, or infants whimper from never having known their mothers. Thus, Ershkigal systematically teaches Inanna/Ishtar the true cost of mortality, so that Inanna/Ishtar, a goddess associated with immortal life, can be educated on all facets of natural life, mythically making her a more relatable goddess to her worshippers. Inanna/Ishtar must respect and understand Ershkigal, not believe she can dominate her, in order for both sisters to serve as a symbolic representation of the life cycle. Inanna/Ishtar learns that she must face death, and this she does by giving her beloved husband, Dumuzi/Tammuz, over to Ershkigal, so that he may reside in the underworld, though Dumuzi/Tammuz symbolically rises from the underworld each spring, allowing the myth to also serve as a mythical explanation of nature's seasons that include a time of dormancy and a time of abundant growth. This myth shows, as the one of Nergal and Ershkigal also portrayed, how even the deities in Akkadian and Babylonian culture are not believed to be far removed from death, so that they may fully represent nature as it is.

In the myth of Nergal and Ershkigal, Nergel, being called by Ershkigal into the domain of the underworld for not showing death respect by bowing in honor of Ershkigal at the feast of the gods, charges past Ershkigal's guards and rushes directly at Ershkigal herself. In sheer defiance, much greater than that displayed by Inanna/Ishtar, Nergal "seized her by her hair and pulled her from her throne, intending to cut off her head" (Kerrigan, Lothian, & Vitebsky 46). Surprisingly, Ershkigal begs Nergal to be her husband. This scene is interesting, and has its counterparts in other classic myths, such as the scene in Homer's *Odyssey* when Odysseus is instructed by Hermes that the only way to defeat the powerful Circe is to immediately overpower her, hold a sword to her throat, and have sex with her, and in this myth too Circe relents and becomes enamored with Odysseus. This Akkadian scene, like the one from Homer, could again suggest a period of male domination overtaking feminine power through the use of myth, but within this story it appears that there may be more to this initial confrontation between the two deities of Nergal and Ershkigal. Nergal, is similar to Inanna/Ishtar and other heroic protagonists who want to defeat death, but they must discover in their respective myths that death can never be undone; instead, this myth continues to show that Ershkigal teaches Nergal about death, not through fearful means, as she did with her sister Inanna/Ishtar, but through tantalizing means.

Ershkigal states to Nergal, "'you shall be my master and I shall be your mistress!'" (Kerrigan, Lothian, & Vitebsky 47). At this Nergal is said to have "wept, then brushed away his tears and kissed her" (Kerrigan, Lothian, & Vitebsky 47). Ershkigal and Nergal apparently, and quite quickly, fall in love. Most versions of the myth show Nergal and Ershkigal having sex, and then Nergal attempting to flee or simply wishing to leave, but all versions show Nergal finding that he is drawn back to the underworld by his own inner motivation. Nergal is then said to choose to stay in the underworld with Ershkigal forever.

This myth does not simply showcase a cautionary tale about learning to respect the magnitude of death, as Inanna/Ishtar had to learn; instead, it reveals Nergal as first attempting to defeat death, but ending up being tantalized by death. The myth finally shows Nergal's willingness to accept death fully and concede that his identity is fleeting and inconsequential in the larger scheme of nature, thus making Nergal a botanical hero.

Gilgamesh and Enkidu—Nature's Lesson of Life

Gilgamesh in the Sumerian *Epic of Gilgamesh* is a prime example of a botanical hero because of his experience transgressing into the underworld. Gilgamesh begins as an unrighteous king who is taking advantage of his people in Uruk. The people demand better from the gods, and in answer to their cries, they are rewarded with a wild man named Enkidu sent by the Earth Goddess Ninhursag. Enkidu is portrayed as a clear representation of nature, as he is in every way wild. Enkidu lives outside of Uruk in the unchartered wilderness; he lives among the animals as one of them, running with them, and drinking from the same watering hole. He is also completely covered in fur. The text interestingly shows Enkidu being stripped of his wildness by a priestess who comes to him in the wilderness and entices him to have sex with her. Once the two copulate, Enkidu is depicted as forever changed away from some aspects of his animal nature into a more "civilized" human being, as he is no longer allowed to reside among the animals, as they all now flee from him.

It is at this point that Gilgamesh discovers Enkidu, and seeing him, Gilgamesh immediately proceeds to fight him. As the two battle, Gilgamesh soon realizes, with the aid of a dream he had, that Enkidu is in fact his equal. The myth evolves to show that Enkidu is an integral part of Gilgamesh himself, as they, together, enter upon their heroic quest into unknown realms. As previously discussed, the archetype of entering into unknown environments is an essential part of the process of stripping the hero of his or her former identity. In this myth, Gilgamesh must enter into a realm that is completely unknown to him, so that he may be receptive towards psychologically changing, since again the quest of the botanical hero is for the hero to find spiritual knowledge within. Gilgamesh is two thirds immortal, and one third mortal; the goal of his conscious quest becomes a journey towards discovering how to eradicate his mortal third. Gilgamesh believes that his heroic quest will involve him freeing himself from the confines of mortality, as he seeks the secrets of immortality, but his botanical heroic journey must instead teach him to learn the important lessons nature holds.

It is significant that Gilgamesh's first task upon his journey places him in the sacred Cedar Forest important to Enlil and the fertility goddess Ishtar, and he takes it upon himself to utterly destroy this environment that serves as an exemplification of the everlasting quality of nature, as cedar trees appear to resist the cyclical pattern of life and death by remaining green all year. It is also important that when Gilgamesh first enters this wilderness, it is so foreign to him that he pauses and marvels at it:

> They stood there marveling at the foot,
>   gazing at the lofty cedars,
> gazing at forest's entrance [*Gilgamesh* 39].

At this early point in the text, Gilgamesh is filled with awe at what to him is an otherworld of unchartered wildness, but instead of revering the land, he adopts a position to destroy it because he fears it, as up until this point in his life, he has remained within the confines of "civilized" society. His impulse to destroy what he fears connects the wilderness to the primary goal of his quest— immortality. Gilgamesh fears death, as he is journeying upon his quest to find the secret of everlasting life; therefore, his fear of nature immediately upon his quest connects the two concepts within the epic. This scene makes it clear that Gilgamesh has no concept of nature, and without an understanding of nature's laws, Gilgamesh will not be able to come to terms with the reality of his own mortality.

Gilgamesh and Enkidu destroy the Cedar Forest that filled them with awe by desecrating it and cutting down many of the sacred trees. As a result, Gilgamesh and Enkidu encounter Humbaba, who is not really harming anyone, but is merely Enlil's guardian of the forest. Gilgamesh's action towards Humbaba shows that he is still the unruly king his own people despised, as he helps to mercilessly kill Humbaba. Enkidu, suggestive of a needed aspect of Gilgamesh's character, is afraid of the ramifications of killing Humbaba, and initially wants to leave Humbaba alone. This fear and reticence on the part of Enkidu shows that he, as a representation of nature, is respectful of life; "Enkidu's fear would reflect his former integration with nature—why go out of one's way to kill another creature who is not threatening you directly" (Van Nortwick, *Somewhere*, 21). But after Enkidu becomes convinced to kill Humbaba, he who once ran free amongst animals of the forest, now sees the protector of the forest as a monster; the "trauma and dissociation Enkidu has been made to undergo begin to make themselves terribly evident. Enkidu here is akin to an enslaved, or at least seduced, former wild animal made to undergo traumatic cultural experimentation. He also may be likened to a wolf who, when domesticated, is used to kill other wolves" (Barron 383). When assaulted by Gilgamesh and Enkidu, Humbaba begs to be spared, but it is, as Barron states "strangely" Enkidu who finally argues to kill him (383). This scene of destroying Humbaba reveals that Enkidu is symbolically dying because the natural state that originally defined him is becoming enmeshed within Gilgamesh. Enkidu, as a gift from the gods, is becoming part of Gilgamesh, transforming him from a ruthless king into a botanical hero.

Ishtar, again the Akkadian/Babylonian Queen of Heaven and the goddess of fertility, warfare, and wisdom, who is derived from the Sumerian Inanna, is depicted as wishing to marry Gilgamesh. Gilgamesh, though, does not want to marry her as he knows quite well what happens to the husbands of Ishtar. In Gilgamesh's firm declaration that he wants nothing to do with Ishtar, he reveals that he does not understand the meaning of the vital role of Ishtar within nature. It is true that Inanna's/Ishtar's male consorts do not fare well; like her story with Dumuzi/Tammuz that is discussed within this chapter, they are sacrificed so the natural cycle of life can continue. Gilgamesh denies Ishtar in his view that she is merely a harsh killer of men, but in running from her, he is only psychologically hiding from the fact that he will indeed one day die. Barron states that "the source of the eventual strife and chaos in Gilgamesh is equally a result of tearing Enkidu from the wilderness as of Gilgamesh and Inanna's [Ishtar's] disunion. Rather than seeing an inviolable sense of ritualized, cultural harmony evident in Inanna [Ishtar] and Dumuzi," the text shows a tension between Inanna/Ishtar and Gilgamesh; "these unresolved tensions lead to the civilizing of Enkidu…. It soon becomes poignantly clear that an accommodating, inclusive … pattern that above all exhibits reverence for (cultivated) nature—as evident in Inanna [Ishtar]—has been usurped by the violent and heroic, tragic plundering of the wilderness and assault on animal life" (382). Because Gilgamesh is unable to comprehend the significance of Ishtar, the text shows a crucial misunderstanding of life on the part of Gilgamesh. His outright denial of Ishtar, as a representative Earth Goddess, further reveals that he has no understanding of the basic functioning of nature, and it is precisely this lack of connection with nature, that has kept him in a place where he does not value life, wrongfully tyrannizing over his kingdom and searching for ways to live forever. Ishtar and Inanna were at one time sacred divine representatives of the cycles of the earth. In Sumerian times, Inanna was viewed as essential towards securing the productivity of the harvest, so that humanity could survive. It is also vital to understand that Inanna's male consort, Dumuzi, is just as essential to the success of the harvest; his position within the myth and correlating ritual reenactments is the same role human beings hold in the face of a greater nature. Dumuzi, as well all living beings, must die, so that the earth, represented by Inanna, can be sustained, assuring the prosperity of the people. Gilgamesh, first as a king, must learn to accept the symbolic role of Dumuzi, which means putting the lives of his subjects before his own pleasure; he also must adopt Dumuzi's acceptance of mortality to spirituality evolve into a botanical hero.

Oelschleger's points to Gilgamesh's and Enkidu's killing of Humbaba as representing "the relentless Sumerian encroachment on the ancient forests and the triumph of civilization over the wilderness" (39), signaling that this myth may also reveal cultural conflict similar to what appeared in Homer, as it perhaps captures a period where more traditional values were being either incorporated into or replaced by new cultural belief systems and practices. The conflict presented in this epic, which was pieced together from many sources found in the region, presents a unique view again into the mindset of a people at a time of cultural transformation. The role of Ishtar within this myth is indicative of cultural conflict, as Gilgamesh outright discredits her and labels her as close to evil for her treatment of men. This theme, of labeling the Earth

Goddess as sinister, appears similar to the treatment of such representatives in the later Babylonian tale of Marduk and Tiamet as well myriad Greek myths as discussed. Oelschleger succinctly connects the *Epic of Gilgamesh* to changing spiritual views of the era, as the roles of gods and goddesses evolved in this long period of cultural evolution, along with the perception and value of the natural world. Gilgamesh's desecration of the untouched Cedar Forest suggests a view of humanity's evolving belief that mankind may no longer need to subserviently bow down to nature in sacrifice; instead, Gilgamesh's actions in cutting down the Cedar Forest as a king, suggests a view that mankind can control nature, and is thus superior to it, and certainly the history of the Fertile Crescent provides evidence of this transition in belief systems as again Neolithic settlements here, along with their earth-based belief systems, gave way to invading peoples and their ideologies. However, this text, like many Greek texts, does not just rest easy in justifying these cultural transitions; instead, this text perhaps questions the validity of these changing ideologies, as Gilgamesh is not shown as dominating the environment. Instead, the *Epic of Gilgamesh* suggests more traditional ideological beliefs that point to Gilgamesh's desecration of nature as wrong, presenting the Earth Goddess he despises, Ishtar, as essential in instructing him of this, thus moving Gilgamesh closer to a realization of the lessons of botanical heroism.

After Gilgamesh denies Ishtar, and Gilgamesh and Enkidu return to Uruk, Ishtar demands that her father, Anu, and mother, Antum, send the Bull of Heaven to the people of Uruk. Anu tries to stop Ishtar by reminding her that the Bull of Heaven will cause seven long years of famine in Uruk, but she states that they have provisions prepared that will save them; she just wants the Bull of Heaven to destroy Gilgamesh. However, once the Bull of Heaven arrives in Uruk, it causes the ground to break open, and hundreds of people perish. Gilgamesh and Enkidu attack the Bull of Heaven and savagely tear it apart. Ishtar, inflamed, curses Gilgamesh and Enkidu, but Enkidu only throws part of the Bull at her and threatens her with the same fate. Gilgamesh then cuts off the Bull's horns and adorns his palace with them, as his people shout the praise of both Gilgamesh and Enkidu. This scene clearly demonstrates similar mythical episodes that deal with the overtaking of a traditional Earth Goddess by a male hero, like that of Theseus and the Minotaur. As discussed previously, the imagery of the bull was often utilized as a representative of Earth Goddesses and their male consorts, so it is highly significant that Gilgamesh and Enkidu kill the Bull and threaten Ishtar with such hostility. It asserts, in this time of cultural flux, that a new order is taking over dominance, putting to rest any semblances of matriarchal power. However, the myth does not end with this scene that leaves Gilgamesh and Enkidu merely societal heroes who hear their names chanted by crowds of approving people after they kill the Bull of Heaven and mock Ishtar. Instead, for Gilgamesh to fully realize his heroic journey towards botanical heroism, he will have to continue on until he learns the lessons of the myths he thought he overcame—the lessons of the mythic Earth Goddess.

In destroying the forest and its guardian Humbaba, as well as denying Ishtar, and later killing the Bull of Heaven, Gilgamesh and Enkidu, unbeknownst to them, bring upon Gilgamesh a psychic underworld that will leave him transformed, as Ishtar orders the death of Enkidu, who, as discussed, serves as Gilgamesh's other half. The scenes of the blatant destruction and denial of nature and its representatives: the Cedar Forest, Humbaba, the Bull of Heaven, and Ishtar, immediately thrust Gilgamesh into facing the one thing he feared most—his own death, which is symbolically brought about by the death of Enkidu. When Enkidu dies, Gilgamesh is referenced in overt natural images, such as an eagle circling the body of his dead friend, or a lioness that found its young killed; these natural images suggest the psychological transformation that is taking place within Gilgamesh in relation to nature. Nature will reveal to Gilgamesh that his own search for immortality is impossible, as everlasting life is just as much an abomination to the natural order as decimating the forest and brutally killing its inhabitants. Therefore, Ishtar kills Enkidu, not necessarily as a punishment for the wrongs done to her, as Gilgamesh interprets, but as a symbolic mythological lesson to Gilgamesh about death within the natural world.

Gilgamesh must learn that his quest for immortality is unnatural, and therefore will not lead to him becoming a capable leader of his people. Instead, Ishtar, in her earlier role as an Earth Goddess, through killing Enkidu teaches Gilgamesh that his own death is imminent and necessary:

> The suffering that Enkidu's passing brought for Gilgamesh is closely tied in the story of the king's quest for a way to escape his own death…. In accepting the inevitability of his own mortality, Gilgamesh by implication accepts the wild man as a part of himself…. Gilgamesh has now accepted, on a deeper level the presence of the wilderness within himself. The loss of Enkidu has, then, made a difference in the way Gilgamesh sees the world: death, once something to be defied, then to be denied, has become a part of life; Enkidu, lost forever, is at the same time found again [Van Nortwick, *Somewhere*, 34].

The myth propels Gilgamesh to proceed alone to continue to try to find the secret to obtain immortality, though of course he will never find it.

Once solitary, Gilgamesh is ready to face the mythic underworld, which in this myth is a tunnel that runs through a massive mountain and is guarded by a scorpion man and his wife. Gilgamesh upon entering the underworld, finds that he has to travel in complete darkness. He has no way of knowing in which direction he is walking; he simply has to continue walking, feeling his way through the confusion on this underworld. Again, the underworld is often a place where the botanical hero must face the death of self, and this is true for Gilgamesh within this symbolic representation of his own death, as he has no way of knowing if at any moment he will fall to his doom, become forever trapped, or encounter an adversary of which he is unprepared to face in this abyss of blackness. Van Nortwick states, Gilgamesh "goes to the underworld ... to discover how to escape being what he is, to escape death" (*Somewhere*, 28), but as is true of the heroic journey, the underworld for Gilgamesh precisely reveals the fact of his own impending mortality to him.

Also, the presentation of this underworld as a dark and seemingly endless cave connects the necessary psychological component the underworld must carry for the botanical hero, as Gilgamesh must contend with only his own mind while transgressing this domain. One's psyche can magnify the terror of any situation, and apparently here Gilgamesh must learn to control his mind if he will be able to resurrect out of this underground chamber. After seemingly unending hours of darkness, Gilgamesh emerges from this underworld into a land that seems magical to him as it is bursting with life. The abundant natural imagery, now viewed by Gilgamesh as beautiful and not a place to despise, like he viewed the Cedar Forest, signals that Gilgamesh has undergone a representational death of his former identity, and has upon emerging from the dark cave, experienced a symbolic rebirth.

In this state of psychological rebirth, the myth presents Gilgamesh as ready to hear the wisdom his journey will provide to him, and in the version of the epic found in Sippar, it first comes from Shiduri, the alewife he meets upon his ascension. Gilgamesh confides to Shiduri about what happened to Enkidu and about his own fear of death:

> Enkidu, whom I loved so deeply...
> He went to the doom of mortal men.
>   weeping over him day and night,
> I did not surrender his body for burial—
>   "Maybe my friend will rise at my cry!"—
> For seven days and seven nights,
>   until a maggot dropped from his nostril.
> After he was gone I did not find life,
>   wandering like a trapper in the midst of the wild.
> "O tavern-keeper, I have looked on your face,
>   but I would not meet death, that I fear so much" [*Gilgamesh* 124].

And here Gilgamesh gets the insightful message from Shiduri that discloses what most myths of the underworld reveal:

"O Gilgamesh, where are you wandering?
"The life that you seek you never will find:
    when the gods created mankind,
death they dispensed to mankind,
    life they kept for themselves.
"But you, Gilgamesh, let your belly be full,
    enjoy yourself always by day and by night!
Make merry each day,
    dance and play day and night!
"Let your clothes be clean,
    let your head be washed, may you bathe in water!
Gaze on the child who holds your hand,
    let your wife enjoy your repeated embrace!
"For such is the destiny [*of mortal* men] [*Gilgamesh* 123].

Still, Gilgamesh continues on his quest to seek out a means to avoid death and arrives at the compound of Utnapishtim, the oldest man alive who survived a great flood that is described in similar terms to the Old Testament tale of Noah's Ark. Utnapishtim tells Gilgamesh that even he, clearly favored by the gods, will one day die. He instructs Gilgamesh to give up his quest for immortality, but seeing Gilgamesh insist, he tells him the means towards securing long-lasting youth, not immortality, through the aid of a magical flower, the natural portrayal of which is significant, suggesting that the cycle of the flower in nature is something that Gilgamesh will need to understand before he can achieve botanical heroism. Utnapishtim tells Gilgamesh that the flower that he seeks is in a faraway place, so Gilgamesh must continue his quest.

Gilgamesh partakes on the final part of his journey alone into unchartered nature, where he eventually finds the flower he seeks, but in an anticlimactic way, Gilgamesh simply falls asleep once having secured the one thing that fulfilled his initial mission. While asleep a snake easily steals the magical flower, thus demanding that Gilgamesh finally accept his fate of eventual death.

The portrayal of a flower serving to show Gilgamesh the final lesson of his heroic quest perfectly signals to him the laws of the cycles of nature. Gilgamesh seeks out a flower that is full of resplendent beauty in order to try to obtain his own everlasting youth, but he finds that his mortal body has weakened as a result of his long and arduous journey, so he must give way to sleep. When he awakens, he learns that trying to obtain the miraculous beauty the flower held in his attempt to secure everlasting youth was an illusory endeavor, as the symbol of the flower teaches Gilgamesh about nature's cycles—flowers reveal spectacular beauty in their prime, but also show that this stage is short-lived as all flowers must wither and decay for new flowers to emerge. Van Nortwick states that "such a realization need not be entirely depressing. If death will take away the world, its prospect also clarifies.... All of this means that the acceptance of one's own mortality, painful though it may be, is one prerequisite for emotional maturity, because without it we cannot really know ourselves for what we are" (*Somewhere*, 12).

Gilgamesh must face his own death multiple times within the myth. He holds in his arms his other half, Enkidu, while he dies; he transgresses a psychological underworld in a dark and endless tunnel, and he symbolically allows a snake to sneak away with his means towards everlasting youth as a sign of his concession that he must embrace the fact of his own mortality.

The myth ends with Gilgamesh returning to his kingdom to stand among his people with his newfound knowledge that will make him a better king. He knows now that he is not better than his people in his semi-divinity, but that he is in fact mortal and fallible like them. Gilgamesh failed his quest to find immortality, and upon returning to his kingdom, he is not initially depicted as receiving any praise for his heroic journey. Instead, Gilgamesh's journey was not a quest that might be found in popular contemporary renditions of a hero, it was a psychological quest, where he faced his own fears and desires for importance and ended the journey knowing his own mediocrity. Gilgamesh's heroic quest taught him to embrace his mortality, and it is the embrace of the thing he feared most—death—that allowed him to be psychologically reborn, so that he may truly live as a botanical hero.

Needing to Cheat Death—American Indian Myths of the Land of Death

The Zuni American Indians recount a legend of a husband attempting to retrieve his wife from the underworld.[3] The myth states that the man, upon losing his beloved young wife, is determined to go to the place that no mortal should enter, the Land of the Dead, in order to bring her back with him. Leeming and Page state that "he waited by her grave one night and she appeared, smiling. 'Don't grieve so,' she said. 'I've merely left one life for another.' 'But I love you,' the young man said. 'I feel I must go with you'" (*The Mythology* 127). The wife tried to dissuade her husband's attempt to cheat death, but he was immovable and followed her when she left. She revealed to him that he would be unable to see her on their journey during the daylight hours, but if he tied a red eagle feather in her hair, he could follow the feather.

For many days, the man struggled to follow the feather that always seemed just out of his reach, and at the point where he reached utter exhaustion and thought he would be unable to continue, he saw the red feather glide effortlessly across a vast chasm of rock. He screamed to his wife that he loved her and wanted to follow; the man slid onto an unsecure ledge on the side of the cliff still calling after his wife, though he could no longer see her feather. Just then, when surely his own death was imminent, a small squirrel appeared and laughed at him, mocking him for his attempt to cheat death. But the squirrel also vowed to help him. This point in the myth provides the man his lesson about life and death. The squirrel shows the man the flimsiness between the two worlds of life and death, which is also what the man's wife tried to teach him.

The squirrel simply pulls out a seed and plants it in the rocky soil, and miraculously a tree bursts forth, giving the man a means to cross the chasm. To the man's delight, he sees his wife's feather fading into the distance, so he again follows it. Continuing his heroic quest, he chases after the feather for many more agonizing days, until he thinks he will soon die from the struggle to keep up. Once again, when he is about to lose hope, he sees the feather disappear into a deep and vast lake, and again he is forlorn. He thinks about diving in, but something tells him that within the lake is the Land of the Dead itself. After having traveled so far to get there, once there, he is terrified to enter it. He simply sits in front of the lake, stares into its depths, and cries until night comes. During the night an owl visits him. The owl inquires why the man cries, so the man tells him his sad story. Out of compassion, the owl instructs the man to come and live with him in the mountains, and if the man does this, he will again be reunited with his wife. The man readily follows. He finds that he is among owl men and owl women, but when the man looks at the owl man who greeted him, he sees the owl man removing his bodily covering to reveal himself in the form of a man.

The owl man tells the young husband to listen closely: "'this medicine will put you into a deep sleep, and when you awake you must follow the morning star to the middle anthill. Your wife will be waiting for you there, and when the sun rises she will live again. But be patient. Do not touch her or embrace her until you both have reached your home'" (Leeming & Page, *The Mythology*, 128). The owl people went down into the lake and recovered the wife and carried her in their wings up to their home, and the man awoke to see his young wife beside him. They both were ecstatic. Happily they left the home of the owls and made their way back towards their village, but on the way, the man could only stare at the beauty of his wife and marvel at how he succeeded in cheating death. Suddenly, overcome by his feelings of love for her, without thinking, he reached out and embraced his wife, and in a flash, crying out, she disappeared. The man's "eyes went blank and he stared into the distance and his mind raced off, never to return" (Leeming & Page, *The Mythology*, 129). The ending of this myth is also similar to the tale of Orpheus, as the Greek myth also shows Orpheus in an altered psychological state at the end of his quest. Some can interpret the state of the young man upon losing his wife forever as tragic, but another interpretation can reveal psychological wisdom, as the young husband finally loses his desire for his own autonomous identity and accepts the laws of nature, portrayed through the acceptance that he cannot retrieve his former life with his wife.

The young husband learned upon his quest, from first the squirrel on the deep rock chasm, that life and death are part of the same cycle; the squirrel showed the man that if he wanted to overcome death, he must see it as merely one stage within an endless cyclical reality. The squirrel revealed this wisdom with his symbolic lesson of easily planting a seed that grows into a tree to bridge the gap between life and death, so that the young husband could see that from death, the seed can produce new life. The man also learns this same lesson from the owl people. They too easily submerge themselves into the lake, the Land of the Dead, and bring out the man's wife, restoring her to life. Like the owl man's ability to transform into and out of his owl coverings with effortlessness, he too shows the young husband the workings of nature's patterns, as he symbolically portrays that one lifetime is merely a fleeting stage within an endless cycle of ceaseless lifetimes. In many American Indian myths, animals often teach mortal heroes the ease of shape-shifting or regenerating, as Manabozho learned from the moose mother being able to feed her children from her own carved flesh knowing that it would reproduce itself instantaneously. Animals often teach mythic heroes this regenerative lesson to show them that by embracing the workings of nature, one finally is able to glimpse a pattern that makes all life and death part of the same cyclical moment. The ability of the owl man to shape-shift, from owl to man, is the same ability the moose mother holds in instantaneously regenerating her flesh; it symbolically teaches audiences that death in nature induces constant rebirth.

The young husband in embracing his wife commits the same act Gilgamesh does when he falls asleep holding the means that would free him from death for many years. They both fail their initial quests, but as a result of their journeys, they learn that their initial quests were foolish. In Gilgamesh falling asleep and the young husband here trying to embrace his wife, they both break the rules that would have given them what they thought they wanted, but instead, they choose to not defy nature, but embrace it as it is. Gilgamesh will then live a normal lifespan and die when his time comes, just as this Zuni man finally accepts that his wife must remain dead, just as he eventually must die in order to perpetuate the necessary natural cycle.

An American Indian Pawnee legend presents another heroic journey into the underworld where a man attempts to retrieve someone he loves. The protagonist of the myth is presented as living what to him is an idealized life; he is married to a beautiful women and has a young son whom he adores. But, in accordance to the heroic mythic cycle, the protagonist is called away from this life, so that he may begin a journey that will leave him transformed. His wife falls ill and dies, and his son too soon becomes ill; the man cares for his son a long time, but ultimately does not have the power to save him, so he loses his son as well. His whole life comes to an abrupt stop; he no longer wishes to remain in his community, and even no longer wishes to remain living. He partakes on a heroic quest to thwart the natural cycles of life and death, as he wishes to find the Spirit World and retrieve his son.

After mourning at his son's grave for four days, the father wanders the wilderness looking for the entrance of the Spirit World. The father hears voices speaking in his own language, and when he sees people, they think that he is a strange tree; "'I have found a wonderful tree. It looks like a man'" (Astrov 112). The man knows that the people he found are spirits. Their comment to him of mistaken identity reveals an important aspect of the myth; to them, knowing intimately the natural cycles of life, a man and a tree are linked as one, no different from one another in the cycles of life and death. The father as yet uneducated on the cycles of nature, however, identifies them as dead, and seemingly insulted, they run away from him. Each time he pursues them, they continue to flee. The father finally comes to a thick grapevine that hides the entrance of a cave, and seeing this, he knows he has found the entrance of the Spirit World. This symbol of the grapevine leading this protagonist into a cave where the dead reside shows again the belief that death is tied to the natural world and its perpetual cycles, because the grapevine is known to live and thrive, decay, and then go dormant below ground, only to annually resurrect each spring.

At first the father is afraid to enter the Spirit World, recognizing the people within as the dead of his own tribe, but he finally does overcome his fear and emerges into the earth. Once there both the spirits of the dead, who fled from him on earth, and the father acknowledge a breaking down of the seeming boundaries between life and death, as they both are ready to speak to one another. The man tells a dead chief his worldly sorrows; he tells mostly of his son, saying that with his son dead, he too wishes to die. The leader understands the grief of the father and asks the gods to take pity on him and let him see his son once more. The leader tells the man that the gods have approved his request, but first he must return to his people and tell them that they all can again see their deceased relatives for four days, but they must not attempt to touch them or speak with them.

The man's journey continues in its mystical tone, as he swiftly makes it back to his people, so fast in fact that he marvels at the apparent leap in conceptual time. The man brings the people of his community back with him to the place where the spirits instructed him to meet them. At first the people are terrified, but as they begin to see again the faces of their deceased relatives, they rejoice, and they keep their promise to not try to speak with or touch any of them. The man's son finally appears, and immediately breaking the mortal pact he swore to the spirits, he reaches out and grasps his son; "He caught his son [;] he spoke to him and hugged him, and in his heart, he said: 'I will not let you go'" (Astrov 116)! Once this transgression occurs, his son and all the dead relatives disappear. The people leave and reenter their community mostly unchanged. But the man, as a result of his journey to the Spirit World is profoundly transformed. His former identity is lost forever. For the rest of his life, the man is deemed insane by his people because he lives outside the confines of his tribe. Instead, wearing a "horse robe," he chooses to live in the wild.

This myth, as stated, follows typical mythic archetypes for the heroic quest, but its ending appears somewhat different. The man is presented as feeling that he was called upon his quest to either secure his son back or die in the attempt; he leaves his familiar community and travels to the mythic underworld, but his overt confidence at breaking through the restrictions of mortality is important. Often mythic heroes enter the underworld, here presented as the Spirit World, to face the fact of death; this is, as discussed, often mythically portrayed as a terrifying and hard experience for the hero, but here, the father is quite willing to die. He has already faced the worst the underworld usually has to teach mortals through the deaths of his loved ones, so he welcomes death for himself. This willingness to die gives him the confidence to try to defy natural law, so that he eventually tries to take back his son. The myth suggests that his over-confidence causes him, and his people, to be punished, as his son disappears and his people are no longer allowed to be reunited with the dead. But the man's unification with nature at the end of the myth is revealing, suggesting that the man was not punished in trying to reunite with his son, but merely learned a necessary lesson about death.

The father's people view him as insane, but in many world myths this is rarely indicative of the true state of the hero, as the community's assessment of the hero seldom matters. The myth could be interpreted to suggest that the man chooses a way that is different from his people because he has accepted natural laws that supersede mortal understandings. In choosing to leave his community and live a solitary life in the wild, suggests that the man has indeed accepted the cyclical aspect of nature, and in doing so has obtained botanical wisdom as a result of his underworld journey.

The Hero Twins Overcome Death

The Maya text, the *Popul Vuh*, recounts their version of creation; it also tells of an adventurous tale involving the underworld, Xibalba, labeled the "Place of Fear." The creator gods of the *Popul Vuh* eventually had two sons, the twins, Hun Hunahpu and Vucub Hunahpu. They were notorious for gambling and playing a ball game called Ōllamalizti. One day while playing they were so loud that they caused the lords of Xibalba to become angry, so they intervened and projected the twins into Xibalba. While immersed within this underworld, the lords of Xibalba told the twins to sit down, but their seat burned them. Then they were instructed to go deeper into the underworld into a region called the Dark House for the night. In the morning the lords of Xibalba returned to the terrified twins and ordained that they would be killed at the sacrificial ball court, which indeed they were.

After their deaths, the head of Hun Hunahpu was cut off and hung on a tree, which became the first gourd tree. The text continues to show the maiden Xquic, daughter of one of the lords of Xibalba, one day reaching out to pick a gourd that hung from this tree, but as she did this the head of Hun Hunahpu spit on her, and she was suddenly impregnated by him. This angered her father so much that he also ordered her death, but she escaped and journeyed to the land of the living to live with Hun Hunahpu's mother, where she later gave birth to the Maya Hero Twins, Hunahpu and Xbalanque.

The Hero Twins, like their father and uncle, loved to play Ōllamalizti, and one day after they were fully grown they learned the fate of their kin, so they decided to journey upon their heroic quest to Xibalba to avenge Hun Hunahpu's and Vucub Hunahpu's deaths. They started the process in the same way that brought about the demise of their loved ones and began to play ball too loudly. The lords of Xibalba again became enraged at this loud sound, pre-sumably because the sounds of one enjoying life was offensive to beings associated with death, so they challenged the Hero Twins to a game of Ōllamalizti. In this challenge, the Hero Twins descended into the realm of death, and like their father and uncle, they too were subjected to many trying ordeals that forced them to face the terrifying fact of death. The Hero Twins were mandated to stay in the Dark House, as well as the Razor House, the Cold House, the Jaguar House, the Fire House, and the House of Bats. Each night they were forced to face their worst fears, but they remained psychologically strong. The Hero Twins faced the sure death that killed their father and uncle and still avoided each trap set forth for them. And similarly they avoided all of the other perils of the subsequent trials while within the underworld.

The Hero Twins, however, could not avoid death for the entirety of their journey, as again the role of the underworld for the botanical hero is to show him or her the fact of eventual mortality. Each day the Hero Twins had to incessantly play Õllamalizti against the lords of the Xibalba, suggesting that in all games of life, death is always close at hand, as even in the religious reenactments of this mythic game, the ancient Mayas would sometimes sacrifice the players of the game, who were often war captives. In the last house the Hero Twins had to endure, the House of Bats, Hunahpu gets his head bitten off by a bat. The next day Hunahpu's head then becomes the ball for Õllamalizti.

Xbalanque, though, remains steadfast to what kept him alive thus far—his psychological wit. He fashions a head of wood for his brother, and reanimates Hunahpu, so he is able to play in this game of life or death with his brother Xbalanque. Eventually as they are playing, Hunahpu grabs his brother's head and puts it back on Xbalanque's frame, fully resurrecting him anew. It is this point in the myth where the Hero Twins are now capable of winning the game against the forces of death, the lords of Xibalba. This aspect in the myth suggests that when they both finally face the fact of death, it is only then that they are capable of moving past it, and again, here death is merely portrayed as a necessary stage that can be overcome. The Hero Twins are not portrayed as stricken with agony over the development of Hunahpu's initial death; they simply accept it, use Hunahpu's head to roll upon the earth, perhaps representative of invigorating the earth through fertilization, and then return Hunahpu's head to his body, so he can be resurrected. It is this newfound knowledge that allows the Hero Twins to master death, sending again a botanical message to audiences, that like nature, death is merely one part of a more continuous seasonal cycle.

To further this necessary acceptance of death, the lords of Xibalba, enraged, take both Hero Twins and burn their bodies, grind down their bones, and sprinkle the dust of their remains in the river. But the myth presents, again, that when viewed in terms of nature's cycles, death is only one stage in an everlasting cycle, as both Hero Twins are again resurrected in six days. They then declare that they put themselves back together from the many pieces scattered about the land by the river's current, and now they know the secret of how to bring the dead back to life. Again, the mythic elements are clear; the death and reduction of the Hero Twins' bodies into nothing but ashes spread throughout the land by the mode of water, followed by their resurrection, shows that in nature death is only a means for regrowth.

Furthermore, once resurrected the Hero Twins proceed to prove their new lesson they learned as a result of their underworld experience by appearing to their murderers, the lords of Xibalba, and showing them the true aspect of nature's cycles. To prove this, Xbalanque held down Hunahpu and cut out his heart in front of the lords; then Xbalanque told his brother to stand, which he did:

> One by one his legs, his arms were spread wide. His arms were spread wide. His head came off. Rolled far away outside. His heart, dug out, was smothered in a leaf, and all the Xibalbans went crazy at the sight. So now, only one of them was dancing there: Xbalanque. "Get up!" he said, and Hunahpu came back to life. The two of them were overjoyed at this [*Popul Vuh* 136–7].

This mythic aspect too may help to explain the practice of Maya sacrifice where victims often had their hearts removed in sacrifice to assure the continuation of survival through the appeasement of the gods. This myth makes it clear that the Maya accepted that the propagation of new life in nature depended on death. The myth also suggests that the Hero Twins learned how to overcome death by their embrace of it, so that when viewed in terms of nature, death is only a part of a continuous cycle that will always be restored with new life. The Lords of Xibalba could only stare in astonishment at the ease in which the Hero Twins could move from death to life. With this evidence, the lords of the underworld ask the Hero Twins to also kill them, so they too can overcome death. So the Hero Twins appease the Lords of Xibalba by killing them and cutting out their hearts, but of course now the Hero Twins do not bring back to life the Lords of Xibalba.

The Hero Twins are good examples of botanical heroes because they are mythically portrayed as losing all sense of their identity upon the fulfillment of their quest by ultimately being transformed into the natural elements of the sun and moon. The lesson that the *Popul Vuh* relates to audiences is that again the theme of death and resurrection for the botanical hero is merely a representation of the seasonal aspects of nature's cycles. The Hero Twins were sometimes depicted alongside the Maya maize god, who was attributed as being a resurrected version of their deceased father Hun Hunahpu; this again recounts the natural explanation that like the harvesting of corn, death and dismemberment is essential for the assurance of a new crop, just as death is an essential part of the lives of human beings. If audiences grasp the message of the *Popul Vuh* that does not elevate the Hero Twins as exceptionally important, but as mere representations of nature, then audiences see that they too can overcome the fear of death by the psychological acceptance of it as natural, becoming botanical heroes themselves.

Kwasi Benefo's Underworld Journey for Love

The Ashanti people of Africa have a myth about Kwasi Benefo, who also made a journey to the underworld. In his life he married four women, and each one died. After the death of his first and then his second wife, Kwasi Benefo, separated himself from his people in grief. The people saw that he never emerged out of his house, so the family of his second wife, seeing how much he had loved their daughter sent him their other daughter to marry, saying "'What is past is past, one cannot go there anymore. What a man has loved in heart, it does not go away. Let the dead live with the dead, and the living with the living'" (Ford 22). Ford states that the family of Kwasi Benefo's deceased wife refer here to the Ashanti belief "that the dead inhabit a world that is a mirror image of the world of the living, only underground" (22).

Kwasi Benefo does marry the sister of his deceased wife, and finds that he is able to experience happiness again, until she also dies when a tree falls on her. When Kwasi Benefo learns of the tragedy, he embraces his wife's body and falls into a state that resembles death to the people of his village; "he threw himself on the ground and lay there as if life had departed from him also. He heard nothing, felt nothing. People said 'Kwasi Benefo is dead'" (Ford 23). The people send for their medicine man who recognizes that Kwasi Benefo yet lives; he only "'lingers between here and there'" (Ford 23). The medicine man is able to awaken Kwasi Benefo, but he is never the same.

Distraught with the events of his life, Kwasi Benefo leaves his village to enter into a life within the isolated bush. Desiring a "wild place," Kwasi Benefo builds himself a crude structure and lives off of the resources nature provides. Over time, his hair grew out; he wore the skins of animals, and he forgot his former life and even his name. This point within the myth is crucial to marking Kwasi Benefo as a botanical hero because the factuality of death, as he was forced to witness through the deaths of his wives, caused him to return to nature, and in doing so, he meets the archetypes of the botanical heroic quest. The deaths of his wives become for him his own psychological underworld, and his return to his wild self, marks him as accepting the natural inevitability of death. His willingness to lose identity is an important marker in identifying him as acknowledging the patterns of the natural world.

However, the myth states that Kwasi Benefo does not remain secluded in his wild hermitage, as after many years, he tries again to reenter a life similar to the one he left behind in a new village. But, the botanical heroic quest seldom lets the hero merely reintegrate back into mundane life after his or her journey, so here too, Kwasi Benefo marries for the fourth time, but finds that he has not fully achieved his quest, so mythically his fourth wife also dies. Kwasi Benefo then prepares to die. He returns to the village of his former home to be buried near the graves of his ancestors. But, one night, he feels called to journey to Asamando, the Land of the Dead, to seek his lost loves.

Kwasi Benefo went to the place of the burial of his wives and then beyond it, passing through a dark, silent, trackless forest where he came to a river. On the far side sat the old woman who greets dead women's souls. She felt sorry for him and allowed him to cross the river, though normally the living are forbidden to enter Asamando. Once in the underworld, he finds that little has changed in this land of the dead beneath the soil. He sees fields and a village, and hears the sound of villagers and farmers carrying on as usual, though he can see no people. Suddenly, he hears the voices of his wives, and they begin to tend to him, feeding him, helping him to finally rest. They tell him that he cannot see them because they are unencumbered by a body. They also tell him that he was a kind husband, and that he should embrace life while he is living, and only die when it is natural for him to do so. They instruct him to return to the land of the living, and to marry again, promising that his fifth wife would live, and that they would be waiting for him in the underworld when his time came to die. Hearing this, Kwasi Benefo fell into a deep sleep and awoke again in the bush, back in the land of the living.

Kwasi Benefo then merely walked back to his home village. Though it is rare for any hero to simply return back to his or her former life and identity, this myth allows Kwasi Benefo to do just this. The myth suggests that he could not do this before fully learning what death meant in natural terms. The four deaths of his wives only made him see one side of death, only as a mortal defines it, as an end. Therefore, when he tried to start a new life in a new village with his fourth wife, before visiting Asamando, his pursuits failed. He had to venture into the domain of death to see it for what it really was—natural. He saw that life there was no different than the life he was used to; he saw that his deceased wives relished the fact that they were not encumbered by bodies. This mythic depiction is suggestive that the Ashanti underworld and perception of death is viewed in terms closely aligned with the cycles of the natural world—when one dies, one merely lives on. The botanical heroism of Kwasi Benefo provides a mythic example that shows this cyclical promise of the underworld.

Marwe's Journey to the Womb of the Earth

In Kenya, there is a myth of a young girl named Marwe, who, with her brother, was responsible for keeping monkeys from eating the family's crop of beans.[4] While guarding the bean fields one day, Marwe and her brother momentarily leave to relieve their thirst, but upon returning they see that the monkeys have eaten all the beans. Marwe, afraid of what her family would do upon hearing the news of their lost crop, drowns herself. Her family is distraught upon hearing the news of Marwe's suicide.

Upon Marwe's death, though, she embarks upon her own heroic quest. She sinks to the bottom of the pool, until she finds herself in the underworld. The direct descent into the underworld from the natural source of the pool reminds audiences that death for all is a returning to the source that propagated new life. She returns into the womb of the earth, where she finds an old woman living with her many young children; the old woman tells Marwe that she will be her guide into the underworld. The depiction of this generational aspect within the myth is crucial.

Marwe as a maiden has died before she has fulfilled her natural role. The representation of the children being watched over by the old woman, might point towards Marwe's natural obligation to be a mother, signaling that her death was unnatural and so may not be recognized as final. Also, the fact that the young children are watched over by the elderly woman of the underworld adds a symbolic element of nature as cyclical to the myth, suggesting that rebirth from the old into the young will come from the underworld. Marwe's experience in dying here is not shocking or horrific, like it is in many heroic journeys; instead, it is represented as just another stage of the life cycle. In this realm of death, Marwe is only depicted as living with the old woman and her children, helping them, for many years.

One day, the old woman can see that Marwe wishes to return to the land of the living, so she again treats this apparently mystical request like a mundane matter. She tells Marwe to dip her hands, legs, and feet into a jar of cold water, and when Marwe pulls them out, she finds that they are covered in jewels. This odd portrayal of Marwe obtaining objects of wealth upon requesting to return to life suggests her underworld transformation. As stated, often heroes leave the underworld spiritually transformed; the jewels Marwe wears represents her spiritual evolution based on her experience of death. But again, what is significant about this myth is that the whole process is represented in a rather ordinary way, which signals its nature-oriented symbolism. Marwe simply wants to return to life, just as she enabled her own death. She is portrayed within this myth as easily going from one life stage into the next, just as spring moves into winter and transforms back into spring.

The old woman allows Marwe to return home, and she does so covered now in jewels, again signaling her new identity. All the eligible men of the village now wish to marry her, but she ignores them, choosing only Sawoye to marry, a man suffering from a horrible skin disease. Ignoring the protestations of her people, Marwe internally knows that Sawoye is kind and therefore the best choice for her. Again this aspect of the myth identifies Marwe as having obtained knowledge in her embrace of the natural cycles of life and death. After they marry, and consummate their marriage, Sawoye's skin disease is fully healed. Marwe through her underworld experience learned the necessity of living out her life roles to their utmost; as a maiden who foolishly chose death before her natural time, she had to return to life to fulfil her natural role as mother in order to perpetuate the cycles of life. Once this role is fulfilled, Sawoye's skin disease miraculously clears up showing mythic confirmation of this natural role fulfillment for both Marwe and Sawoye, so they both can grow into their next natural roles.

Both husband and wife live in wealth and prosperity for a little while, until the men of the village grow jealous and kill Sawoye; "But Marwe having herself already died, knew the secrets of the Underworld, including how to revive the dead. She took her husband's body inside their home and recited magic incantations that she had learned from the old woman in the land of the dead" (Bierlein, 204). Sawoye again easily comes back to life, as Marwe herself did, and he kills all of their enemies. Marwe and Sawoye live happily together for many more years growing old, "and since both had died, they met their ends without fear" (Bierlein, 204). Death within this myth is portrayed, not in a terrifying way, but as a natural part of a greater cycle.

This myth precisely shows the necessity of the archetype of the underworld to the botanical hero's quest because it portrays Marwe as having learned essential knowledge of her role in nature. The fact that Marwe can bring her husband back to life because of what she learned from her underworld guide shows the myth's embrace of life and death as an endless cycle. The plant fears nothing in decaying back into the earth, and so too Marwe feels only peace in her new underworld surroundings. She buds again into a beautiful and radiant maiden, desired by all the men within her community, but she quickly moves away from this role into fulfilling the next stage of her life cycle—motherhood. In her using the magic the old woman taught her to resurrect her husband, she is getting closer to taking on the role of the old woman herself, signaling her own impending demise. Marwe has learned the wisdom of the old woman of the underworld, and therefore, she is now a representation of all aspects of the cycles of life. Marwe willingly died and returned mundanely, not spectacularly, into the symbolic womb of the earth, and just as matter-of-factly she sprouted forth again from the earth as a botanical hero enlightened with a wisdom to only continue her cyclical role in life—the role of all living beings.

The mythic underworld, therefore, provides the hero with an essential experience that allows him or her to face the fact of mortality. If a hero does this, and sees that his or her death is in actuality not a monumental event, but just a natural occurrence, then the hero has obtained many of the necessary elements needed to achieve the apotheosis of a botanical hero.

Many world myths present heroes who are not permitted to so easily transgress into and out of mythic underworlds. In these myths, often the heroes are called upon to accept their death, not symbolically, but actually. Mythic sacrifice and death raises the bar for the hero facing the decision to be sacrificed, but like the myths where a living being enters and emerges from the underworld, the myths that showcase sacrifice in a physical death, still present similar aspects found in the myths of the underworld, where heroes must resign disillusions of grandiose selfhood in conciliation of the workings of the environment in order to become representatives of botanical heroism. True sacrifice that leads to a physical death of a mythic being only better allows audiences of myth a chance to see the mythic character as a representation of the natural life cycle. Therefore, the next chapter will look towards the role that death and sacrifice within myth plays in further identifying heroes as botanical heroes.

CHAPTER 3

Death and Sacrifice

"Didn't you know
It's the severed head
That speaks the loudest,
The scattered remains
Of the dismembered hero
That become the seeds of future salvation?"—Michael O'Ciardha

"You have to die a few times before you can really live."—Charles Bukowski

Since Paleolithic times, early humans realized that the death of other living beings was essential to their survival; Paleolithic man:

> had to learn a hard lesson. In the pre-agricultural age, they could not grow their own food so the preservation of their own lives meant the destruction of other creatures to whom they felt closely akin. Their chief prey was the great mammals, whose bodies and facial expressions resembled their own. Hunters could see their fear and identify with their cries of terror. Their blood flowed like human blood. Faced with the potentially intolerable dilemma, they created myths and rituals that enabled them to come to terms with the murder of their fellow-creatures [K. Armstrong, *Short History*, 29].

Many nature-dependent cultures believed that in order to ensure the continuation of their people, they must understand their place within the environment. Myriad myths show veneration for the animal kingdom and explain that the animals that are killed in the hunt allow humans to kill them based on mutual respect. For example, the nature-dependent cultures of the extreme Arctic had to respect the limited resources presented to them, and as a people required to hunt for their food supply, a respect for the animals they must kill to remain alive was crucial. As Allan, Phillips, and Kerrigan state "The Arctic environment was much too harsh for its human inhabitants to dream of mastery, for other creatures often had the edge when it came to survival. No man could claim to have the strength of the white bear, the awesome bulk of the whale or the tough resilience of the reindeer. If anything, animals seemed more dominant than the puny, helpless humans" (52). A hunter was viewed as having "to earn his right to his prey ... he was careful to give all due thanks for his success and deal respectfully with the carcass. He had to share his good fortune fairly with the other members of his community—otherwise he would find himself hunting fruitlessly next time.... In innumerable little acts of respect the hunter affirmed his awareness that he was taking the life of his spiritual equal" (Allan, Phillips, & Kerrigan 53).

Swan discusses the perception that the animal prey is a willing sacrifice within many nature-dependent cultures; "from all around the world, much the same story is told—in the beginning, prey animals negotiated blood contracts with human predators. Seers, wizards and shamans, who communicated directly with the spirits of animals ... uniformly report that prey animals understand that being killed and eaten is likely. Accepting the reality of their place in the food chain, the animals in turn set down the conditions under which man may hunt and kill them" (33). Therefore, myths and sacred rituals were created to explain how first the killing of other living beings was necessary, but also how mankind fit into this world view. If the animal must be sacrificed so that the hunter and his community may live, then mythology served to remind audiences that the lives of human beings must also be sacrificed to maintain the wellbeing of the same ecosystem; "In the shamanistic hunting cultures, the killing of game was in accordance with the cosmic order. To kill was actually an act by which the men preserved life, comparable with childbirth for women. Without hunting and killing, no life was possible. Without game, humans would perish and life cease" (Swan 102). Sacrifice became not an act for a chosen few, but a reminder to all involved that they too will one day be sacrificed for the greater cycle of nature to continue.

In some cultures, moving from hunting and gathering to agricultural subsistence, as in the Neolithic period, the sacrifice of the animal in the hunt became a ritualized sacrifice of living beings for the assurance of continued success in the crucial harvest. Ritualized sacrifice allowed human beings to feel that they had an active role in assuring favorable natural conditions. Domesticated animals were sacrificed in most ancient civilizations around the world; the Sumerians, Greeks, Romans, Africans, Hebrews, etc. were all known to hold the sacrifice of animals as a sacred endeavor. K. Armstrong states that animal sacrifice "was a way of recycling the depleted forces that kept the world in being. There was a strong conviction that life and death ... were inextricably entwined. People realized that they survived only because other creatures laid down their lives for their sake, so the animal victim was to be honored in its self-sacrifice" (*Great Transformation*, xx). For instance, in ancient Greece the animals who were to be sacrificed were viewed as needing to agree to their own sacrifice, so the ritualists would throw water upon the head of the animal, so it would bow its head, providing a signal to onlookers that it agreed to be sacrificed.

Sacrifice often is envisioned as an act that must have allowed ritualists to believe that they were appeasing a particular divinity, so that they may win favor from this divinity. The Indo-Europeans who practiced substantial animal sacrifices believed first that they could obtain favorable natural conditions from their gods who were representations of the elements of nature, but as their civilizations continued, some participants believed that sacrifice could result in personal benefit coming to them in an afterlife among the gods (Armstrong, *Great Transformations*, 7). Certainly many examples of sacrifice show participants enacting these sacred rituals to appease divine beings and to win personal favor, but arguably, at the core of the act of sacrifice for participants and onlookers is the witnessing, and therefore internalizing, of the inevitability of death. The sacrifice of any living being is a sonorous, and even horrific, event to be witnessed; its nature forces participants to accept that death is a natural process, and from the initiation to perform this task, the participants are acknowledging that death is necessary to produce a successful continuation of the cycles of nature. But, sacrificial rites were also "intended as the ultimate celebration of life" (Allan and Phillips, *World*, 126), as they confirmed belief systems that centered on the process of death assuring new life; "the abundant and repeated message ... was that the natural order tends to regenerate life from death" (Barnes 31). Therefore, ritualized sacrifice allowed participants to view their own lives in regenerative terms, as Campbell states of the Neolithic era, "a new insight ... was opened by the lesson of the plant world itself ... which dies and is resurrected" (Campbell, *Primitive Mythology*, 180).

In some nature-dependent cultures, human sacrifice was also performed to revitalize nature. For instance, in ancient India, kings used to be expected by their people, at a designated time period at the end of their reign to self-mutilate their bodies—cutting off an ear, their nose, fingers, etc., and throwing the severed pieces onto the earth, so their sacrifice would nourish the harvest and bring forth new life to the people (Frazer 224). In Celtic belief the king was "sanctioned by the elements, the manifestations of the gods of the land" (Matthews 32); "the state of the land was always a reflection of the kingly rule. If the king was in harmony with his duties and obligations, then the land flourished. If, however he neglected his duties, the land subsequently fell into wasteland and desolation" (Matthews 32). The king then would be ceremoniously sacrificed, as evidenced in some of the bog bodies of Ireland, so that a new and younger king could take over the rulership, and thus renew the land as an embodiment of youthful vigor. In addition, the Aztecs would annually sacrifice a young man "in order to revitalize the sun" (Rosenberg 601).

The discussion of animal sacrifice in religious practices usually supersedes that of human sacrifice, and scholarship that focuses on human sacrifice, usually concentrates on the act in negative terms, such as defining the act of human sacrifice as sadistic (Porter & Schwartz 3). But as René Girard contends "the separation from human to animal sacrifice presumes that one category of victim is unsuitable while the other is eminently sacrificable. But it is inappropriate to proceed *a priori* with such a notion, however distasteful the idea of human sacrifice may be" (qtd. in Porter & Schwartz 3). Porter and Schwartz discuss that in cultures that perform sacrifice there tends to be little differentiation between the type of sacrificial victim, animal or human (3). As stated, animals and humans in many societies are viewed as intrinsically related to one another; myriad creation myths from nature-dependent cultures showcase humans and animals being created together as equals, and many myths also show animals as serving to propel the success of human life by educating human beings on ways of survival or producing a habitat for humans to thrive in. This apparent connection between the human and the animal sacrificial offering also suggests that the act of sacrifice serves to connect all living beings within nature's processes. In contending that the animal and the human are equal, not separate, there is a suggestion that the act of sacrifice serves to offer commentary on the nature of life and death—that for life to continue there must be a conciliation to death regardless of species.

Over time, many civilizations moved away from the need to sacrifice living beings towards a preference to perform sacrifice through symbolic representations, such as giving food, like grains or wine, or votive offerings. In the Shang and Early Zhou periods in China, thousands of animals were ritually slaughtered because the people held a view that their natural resources were inexhaustible, but later times revealed a need to transform the physical slaughter of living beings into the realm of symbolic sacrifice, which continues today (K. Armstrong, *Great Transformations*, 136). Similarly, in many religions there is discussion within their sacred texts of a specific time where religious devotees were instructed that physical sacrifice through killing was no longer required by the divine being, such as the Biblical representation of Abraham being spared from killing his son Isaac. In India, ritualized sacrifice of living beings, as seen with the arrival of the Indo-Europeans for instance, also moved to symbolic forms of sacrifice that still promoted the message that sacrifice must be done with an intention of not just seeking favor from divinities, but to acknowledge that the loss of self was the intent of the sacrifice. As K. Armstrong discusses of India in the Axial Age (900–800 BCE), ritualists conducted the sacrifice of living beings so that they may internalize the act of death as a concession that all life must cease (*Great Transformations*, 100); this recognition allowed

participants to see that the same natural cycle that demanded death also provided a constant source of rebirth. This act of internalizing sacrifice within
one's own psyche allowed for the transformation from physical sacrifice to that
of spiritual sacrifice; "the ritualists were demanding that everybody reflect upon
the rites and become aware of the implications of what they were doing; a new
self-consciousness had been born. Henceforth, the spiritual quest of India
would not focus on an external god, but on the eternal self" (K. Armstrong,
Great Transformations, 100). Spiritual sacrifice then allowed for the evolution
of faiths like Hinduism, Jainism, and Buddhism to understand, like the witnessing of physical sacrifice evidenced the necessity of accepting the inevitable
death of the participants, that the psychic death of the belief in an overly important autonomous self was also a necessary act to reach a heightened spirituality.

Many cultures and religious traditions connect the sacrifice of the physical
body, through deprivation or pain, with the seeking of spiritual knowledge.
For instance, the Hindu practice of asceticism has been applied in many ways:
abstaining from food, eradicating physical comforts, like choosing to only sleep
on the floor, wandering through the wilderness without the protection of clothing, or vowing not to use a limb, etc. In the Roman worship of the Phrygian
goddess Cybele, the Galli often castrated themselves to join in symbolic union
with the spirituality of the Mother Goddess. Many of the Plains American Indians practiced the sacred Sun Dance that often included a young male being
pierced through the chest with thongs that held him fastened to a pole in which
he would dance around for a long period of time, sometimes days, to seek wisdom in connection with nature's patterns. As Brown and Cousins state "The
Sun Dance honors the source of all life so that the world and humankind may
continue in the cycles of giving, receiving, bearing, being born, growing,
becoming, returning to the earth, and, finally, being born again" (13). Adherents
of Christianity in the Middle Ages sometimes practiced flagellation with the
use of metal barbs on the end of their whips to tear into their flesh, the pain of
which was said to help them find divine wisdom. Also in many contemporary
religions, practices like abstaining from sex or food are quite common to reach
a heightened spirituality. This process of inducing physical pain upon oneself
in order to attain enlightenment is an aspect of many mythological tales as
well, such as the Norse myth of Odin's self-sacrifice for wisdom in which he
hung himself for nine days and nights on a tree, without food or water, while
being stuck by a spear, so that he could earn, through suffering, the knowledge
of the runes.

The Sacrificed Divinity

Many of the examples in this chapter present divine representations of heroic sacrifice, and though these mythic characters are divine and not mortal, they serve to show a heightened depiction of sacrifice because if a divine being must concede to death, all mortals can more readily accept their own place within the sacrificial myth. The Japanese Izanami as divine creator helps to ensure a prosperous environment for all living beings, but her creation of fire, that is vital for the survival of all, kills her. The Greek Titan Prometheus also created human beings and then sacrificed his welfare to provide them with fire. The Chinese creation myth of P'an Ku and the Norse creation myth of Ymir additionally show divinities who must be sacrificed so that creation can continue. The Egyptian Osiris and Greek Dionysus must experience the mutilation of their bodies by having their corpses cut into many pieces and spread throughout the land to ensure fertility for the people. And finally, many religious divine figures are also presented as needing to experience the sacrifice of death, such as Jesus Christ.

These mythic portrayals of divinities who must experience death and sacrifice are conceived by their worshippers to seemingly make the divine being more relatable to the humans who revere them. But, perhaps, if viewed in botanical terms, there is more to the consistent portrayal from around the world of mythic divinities needing to experience death through sacrifice than merely connecting them to a commiseration of mortality. When looking at nature-dependent cultures, myriad divine beings allow themselves to be sacrificed, often in what appears a gruesome way, but there is little indication that the divine being is deserving of acclaim for his or her sacrifice. Instead, the divine being experiences death through sacrifice to serve as an example to the audience, showing them that sacrifice of self and individual death are only natural acts that each person must eventually experience. The divine sacrificial character superbly provides an example of nature's cycles of life because when a divine being openly steps forth into sacrifice, dies, and then oftentimes lives again, even in another form, such as an animal or plant, he or she has become a mythic embodiment of the natural seasons. For example, the American Indians have many legends that showcase divine heroes who sacrifice themselves; however, these heroes do not ask for or receive acclaim for their sacrifice because the giving of their life is viewed as just one part of the natural cycle.

Coming out of antiquity, western culture placed identity-tied significance on the act of sacrifice as an essential component for many heroes. The concept of martyrdom, for instance, places great importance on the individual willing to die for a "higher" cause. The identity of the martyr becomes societally revered for his or her important sacrifice, such as Joan of Arc's willingness to die to maintain her belief that she had direct correspondence with God. The popular heroes of many contemporary films, books, and television shows who sacrifice themselves are often viewed as martyrs because their sacrifice of self maintains a view that their identity was of great value, and in relinquishing their lives, they should receive great acclaim. In contrast, in the mythology of many nature-dependent cultures, mythic characters often did not receive acclaim, even for sacrifice, because one individual life in the greater scheme of nature was perceived as fleeting. Death was viewed as part of the process of life. Therefore, when mythic characters realize that death, sometimes symbolically portrayed as the psychological sacrifice of self, is only natural and quite necessary for the continuation of his or her people, and for the continuation of the whole ecosystem, then those characters becomes botanical heroes.

Sacrifice as Concession of the Botanical Cycle—Sedna

The Inuit have a legend involving their belief in the Goddess Sedna.[1] Her myth unflinchingly portrays the necessity of death and sacrifice within nature. Sedna was said to be a beautiful young maiden; her beauty struck the young males in her village with desire, and they all wished to marry her. But, Sedna refused all mortals. One spring day, when the ice finally broke over the waters, a fulmar came to Sedna and sang her an enticing song: "'Come to me,' it said 'come into the land of the birds, where there is never hunger, where my tent is made of the most beautiful skins. You shall rest on soft bearskins. My fellows, the fulmars, shall bring you all your heart may desire'" ("Sedna" 64). Sedna couldn't resist the fulmar and went with him. Soon, though, she realized that she had made a terrible mistake. The fulmar deceived her; she was forced to live in poverty, struggling to find sustenance to survive.

After a year passed of Sedna surviving the long winter, her father came to visit her; when he saw how his daughter was being treated, he killed the fulmar and stole Sedna away with him in his boat. However, the other fulmars, upon seeing their dead friend, pursued Sedna and her father. The fulmars stirred up such an intense storm within the sea that her father understood that both his and Sedna's death was imminent. He perceived that he had no other option but to sacrifice his beloved Sedna to the birds, so he pushed her out of the boat into the dark sea.

Sedna, though, would not allow herself to be sacrificed without cause. She held onto the side of the boat with trembling fingers, refusing to die. Her father, seeing this, still fearing for the death of them both, took out his knife and cut off Sedna's fingers at the first joints. The tips of Sedna's fingers became whales. Still Sedna refused to let go of her life, so she continued to hold onto the side of the boat. Her father then cut off the second joints of her fingers, which again fell into the sea and became seals. The fulmars saw what happened, and seeing the strength of the storm they created, they assumed by now that Sedna finally drowned, and so they were pacified and went home.

Sedna, though, was not dead. The father, seeing the storm subside and the fulmars leave, allowed her to climb back into the boat. Though, now, Sedna hated her father, and she swore revenge. The two made it back to their village, but at night, Sedna called her dogs to eat the hands and feet of her father while he slept. He awoke in dreadful pain and cursed Sedna and the dogs; "whereupon the earth opened and swallowed the hut, the father, the daughter, and the dogs" ("Sedna" 65). Sedna, her father, and the dogs all continued to live in Adlivun, the underworld, where Sedna reigned supreme.

It is said that because the whales and seals came from Sedna's sacrificed fingers:

> she can call them and tell them where to go. So it is that when the people wish to hunt, they have their *angakok,* the shaman, descend in his dream-trance to the land under the sea where Sedna lives. He combs out Sedna's long hair, for without fingers she is unable to do it herself. Then he can ask her to send the whales and seals back to the places where the people can hunt them. Thanks to the blessings of Sedna, who is always generous to those who remember to ask for her help in the right way, the people no longer go hungry [Bruchac 71].

Sedna represents the struggle for survival. Nature can be harsh, especially in the Arctic environment of the Inuit. To live, one must sacrifice. Nature requires a constant system of death and decay, so that regeneration can be possible. Sedna is not immune to this within her myth. She is portrayed as an integral part of a larger, sometimes merciless, natural order. The portrayal of her being deceived by the fulmar with a life of ease reveals a mythic message of the reality of life. The Inuit, like Sedna's winter alone with the fulmars, must accept that survival has a cost. Sedna's sacrifice of her fingers to make the necessary food staple of the Inuit, whales and seals, reveals the mythic message that all people are inextricably connected with every natural element. Her sacrifice teaches that mankind is a part of nature, not dominant over it.

Though Sedna loses her fingers, she refuses to die in the myth; this reveals an important lesson. Her sacrifice is significant; she loses independence when she loses her finger, as they are her mode of self-sufficiency. This sacrifice of a large part of her selfhood signals a change in Sedna from the start of her myth. At the beginning, she is wooed by disillusioned visions of a life of ease, but her ordeal at facing demise teaches her to symbolically let go of her need to hold on to an autonomous existence. She gives her body to nature, ensuring the survival of her people. This giving away of her independence for the survival of the community directly counters the act of her father; the natural cycle requires that the father protect the offspring, but her father misjudges his duty. He becomes mythically impotent then, as Sedna takes over dominance enabling her dogs to disable him. Sedna does not die with her sacrifice but is portrayed as becoming stronger. Her journey led her to hold her rightful place as overseer of death in her underworld chamber in Adlivun.

The Inuit people often recreate Sedna's descent into the sea in ceremony where shamans willingly make this journey to help the community; "the shamans ask their helping spirits to clear the way to the sea …. The spectators hear the shamans' voices recede, and they know that they are now facing the obstructions that are placed in the path to Sedna: large stones, a vicious watch dog, and Sedna's angry father. Finally, once the shamans enter her home, they can see Sedna, sitting with her back to the light, her hair tangled with dirt and slime of human wrongdoing …. Gently, the shamans take a comb and draw it through the hair Sedna cannot comb" (Brown & Cousins 104). Her role for the Inuit is that of provider, but it comes with a lesson of the natural world. For the Inuit to be able to kill whales and seals in order to survive, they must remember Sedna in her underworld, thus recognizing that each death of a whale or a seal comes with a cost and a reminder that the hunter must one day succumb to the same fate as his prey.

There Is No Sacrifice Because There Is No Self— Purusha and Prajapati

The *Rig Veda* was believed to have been composed about 2,000–1,000 BCE by Indo-European invaders into the Indus Valley, and it was closely aligned with the natural world, assigning divinity to the various elements found within nature. K. Armstrong states that audiences of the *Vedas* "felt that they were in touch with the power that made the seasons follow one another regularly, the stars remain in their courses, the crops to grow, and enabled the disparate elements of human society to cohere. Scripture, therefore, did not impart information that could be grasped notionally but gave people a more intuitive insight that was a bridge, linking the visible with the invisible dimension of life" (*Great Transformation,* 19). The *Rig Veda* was embraced by the Indo-European/Aryan community who valued raiding and war as a means of survival; for them the violence associated with raiding often allowed them to intertwine the exuberance of battle with their feelings of spiritual experience; "a warrior knew he would have to fight his way to vision and insight" (K. Armstrong, *Great Transformations*, 20). Since warriors who died in battle or raiding were believed to receive enlightenment, spirituality was often connected with violence. K. Armstrong contends, therefore, that out of this connection with violence and spirituality arose the need to sacrifice; "the sacrifice reenacted, in a heightened, ceremonial setting, the glory and terror of the Aryan heroic code" (*Great Transformations*, 22). The sacrifice would therefore showcase violence, and the "climax" was the "dramatic decapitation of the animal victim" (K. Armstrong, *Great Transformations*, 92). The Aryan sacrificial offerings mimicked the cattle raids that provided them their means of sustenance; the raja, or chief, would provide a grand banquet of the items he had obtained through successful raiding, and in a "riotous" manner, the people consumed them, sacrificing some of the cattle to the gods of the *Vedas*. Often, the celebratory sacrifices, that involved much pageantry and competition, would invoke violence among the onlookers. However, in the late Vedic period, there was a transition from the violence of the raiding communities, into a more docile existence of farming. It is in this period that the myths of Purusha and Prajapati were created.

The tenth book of the *Rig Veda* presents the "Purusha Sakta" hymn that shows sacrifice as a means towards spirituality. It discusses the concept of sacrifice in accordance to natural creation; "The importance of sacrifice as a creative event is stressed as Purusha (Primal Man) is sacrificed to become the world.... Through the destruction of a body in one form, accomplished in a spirit of offering, that greatest creation of all forms took place. In recognition of this fact and in hopes of imitating the event and thus reestablishing its sacrality, religious rites were born" (Sproul 179–70). It is out of Purusha's sacrifice that spirituality in India was vastly transformed.

The *Rig Veda* states that Purusha, "Primal Man," was composed of one thousand heads, eyes, and feet, so that he was said to encompass the whole universe. Three quarters of his being were "immortal in heaven," but one quarter of his body was used to create all aspects of the earth. In this myth, Purusha is described as:

> walking of his own free will into the sacrificial ground, lying down on the freshly strewn grass, and allowing the gods to kill him. This act of self-surrender had set the cosmos in motion. The Purusha was himself the universe. Everything was generated from his corpse: birds, animals, horses, cattle, the classes of human society, heaven and earth, sun and moon.... Unlike the agonistic rituals of the warriors, there was no fighting in this sacrifice. Purusha gave himself away without a struggle [K. Armstrong, *Great Transformations*, 29].

Out of this sacrifice of Purusha in giving part of his being to enable life on earth, the myth discusses how this first sacrifice allowed for the interconnectivity of life:

From that universal offering ... sprang horses and all the animals.... When (the gods) divided Purusha, into how many parts did they cut him up? The Brahman was his mouth, the Rajanya was made his arms.... The morn sprang from his soul (manas), the sun from his eye.... From his navel arose the air, from his head the sky, from his feet the earth ["Purusha"].

The seasons, spring, summer, and autumn, are presented as part of the sacrifice, and winter presumably is Purusha's death, but as with other myths of sacrifice presented throughout this text, death, when portrayed in mythic terms associated with the cycles of nature, is momentary. Here too Purusha's death is only one component of an everlasting cycle, as all creation comes forth directly from him, and will continue to do so. Because Purusha willingly sacrificed himself to create life, it helps to explain to mortals the contract of life on earth for living beings—everything that grows must eventually die, but as this myth is clearly tied to the natural cycles of life, his sacrifice also assures that what the natural cycle takes away, it always replenishes.

This myth portrays Purusha as willing to become the sacrifice, and yet there is no prolonged details about him struggling to make this decision or lamenting over his impending doom. This lack of lamentation reveals a psychological acceptance about his lack of self-importance, and it is key to understanding sacrifice in the upcoming myths of the quests of the botanical heroes in the next chapter. Purusha willingly sacrifices himself without grandiose showmanship because it is precisely a natural action. He willingly gives his body over, so that new creation can occur because this is merely the way that the system of nature operates. Like seasonal change, Purusha is depicted as continuing on in each new creation that emerges from the pieces of his body, but also the two thirds of Purusha not used for the sacrifice is depicted as rising to the "heavenly" cosmos, which mythically shows audiences that death, for all worldly inhabitants, is only one part of a continuous natural cycle. Therefore, when analyzed according to natural terms, one's life and death serve an everlasting, regenerative cycle of wholeness, so like Purusha, when one being dies, manifold others are created. This portrayal of the mundane sacrifice of one's life introduces the spiritual concept that singular life, and also death, are part of an illusion of self-importance. The myth shows that life and death are part of an uninterrupted cycle—that in nature there is no death.

Purusha's sacrifice transformed the idea of sacrifice in Indian conception; Purusha, now, offered a means for everyone to enter into the spirituality that sacrifice invoked, even if the sacrifice was achieved in symbolic terms. With Purusha, sacrifice, if willingly accepted, could allow one the means towards spiritual enlightenment. The component of his sacrifice being self-ordained is central because in his willing death, he is accepting the natural order that will always exist for all of earth's inhabitants. He mythically shows audiences that if they view their own deaths in these natural terms, then they too do not altogether cease to exist. This text combines the idea that death is simply a step in a never-ending, natural cycle to the concept of the spiritual belief in the immortality of the soul.

In another section of the tenth book of the *Rig Veda,* it explains the belief that all separate divine entities were united in one deity called Prajapati, "The Golden Embryo," "the life-force of all the gods" (Sproul 181). Prajapati is formless, though he is responsible for creating all life, and in this, the myth presents him as sacrificial. He is the:

> "Giver of life (atman), giver of strength,
> Whose behest all [must] obey,
> Whose [behest] the gods [obey],
> Whose shadow is immortality,
> Whose [shadow] is death" [*Rig Veda* 182].

The text repeatedly asks to whom do the people and gods give their oblations in sacrifice, as the work reveals that the essential quality of Prajapati is formless; "Prajapati was identical with the universe; he was the life force that sustained it, the seed of consciousness, and the light that emerged from the waters of unconscious matter. But Prajapati was also a spirit outside the universe, who could order the laws of nature. Immanent and transcendent, he alone was 'God of gods and none beside him'" (K. Armstrong, *Great Transformations,* 28). Therefore, he is and he is not all that exists and all that does not exist. His description again reminds audiences that they too must realize themselves in such natural terms. Furthermore, the myth ties creation inextricably to immortality and then immortality to death; this again pushes the reader to grasp an understanding that life and death are merely part of nature, realizing this gives one, not a singular immortality, but an immortality like that of Prajapati.

Prajapati was mythically understood to have created all existence from his own creative devices; he found himself alone, so he simply divided himself into all existence. The myth of Prajapati[2] allowed worshippers to move past sacrifice as a brutal affair, as his myth states that he performed a sacrifice with Death itself. The myth states that Prajapati defeated Death, not through violence, but through simply swallowing him. His taking into himself Death allows him, and mythic audiences to see that death is something that can be transcended through acceptance, not defeated through countless killings of "enemies" or sacrificial libations. With Prajapati's victory, he mythically allowed audiences to transform the means from which they found meaning in their rituals of sacrifice. In this later Vedic period, sacrifice became less violent; animals were killed as painlessly as possible, or even spared. Aggressive behavior towards humans, even though competition, was no longer deemed acceptable in sacrificial ritual; now:

> a sacrificer could conquer death only by assimilating it and taking it into himself, so that "Death has become the self (atman)." It was a striking image; by making Prajapati swallow Death, the ritualists were directing attention away from the external world and into the interior realm. By making Death a part of himself, Prajapati had internalized and therefore mastered it; he did not need to fear it anymore. Human sacrificers must do the same [K. Armstrong, *Great Transformations*, 93].

After this mythic realization, the ritual of sacrifice changed even more. Ritualists began to associate themselves with the dying animal of the sacrifice, so instead of killing another being to make a sacrifice, the practice shifted to symbolic sacrifice. The ritualist became the symbolic sacrifice, accepting the natural fact of death, and thus became free from the fear of death, which enabled him or her to embrace the concept of spiritual immortality.

Finally, the progression of these Vedic myths allowed for the conception that ritualistic sacrifice, even if done symbolically, was no longer necessary to achieve the same wisdom that came as a result of the ritual; "solitary meditation could be just as efficacious as the external rites…. If the sacrificer *was* Prajapati, he must also have Prajapati's creative powers. At the beginning of time…. Prajapati had brought forth from his own form, the gods, human beings, and the material world simply by his own mental exertions. Surely the lone ascetic would at the very least manage to create his own divine atman" (K. Armstrong, *Great Transformations*, 99).

Thus, Indian philosophy and religion were forever transformed into the practices and concepts adopted by Hinduism, Jainism, and Buddhism. The concept that the sacrificer is in actuality the sacrificed allows the person to embrace death as natural, as part of an everlasting cycle. Embracing this fact of death allows one to connect his or her own death to this understanding; therefore, sacrifice becomes a psychological concept of accepting the world as it is. Sacrifice when viewed according to some conceptions in India allows it to become a vehicle for letting go of the desire for an autonomous identity; it forces one to let go of the belief that one should fear or attempt to escape death. It places human conceptions of death in connection with death seen every day in myriad natural examples.

Nature shows people that death is only one part of an unrelenting cycle; when spiritual philosophies make this same connection, then sacrifice becomes something that is not grandiose, as presented often in western terms, but something that is mundane. Accepting death and the sacrifice of self in Buddhism, for example, is a central part of the process towards spiritual enlightenment.

As Webb states "The whole purpose of Buddhism is to assist the individual held in this bondage to discover, through meditative practice leading to inward realization and transformation, the truth of 'anatman': that there is no such self. Although Buddhists, having dropped the theistic language of Hindu religion, do not use the symbolism of sacrifice, the Buddhist radical relinquishing of the individual atman through realization of anatman could also be called a kind of sacrifice of the self."

Buddhism and many other philosophies maintain that the self is not important; in fact, it is believed to merely be an illusion of singular importance that is not at all in connection with the natural world. Holding onto the concept that the self is imperative, only binds the person to an elevated sense of egotism. Instead, for a mythic character to achieve botanical heroism, the self must be embraced as any other element within the natural environment—like a leaf that will someday wither and fall to the ground to provide nourishment for the soil in order to produce the next year's stage of growth, so too should one view the sacrifice of the self. With that said, the concept of sacrifice in many tales of the botanical heroic quest eventually too become viewed as illusory. If there is no self to sacrifice in such tales, then attachment to the belief that the giving away of one's self through sacrifice is important, also fades. Sacrifice for the botanical hero becomes less of a struggle, and is defined for what it is—an embrace of the natural order that affects all living creatures.

The Natural Resurrection of Christ Each Spring

René Girard discusses the act of sacrifice in ancient civilizations throughout the world. Webb contends that Girard's analysis of ritualized sacrifice found that the act of sacrifice "simultaneously commemorate[s] and mask[s] the real collective violence and victimization that gave rise to human society.... 'All religious rituals spring from the surrogate victim ... for the working basis of human thought, the process of 'symbolization,' is rooted in the surrogate victim'" (306). Girard argued that later religious traditions placed the concept of the symbolic sacrifice on the story of Jesus Christ, where instead of sacrificing a component outside of the self, the story of Christ portrays him as sacrificing himself; "'This revelation, however, was more than its recipients could bear, and they soon buried it again under a 'sacrificial reading' that interpreted Jesus' death not as the unmasking and exploding of the victimizing mechanism but as itself the ultimate satisfaction (and confirmation) of its exigency'" (qtd. in Webb). Webb agrees in part to Girard's assertion that Christ serves as a representation that the act of ritualized sacrifice serves to connect ritualist or onlooker with the natural factuality of death for all individuals, including themselves. Therefore, Webb states that the intention of Christ's sacrifice of self, and subsequent resurrection, speaks not of a message that showcases a singular achievement deserving of praise, but instead, shows Christ's sacrifice of self in terms of a conciliation to nature that all must also undergo.

Webb continues his discussion of Girard's commentary on Christ stating that "the experience of spiritual transformation Christ's sacrifice and resurrection represent may be understood more deeply and more favorably than Girard may have realized, through a comparison with Hinduism and Buddhism." Webb agrees with Girard's view that Christ's sacrifice is "genuinely 'anti-sacrificial.'" Webb contends that instead of Christ's sacrifice being viewed as a means to appease God, so that the sins of human beings can be forgiven, as some interpretations of ancient ritualized sacrifice view it as an act to appease a particular divinity, Christ's sacrifice of self is indeed more connected to ancient views that show sacrifice as merely the acceptance of death and rebirth as natural. Webb argues that the story of Christ's death serves to help Christians face death without fear, not because it promises a reward of an afterlife in heaven, but because it shows a concept of rebirth in psychological terms, which arguably follows an adherence to the botanical cycles of nature; "To someone who believed in Jesus' resurrection, it would have shown in the most dramatic and convincing way that the conquest of death was no longer merely a dream or hope for the future, but had actually become, in the life of one concrete human being, a reality. And as such it was also a token of future resurrection for others" (Webb).

Webb states that Christ's sacrifice of self showed Christian believers that "freedom from the fear of death comes from their faith in Jesus' resurrection and the hope for their own to come. The renewal of their consciences comes from the breaking of that fear's power to make them cling to the life of the illusory desire-self that must be given up. This means they are called to undergo their own metaphorical but very real deaths" (Webb). Therefore, Christ, and other botanical heroes who will be discussed later in this book, often relate a message that the sacrifice of self is merely a necessary conciliation that all living beings must make in accordance to the cycles of nature.

Viewed in botanical terms, Christ quite readily serves as a symbol of the patterns of nature. His crucifixion story, celebrated in the spring, shows Christ choosing to be sacrificed, experiencing death, and then resurrecting—a pattern that itself mimics the cycle of nature from the death or dormancy of winter to the natural rebirth presented in spring.

As stated, myriad myths, before and after the creation of Christianity, portray characters who live, die, and resurrect, similar to Christ. Many scholars of mythology, like Campbell and Leeming,[3] discuss the story of Christ as holding qualities that connect it to numerous heroic myths. S. Baggs and J. Baggs connect the story of Christ's death and resurrection to many myths from around the world that present heroes who journey into and out of the underworld, as in many of the myths discussed in the previous chapter; "Part of the Underworld myth common to many cultures is the process of restoration to life after death. This is seen in the familiar example of death and resurrection in the Persephone myth…. In the Christian religion, the concept of the resurrection of Jesus as Christ is not new. It could have been absorbed from a Greek or Near-Eastern tradition. Similar themes occurred in the ancient Near East some two thousand years BCE" (11–12).

In addition, the world myths that showcase the death and resurrection of mythological characters, similar to the story of Christ, present the seasonal patterns of nature through the device of mythology, showing not the singularity of the achievement of resurrection, but the commonality of rebirth for all living beings in nature. Leeming contends that often myths of resurrected beings are connected to issues related to the fertility of the earth and come from ancient agriculturally-dependent communities. Leeming identifies a pattern common to such resurrection myths where the mythological character dies, is lamented by women, and then resurrects, most often with the help of the women who lamented them, as seen in such myths as Baal and Anat and Osiris and Isis, where the female characters are represented in quintessential Earth Goddess form and are therefore quite capable in aiding the deceased back to restored life; "Mythologically these women must be seen in connection with the ritual sowing of the seed by fertile women in planting cultures. The death of the hero and his association with the female forces hold promise of new life. Thus, out of the bodies of Attis, Adonis, and Dionysus springs flowers and the vine; the body of the dismembered Osiris is literally planted by his sister-wife, Isis, and the world is renovated…. Attis is buried in the chambers sacred to the earth mother, Cybele, and thus returned to his mother he can be reborn as Spring" (*Voyage of the Hero,* 180). Eisler also portrays the story of Christ's resurrection in similar terms to these more ancient, agriculturally focused myths, stating that Christ is an exemplification of the promise of renewed life that comes to all living creatures when viewed in terms of nature's seasonal laws; Christ "symbolizes the regeneration of nature by his resurrection every spring at Easter" (102–3).

Furthermore, Leeming points to the importance of the tree in many myths of the dying and resurrecting mythological divinity[4]; "Osiris is buried in a tree; Adonis is born of one; Attis, Odin, and Jesus are hanged on trees; the Norse god Balder is killed by the mistletoe from a tree; and Dionysus … was called in Boetia, 'he in the tree'" (*Voyage of the Hero*, 181). The tree so often features in these myths of resurrecting characters, like Christ, because it is a symbol for the meaning of the myth in general—as a tree only appears to die each year, but easily resurrects each spring. Leeming states that these myths of the resurrected mythological divinity teaches audiences that the hero "holds out a promise of a new life through his sacrifice. He thus ... teaches us something of the positive nature of death as the catalyst for a new birth" (*Voyage of the Hero*, 181).

Viewing the story of Christ's death and resurrection for its tenets that are connected to the seasonal patterns of nature allows audiences to fully understand the significance of sacrifice in the stories of the botanical hero. The botanical hero, like Christ, readily sacrifices him or herself to show that death is merely a momentary process in the natural cycle of life. Christ's resurrection, like Persephone's, Baal's, Osiris,' Dionysus,' etc., shows audiences that though one must succumb to the laws of the environment, nature assures a ceaseless cycle of rebirth upon its demand of death. Therefore, the concept of sacrifice as monumental is minimized, because it becomes defined, through mythic resurrection, as a means to show audiences that death and rebirth are the most natural of events.

Quetzalcoatl Sails to the Sun

The Aztec myth of creation also ties the theme of sacrifice to their chief god, Quetzalcoatl, with his act of sacrifice to create life. The myth describes the belief that there were four worlds before the creation of the existing fifth world. Each of the four worlds were inept in different ways: the first world housed people who acted improperly, so jaguars ate them; the second world had people with no wisdom, so they were turned into apes; the third world held people who didn't honor the gods, so volcanoes and earthquakes killed them all, and the fourth world displayed only greedy humans, so a great flood drowned them. The gods, though, were said to have saved one couple,[5] in a tree, and they were instructed to only eat corn, but they ate fish, so the gods cut off part of their heads and turned them into dogs. Finally, the fifth world was created because a god, Nanautzin, who was described as being physically "misshapen, ugly, covered with disgusting-looking sores, and dressed in plain clothing from woven reeds" volunteered himself to be sacrificed so that a successful people could be born. Nanautzin jumped into a sacred fire and burned to death; it is significant that "Nanautzin was a form of the great god Quetzalcoatl" ("Creation Cycle" 603).

Another variation of the Aztec creation myth[6] states that in the beginning Quetzalcoatl and Tezcatlipoca looked down from the heavens and saw earth hidden in only water, and again the common theme of a primordial goddess is discussed as floating upon the sea "eating whatever she could find with her many mouths" ("Creation Cycle" 604). The two gods realize that life on earth will be impossible if this primal goddess remains, so they descend to earth, and to them, as divinities, it can be described as their underworld journey, though their underworld is the existing earth. The two gods transform themselves into two giant serpents and tear the body of the sea goddess apart. However, the two gods understand that though they killed the goddess, she still has provided an essential sacrifice to assure the creation and survival of the inhabitants of earth; this killing of the goddess mythically represents the same pattern that will continuously be repeated on earth for the obtaining of food.

In Quetzalcoatl and Tezcatlipoca killing the goddess they know that they must respectfully acknowledge her sacrifice; they decide "to give her gifts to compensate for her mutilation. They decreed that whatever human beings needed for survival, she would provide. They created trees, tall grass, and flowers from her hair, fine grasses and tiny flowers from her skin, small caves, fountains, and wells from her eyes, large caves and rivers from her mouth, hills and valleys from her nose, and mountains from her shoulders" ("Creation Cycle" 604). Even though the gods compensate the goddess by using her form to create life, which again represents the interconnectivity of all living beings, she mythically reminds audiences that as an essential part of this cycle, death is required as she had to die to initiate creation. This myth, though, does not end with her sacrifice, as it presents the goddess as still alive after this mutilation, in her many parts, and she is unfulfilled. She requires the inhabitants of earth to make the same sacrifice that she was forced to make:

> The goddess is often unhappy. Sometimes in the night, people can hear her crying. Then they know she is filled with a ravenous thirst for human blood. Whenever this thirst comes upon her, the goddess will not provide the fruits of the soil and will not stop crying until the blood from human hearts has quenched her thirst. She who provides sustenance requires human lives in return for her sustenance. So it has always been, so it will always be ["Creation Cycle" 604].

Though this analogy of requiring human sacrifice to assure the continued propagation of nature can seem harsh, it is still tied to an understanding of the natural cycles of life and death. One sees that death ensures the survival of all species, so it is not hard to see a civilization acting upon a sense of obligation to ensure the continuation of these natural processes.

Aztec myths of the divine hero Quetzalcoatl must be considered along with the creation myths and their explanation of the need for sacrifice within

Aztec civilization. Quetzalcoatl's most famous heroic myth relates how Tez-catlipoca, though presented as the other creator god when the primordial sea goddess needed to be defeated, is now portrayed as Quetzalcoatl's enemy, but also he is depicted as the darker side of Quetzalcoatl himself; "According to the Aztec tradition, Tezcatlipoca is invisible and intangible, which is most appropriate because his temptations represent all the evils that test the moral fibers of human beings" (Rosenberg 610). Whatever gifts the divine Quetzal-coatl gives to humans, Tezcatlipoca turns them into excess, which ends up destroying the gifts themselves; this helps define the message of the myth, as Quetzalcoatl initially represents only times of plenty, but the myth teaches him and the audience of the myth, the necessity of loss.

Quetzalcoatl is presented as both a man and a divine being, as son of the goddess Coatlicue and the Sun. The Sun tricks Coatlicue and secretly impreg-nates her with Quetzalcoatl, so the stars murder and bury the Sun after Quet-zalcoatl is born, but Quetzalcoatl gathers the animals of earth to resurrect the Sun. As a man, he comes to the city of Tula, the center of the Toltec Empire from 900–1200 CE and teaches the people the skills of survival. The myth states that in Quetzalcoatl's presence, resources were always abundant. He also teaches the people about the significant cost of morality, as "he had a great respect for all forms of life. He did not believe in killing flowers by picking them, or killing any of the animals of the forest" ("Quetzalcoatl" 611). He for-bade human sacrifice while he lived among the Toltecs. This mythic episode is thought to have been based on true events in Tula, as priest-kings, who called themselves "Quetzalcoatls" invented the myth to replace their former embrace of violence and war. Longing for a more peaceful existence they explained the coming of Quetzalcoatl in order to establish a more peaceful religion. The Quetzalcoatls "challenged the established tradition, as upheld by the warrior elite, of human sacrifice …. Instead of blood and hearts, claimed the new priest-hood, the great god wanted offerings such as flowers, birds, and butterflies" (Allan & Lowenstein 77).

However, this attempt at reformation did not last, and in time "Tula reverted to its old ways and the bloody frightening rituals began again" (Allan & Lowenstein 77). The myth presents this change by stating that in a time of only abundance, Quetzalcoatl, unbeknownst to him, calls forth the contrary actions of Tezcatlipoca, who forces Quetzalcoatl to look at his own face in a mirror, and knowing the inner fear of Quetzalcoatl, Tezcatlipoca makes Quet-zalcoatl see himself as an aged man. This image of mortality stays with Quet-zalcoatl, haunting him, and so Tezcatlipoca knowing this, tricks Quetzalcoatl into pursuing means to maintain youth and vigor. Tezcatlipoca tells Quetzal-coatl to drink what he tells him is a magic potion that will keep him young, but instead it is merely alcohol, and Quetzalcoatl only gets very drunk, becoming the darker side of his own personality that always resided within the moral teacher. When Quetzalcoatl sobers up, he worries that he is unable to continue to rule over the Toltecs, but thinking they would be worse off with Tezcatlipoca, he decides to stay.

Tezcatlipoca also stays with the Toltecs, and he proceeds to kill them through deceiving means. Finally, when few Toltecs remain, he convinces them to stone him, which they do, but Tezcatlipoca's body emits a horrible smell, and the people find that they cannot remove the corpse. The smell invades the crops, and the people cannot eat because the food becomes permeated by the smell. The people begin to starve, and many more die, until Tezcatlipoca comes back to them disguised as an old woman who begins to cook corn over the fire; the remaining starving people come to the aroma, but Tezcatlipoca, knowing that they would come, kills the last remaining Toltecs.

Quetzalcoatl, seeing that all his people have died, knows that he has to move on. He retreats to the wilderness, and like most botanical, and archetypal, heroic journeys, this reflects that he is forced to leave behind his former identity to partake on a quest that will psychologically transform him. In the wilderness, Quetzalcoatl again sees his reflection and notices that indeed now he has grown old; he has become what he always feared before. His fear kept him from maintaining his morality, and so, true to the heroic quest, Quetzalcoatl must face the things that terrify him, and for him, his aging is directly tied to a fear of death. He knows now that he must find his father the Sun.

Quetzalcoatl's journey to find his father is described as a psychological underworld. Also, like the archetypes of many heroic journeys discussed in the last chapter, Quetzalcoatl finally comes to face quintessential underworld imagery. Quetzalcoatl encounters demons, and they tell him that he must strip away all that defines him as divine; "'You may proceed, but only if you will agree to our conditions.... You must toss away all your jewels and all your wealth. You must leave every skill that you possess with us'" ("Quetzalcoatl" 613). Quetzalcoatl complies and continues to lose his identity upon his underworld experience, which connects him to the botanical heroic journey.

This myth fully discusses the purpose of the underworld for Quetzalcoatl; the mythic underworld strips him of the ties that made him believe in his own self-importance. Quetzalcoatl, after having been proven vain and capable of the immorality he spurned in others, knows that he has much to learn. When he reigned over the Toltecs, he believed that he could only give them an abundance of resources, but the myth recounts how this is impossible as it is unnatural. Tezcatlipoca is presented to Quetzalcoatl as a darker aspect of himself.

Therefore, the myth explains the necessity of embracing the harsher sides of natural existence, as Quetzalcoatl realizes that his own insecurities were revealed by Tezcatlipoca, just as he also knows that Tezcatlipoca will never leave humanity, as death and starvation will always exist.

Quetzalcoatl, knowing that death and strife are inevitable for all living beings, makes the journey himself towards his former worst fear—death. Quetzalcoatl reaches the end of his quest by coming to the shore of the sea, climbing aboard a raft made of snakes, and sets off towards his father the Sun. This decision is a sacrifice, as his body, gaining upon his father, burns away. The people say "that his ashes became transformed into a colorful array of birds. The birds rose high into the air and carried his heart into the heavens, where it became the morning star" ("Quetzalcoatl" 613). The mythic portrayal of his sacrifice is not overtly discussed. This portrayal is one of the best representations of the vital component of sacrifice in the botanical hero's journey, as it spells out that Quetzalcoatl's heroic quest only leads to his death. In death, Quetzalcoatl embraces what all mortals must accept. His quest mythically teaches him, and more so audiences of the myth, not to fear aging and death, but to accept them, which he fully does, and his sacrifice allows him to be resurrected in the natural form of the everlasting star.

The Staple Crop—Sacrifice as Rebirth

Many myths portray divine beings as instructing others to sacrifice them in what appears to be a brutal manner; often the characters of such myths are resistant to kill the divine being, but their deaths, which are reluctantly carried out often by mortal characters, serve to show audiences that human life must also follow the same patterns of botanical nature. Linking the lives of mortals to the seemingly indifferent or even harsh botanical cycle of plants can be a hard lesson to embrace if conceived of in connection to human life, but the mythic sacrifice of a divine being shows again that out of death comes the promise of natural renewal for all beings. What is vital to understand in these myths where a divinity transforms into a botanical element through a physical and seemingly painful death, is that the sacrifice is not one where the divine being should be held upon a pedestal; instead, the mythic message serves to reveal that death is natural, and the act of self-sacrifice is only a concession of this fact. It is thus these following myths that will serve as the most important archetype for the identification of a botanical hero, as spiritual apotheosis for the botanical hero requires that he or she readily become nature through his or her physical or psychic sacrifice and death.

The Cherokee Corn Mother and Other Tales of the Illusion of Death

The Cherokee American Indians recount a myth of primordial Man, Kanati, and Woman, Selu.[7] They have all of the corn and wild game they need to feed their large family. Each day Kanati would go out and always come back with an unending supply of game, and Selu would come back each day with her basket forever filled with corn. The children of the primordial parents grew curious about the unending supply of resources, so some of them decide to follow their father; they discover that he walks each day to a cave where many different animals reside. They are surprised to see that Kanati simply calls to a deer, and it willingly comes to him. Kanati walks out of the cave with the deer following and heads towards home; the children sneak to the cave and push the rock blocking the entrance of the cave aside, but find that all the animals rush out into the world. The other children followed Selu and find that she goes to a hidden cabin each day and dances until "plump ears of corn began to drop into the basket until it was full" (Humphrey 65).

That night Kanati and Selu tell their children that they indeed know what the children did. Kanati tells them that now he will have to die, but to ensure his children's survival, he gives them hunting weapons. Selu also tells her children that she too will now need to die, but she instructs her children to take her corpse and drag it over the earth, so that her flesh will nourish the soil, and wherever her body was dragged, corn would be assured to grow, so that the next generations would not starve. She also instructs them that they forever must save some seeds and replant them to assure the survival of all the generations to come.

This myth portrays a guide to a mythic understanding of sacrifice as natural and therefore mundane, as the parents readily give their bodies over for the survival of future generations. Explicitly, Selu, the Cherokee Corn Mother, teaches audiences of the myth that the earth is nourished by an endless cycle of life, decay, and renewal. No regeneration is possible without sacrifice. The Corn Mother depicts in botanical terms that the concept of grandiose sacrifice is an egotistical concept. She, like other botanical heroes presented thus far, does not lament her death in the myth; instead, she mundanely instructs her children what to physically do to her body, and to the vegetable matter, once she dies. In addition to teaching them a method of survival, she also instructs them that the cyclical nature of life and death for plants is similar for human beings as well.

The Polynesians have a similar myth regarding their staple crop of breadfruit.[8] The myth states that in the beginning the people only ate the red earth itself, but primordial parents had one son who they found could not eat the earth, and thus began to starve. The father seeing his son dying told his wife that he would die and change into the proper food that their son needed in order to survive; "'I will die soon. This is what you must do when I am dead: break my body up into pieces and bury them in different places around our yard. When you hear a sound like a ripe fruit falling on the ground, it will be me; I will have become food for the boy'" (Humphrey 67). After the husband indeed dies, the mother hears the breadfruit fall and walks her starving son outside where they see that a glorious tree has sprouted, producing the first breadfruit. The boy eats the breadfruit, and along with him, mankind is provided sustenance in order to survive.

This myth, again, recounts sacrifice as mundane; it also reveals the father's willingness to sacrifice himself as necessary, and thus makes him, like the Cherokee Corn Mother, an ideal example of a botanical hero. The myth strips away the concept that the sacrifice of one individual is a monumental affair in order to reveal a natural mythic message that one generation, like the life cycle of botanical agents, must cease for the assurance of the prosperity of the next generation. The myth also recounts tenets similar to a belief in reincarnation in natural terms, as the father here never completely dies; he simply transforms into a staple food that will directly assure the life of his son, mimicking a process that in other cultures might be defined as reincarnation. The necessity of the father dying is clearly related here to the survival of the son in immediate terms, and subsequently the son's life will assure the survival of the Polynesian people to come, as they grow to depend on the breadfruit as a staple crop, and in this way, the father lives on in nature. The Polynesians "also had similar traditional tales for the origin of the coconut (grown from a man's head), the chestnut (from human kidneys), yams (from a man's legs), and other food plants" (Humphrey 67).

In addition, the indigenous people of Brazil tell of a myth where Mani,[9] an elder leader of the tribe, near death instructed his people to bury his body, and one year after his death to dig up his decayed corpse. His people do this and find the first manioc root. As a tribal leader, Mani's obligation is to provide for his people, which he willingly does.

The American Indian Wabanaki people also recount a myth of sacrifice to provide for the future generations of the Wabanaki.[10] In this myth First Manitou made Kloskurbeh, "the first teacher" (Bierlein 109). One day a boy appeared to Kloskurbeh having formed from the ocean's sea foam that was heated by the sun. They both then meet a girl the next day who had come directly from the earth as a plant, which produced her as fruit. Kloskurbeh knows that these beings are sacred, and because they come directly from the elements of the earth, he understands that their role is to create life. The boy and girl grow and have many children, but they find, sadly, that they cannot feed all of their children with the nascent stage the earth resources are in. The woman goes to a river and enters its waters; feeling desperate when she entered, she mythically feels transformed within the water. She looks down and notices that "a green shoot had come out of her body, between her legs" (Bierlein 110). Again, the myth is connecting her role as a mythic representation of the female with the regenerative powers of the earth; just as she came directly from the soil as fruit ripened by a primordial plant, and just as she understands that she must connect with water, she now concedes that her role is to assure the cyclical aspect of nature.

The woman returns home to her family and tells her husband that he must kill her. The husband refuses, but she remains steadfast that her death is the only way to ensure the survival of their children. She instructs the husband to plant her bones in two piles after he has killed her. The husband seeks the advice from Kloskurbeh, who prays to First Manitou, and comes to understand that the woman is fulfilling her role as a botanical mythic representation.

The man then murders his beloved wife and buries her bones as instructed. After time, he realizes that directly out of the area he buried his wife's remains, there grew two plants: tobacco and maize. The myth states that "Kloskurbeh explained to the man that his wife had never really died, but that she would live forever as these two crops" (Bierlein 110). This myth perfectly captures the mythic portrayal of sacrifice for the botanical hero. Her representation of being mythically transformed, or reincarnated, into two staple crops shows audiences their own role in the same natural processes. When she steps into the water, she realizes that her body must nourish the earth to enable her own children to survive, and subsequently, according to the incessant cycle of life, her death will ensure the survival of all the future generations of the Wabanaki, as she, not in true death, will sprout forevermore as a vital food staple for her people, and serve her people, perhaps more significantly, as a prime mythic example of a botanical hero.

Wunzh and the Rebirth of the Great Spirit

The Ojibwe recount a myth of Mon-daw-min or "the Origin of Indian Corn"[11] where a young man named Wunzh was about to partake on his Ke-ig-uish-im-o-win, a fast to see what kind of spirit would be his guide through life. Wunzh had come from a poor family, and though they were good people and valued the Great Spirit, they found it quite hard to find the means needed to survive. The first few days of his fast Wunzh spent outside admiring his natural surroundings; "while he rambled through the woods, he felt a strong desire to know the plants, herbs, and berries that grew, without any aid from man, and why it was that some species were good to eat, and others possessed medicinal or poisonous juices. He recalled these thoughts to mind after he became too languid to walk about, and had confined himself strictly to the lodge; he wished he could dream of something that would prove a benefit to his father and family, and to all others" (Schoolcraft 88). Soon, Wunzh grew too weak to attempt leaving his bed, and while lying there he saw a young man come to him who he immediately recognized as sacred, as the man wore garments of the many colors of nature, and his head was adorned with beautiful feathers of every natural hue. The sacred man spoke to Wunzh, "'The Great Spirit ... has seen and knows your motives in fasting. He sees that it is from a kind and benevolent wish to do good to your people.... I am sent to instruct you'" (Schoolcraft 89).

The sacred man instructed Wunzh to rise from his bed and wrestle him. Wunzh felt empowered to accomplish this task, though his body was quite weak from fasting. He stood before the sacred man and commenced in wrestling him, but before too long, he grew weak again. The man told him that they would stop for now, but that he would return. The man returned the next day, and they commenced again to wrestle, but this time Wunzh's body was even weaker; still, Wunzh noticed that his mind had grown stronger, as it became more determined to accomplish his mythic task. The sacred man noticed Wunzh's weakened state and left with a promise to return the next day.

Wunzh rose the third day, considerably weakened from his efforts of wrestling and fasting, but still he rose, determined this time to accomplish the task of defeating this sacred man or die in the effort. This determination of mind is what it took for the man to stop the new wrestling match and declare himself defeated by Wunzh. The man told Wunzh that he had won, but also told him that his task was not yet complete:

> "Tomorrow.... I shall meet you and wrestle with you for the last time, and as soon as you have prevailed against me, you will strip off my garments and throw me down, clean the earth of roots and weeds, make it soft, and bury me in the spot. When you have done this, leave my body in the earth, and do not disturb it, but come occasionally to visit the place, to see whether I have come to life, and be careful never to let the grass or weeds grow on my grave. Once a month cover me with fresh earth. If you follow my instructions, you will accomplish your object of doing good to your fellow-creatures by teaching them the knowledge I now teach you" [Schoolcraft 90].

Wunzh, though fearful and saddened at hearing the task he must accomplish, agreed, and when the sacred man arrived the next day, Wunzh defeated him, killed him, and buried his body in the earth.

Wunzh returned back to his family and meagerly began to eat again, but he never forgot about the promise he made to the sacred man. Wunzh continued to go to the grave and meticulously watched over it, keeping it free from weeds, until the summer drew to a close. Finally, at the time of harvest, Wunzh found "a tall and graceful plant.... 'It is my friend,' shouted the lad; 'it is the friend of all mankind. It is *Mondawmin*. We need no longer rely on hunting alone; for, as long as this gift is cherished and taken care of, the ground itself will give us a living'" (Schoolcraft 91). Wunzh pulled an ear of corn from the plant and showed his people the new staple food.

The willing sacrifice and transformation of the sacred man again makes him an ideal example of a botanical hero because his mythic actions provide spiritual meaning to audiences of the myth, which is in correlation to the tenets of many nature-dependent cultures, showing death as illusory, time as cyclical, and all living beings as inextricably intertwined.

Milomaki's Song of Cyclical Time

The Yuhuna Indians of South America have a myth about Milomaki, the sun boy,[12] another botanical hero, who shows that death, again, need not be viewed as a singular and grandiose affair, but merely a botanical, necessary episode for continued propagation. From the Land of the Sun, there appeared a little boy who sang so gloriously that it enticed people to travel long distances just to hear his songs. But, upon returning to their homes and eating fish, the people who heard Milomaki's mysterious music all died. The relatives sought him out in order to avenge the deaths of their loved ones. They captured Milomaki, built a funeral pyre, set it aflame, and put Milomaki on top. Mystically though, Milomaki continued to sing: "the youth continued to sing beautifully to the very end, and even while the flames were licking his body he was singing: 'Now I die, now I die, now I die ... now I depart from this world!' And when his body was swelling with the heat, he still was singing in glorious tones: 'Now my body breaks, now I am dead!' And his body burst" (Campbell, *Primitive*, 221). The remains of Milomaki's body burned fully in front of all the onlookers.

From the ashes of Milomaki's body, a green blade shot up immediately, and it continued to grow, until the next day it was an enormous tree—"the first paxiuba palm in the world" (Campbell, *Primitive Mythology*, 221). The people were amazed by this sight, and they instantly knew that the tree was sacred. They created flutes from its wood that sang the same mystical song that Milomaki first enticed them with. When the food staple of the Yuhuna people is ripe, they always blow on their flutes in remembrance of Milomaki and his lesson of death.

Again, this myth shows death as mundane. Milomaki is calm as he suffers a bodily death; his myth signifies that botanically he will not die, as from his necessary death, one that he seems to have enticed the people into enabling, he provides for them their source of sustenance. His lesson of botanical heroism teaches the Yahuna people the means to connect their own lives to an appreciation of the same botanical cycle Milomaki represented.

Therefore, it is precisely the acceptance of one's link to the natural vegetative cycle that allows a mythic protagonist to attain the status of a botanical hero. As discussed, there are many myths that focus on a hero dying or sacrificing him or herself in what might appear to be a brutal manner, but what should be understood is that these myths are fictional; they are symbolically meant to portray mythical characters who show a willingness to be sacrificed in order to reveal to audiences spiritual tenets often embraced by nature-dependent communities. The mythic sacrifice of botanical heroes who allow themselves to be sacrificed because they seemingly hold a wisdom that tells them their individual deaths are not an end at all, but another beginning, relays to audiences a message that though death is eminent for all living beings, viewing it in botanical terms, allows one to become privy to the same spiritual wisdom that enabled the botanical hero to willingly step into sacrifice. This botanical spirituality in relation to sacrifice and death carries with it the botanical concept of rebirth.

Rebirth, reincarnation, or resurrection are often integral elements of a variety of world myths, and without understanding death and sacrifice in the terms that many nature-dependent communities may have defined them within their mythologies, then arguably little transformative sense can be made from the myriad myths that showcase such miraculous elements. But, if death and sacrifice are understood to be natural, then the door is opened to present rebirth as also natural. This concept of mythical rebirth, as a result of botanical apotheosis, will be the focus of the next chapter.

CHAPTER 4

Natural Apotheosis and the Resurrection of the Botanical Hero

"Each night, when I go to sleep, I die. And the next morning, when I wake up, I am reborn."—Mahatma Gandhi

"The phoenix must burn to emerge."—Janet Fitch

"In the depth of winter, I finally learned that within me there lay an invincible summer."—Albert Camus

The belief in reincarnation is paramount to many cultures around the world. Through witnessing decayed matter appearing to generate new life, early cultures conceived that elements were never fully destroyed. Many cultures, such as the American Indians, Aboriginal Australians, Celts, Greeks, Romans, etc., developed myths that fully embraced concepts related to the transformation of forms upon death, from humans to animals or plants, or vice versa. Often, in Aboriginal Australian mythology, for example, characters metamorphose into aspects of the landscape upon their deaths. Many Celtic tales also describe one being mythically transforming from one species into another after death. In myth, the explanation that a human transformed into a different being, plant, animal, or piece of landscape was a way of embracing the interconnectivity of human beings with the natural world. As civilizations developed different religious and spiritual concepts, the explanation for the transference of matter upon death was put into more abstract terms involving a belief in concepts such as souls that maintain singular identity in various types of afterlifes. The view of what happens to human identity after death depends on what the culture values.

Rebirth or reincarnation within myth also can be presented as psychological. The African San people "use the word *death* to describe shamanic trance, for in their words, shamans 'die when they cross over into the spirit

161

world'.... [They] shake violently, stagger, lower their heads, bleed from the nose, sweat profusely, and ultimately, collapse unconscious" (Ford 106). This process is quite similar to the heroic quest of the botanical hero, because, as discussed, an embrace of death is psychologically vital to the spiritual evolution, or psychological rebirth, of the botanical hero. Psychological rebirth and apotheosis for the botanical hero comes in both knowing that death is imminent and natural, but also that all deaths within nature assure a natural rebirth or a symbolic form of reincarnation. Therefore, when botanical heroes psychologically die, willingly letting go of false beliefs in the importance of their ego-driven identity, then they are able to experience a psychological rebirth, or symbolic reincarnation, that presents to them a renewed vision of the value of life.

In various world mythologies, the psychologically reborn or reincarnated botanical hero may be depicted, after having experienced a psychological death, as metamorphosing into a plant or animal, willingly dying a physical death, or living on and passing their newfound wisdom on to others—all possibilities are equally valid, because the botanical hero who has attained apotheosis knows that all options are really the same thing when viewed in terms of nature's systems. Life becomes defined, for the botanical hero who has achieved spiritual apotheosis, as all-encompassing; death, life, and rebirth are but momentary parts of the natural cycle of life. As a result of this spiritual wisdom, the enlightened botanical hero more acutely realizes the importance of thriving in life while one is permitted to take part in this vital stage of life.

Myths of the botanical hero present an unadorned outlook on the reality of life and death, articulating a view that puts human beings as equal to any biological element within the natural world. This outlook can be a painful and terrifying concept for humans to embrace, but the botanical hero teaches audiences that if they indeed accept this view, they will find everlasting life—not in the preservation of one's specific identity, but in the balanced system of nature. The botanical hero also teaches one to embrace each of the life cycles, as in accepting death, the botanical hero shows the equally important significance of revering every moment of life.

The Natural Apotheosis of the Botanical Hero— The Buddha

The legend of the Buddha provides a prime example of a botanical hero, as he experiences the heroic loss of self, and by doing this secures an understanding of natural concepts of rebirth, thus allowing him to reach apotheosis.

The ancient tales of the *Jātaka* present the previous lives of the Buddha before he attained Enlightenment. One tale, entitled "Hare's Self Sacrifice," tells of the Buddha living as a rabbit with three animal friends: an otter, a jackal, and a monkey. The hare, as the Bodhisattva, tells the three animals that there must be a day of fasting for them, and that on this day, they should not take another animal's life; however, they should still give alms to anyone who comes asking for food. The three animals find a way around these measures by stealing meat from animals killed by others and saving it within their separate abodes, planning to eat it after the day of fasting. Sakka, an incarnation of the Hindu god Indra, comes to each animal and asks them for food, and the animals offer the food they procured for themselves, but the story concludes showing the sacrifice of hare as truly remarkable.

Hare, when tested by the Hindu Sakka, tells him that he indeed will honor his fast by not taking any life of an animal, but he will feed Sakka by sacrificing his own life by stepping into a cooking fire, so that Sakka may consume his flesh. The Buddhist tale presents the future Buddha as not sacrificing himself to pay homage to the Hindu Sakka as superior to himself; instead, his sacrifice is mythologically depicted to present a view that the life of an individual is part of an illusion of importance. The hare, as the future Buddha, willingly offers his life, not for reward, but because he recognizes the loss of his life as a momentary pause in an endless cycle of rebirth. His death as a hare will feed Sakka and result in his rebirth with better karma. This mythic portrayal of the Buddha living as an animal who willingly offers himself to die in recognition of the assurance of rebirth, clearly shows the Buddha as a botanical hero because even as a rabbit, he accepts that he is merely a small part of an endless, natural cycle; it is this knowledge that permits him to indeed be reborn. The ideal botanical hero not only necessarily accepts sacrifice, loss of selfhood, and even death, he or she must also reach the final state of spiritual apotheosis by the mythic tenet of rebirth. Botanical heroes let go of selfhood, and by doing this, gain natural immortality; therefore, the legend of the Buddha's quest towards enlightenment serves as an exemplar example of apotheosis for the botanical hero.

The story of the Buddha, in his final lifetime as a mortal, often presents him as a young prince in India leading a sheltered life of abundance and ease. His parents, wishing to prevent from him the painful realities of life, like poverty, suffering, illness, and death, kept him locked within the confines of their kingdom. However, one day, the Buddha left the comforts of his childhood and began his heroic quest. Upon his journey to what was to him an otherworld, which for everyone else were just the streets of his city, he saw all of the suffering his parents tried to hide from him. The Buddha, having had his former false reality stripped away, saw clearly now that life was indeed full of suffering. The

Buddha vowed to never return to his kingdom and renounced his family and his life of ease.

The Buddha tried many paths to seek enlightenment; he followed the Hindu methods he saw practiced by many around him of deprivation and meditation. He was said to have spent years in attempting these methods until he "acquired and transcended the eight stages of meditation" (Campbell, *Hero,* 31); then he "retired to a hermitage, bent his powers six more years to the great struggle, carried austerity to the utmost, and collapsed in seeming death" (Campbell, *Hero,* 31). The Buddha eventually admitted that none of these traditional methods entirely worked for him in attaining enlightenment, so he moved away from these techniques to find his own way, and in this, the legend portrays the Buddha as moving beyond the confines of his existing society, as he did by shedding his former, limited perception of the world while he lived a life of abundance within his parents' kingdom. When a mythic hero paves a path that is different from the norm, it is a signal that he or she is experiencing a psychological or spiritual transformation, as was discussed often with characters like Achilles, Gawain, and Gilgamesh.

The Buddha, tired of attempting to find meaning for his own life through the means of others, discovered a Bo Tree and simply sat beneath it. Campbell describes this scene as firmly connected with the natural world, as all of nature responded with the knowledge that the Buddha was about to attain enlightenment; "The snakes and birds and the divinities of the woods and fields did him homage with flowers and celestial perfumes ... the ten thousand worlds were filled with perfumes, garlands, harmonies, and shouts ... for he was on his way to the great Tree of Enlightenment, the Bo Tree" (*Hero* 32).

It is significant that the Buddha attains enlightenment while sitting underneath the natural element of a tree. Trees are often portrayed in world mythology as the key element that aids a hero in attaining wisdom, as stated, the Norse Odin willingly hung himself from a tree for nine days in order to gain wisdom, and similarily the Hebrew Eve attained knowledge after eating the fruit from the Tree of Knowledge. It is important that both Odin and Eve had to suffer in order to achieve spiritual wisdom, because the tree in mythology often presents a realistic view of nature, one that encompasses all aspects of the natural world, as a tree exists both above ground in our mortal world, and below ground in the underworld. Trees also provide clear evidence of the cycles of life apparent in seasonal change. Therefore, when a botanical hero is portrayed as attaining knowledge in a mythic scene that is connected to a tree, this is an indication that the knowledge the hero will achieve is in connection to the wisdom of nature. In this myth, the Bo Tree serves as a microcosm of the natural universe, as Campbell states that the Tree of Enlightenment in many myths, like this one, sits in "the center of the symbolic circle of the universe, the Immovable Spot of the Buddha legend, around which the world may be said to revolve. Beneath this spot is the ... world-generative aspect of immortal being. The tree of life, i.e., the universe itself, grows from this point .... The hero ... is himself the navel of the world" (Campbell, *Hero*, 41). Thus, the Bo Tree within this legend directly connects the Buddha's upcoming spiritual apotheosis to nature and its seasonal cycles.

Sitting beneath the Bo Tree, the Buddha underwent a psychological heroic journey, facing every representation of terror that his mind could produce. As discussed in chapter 2, when the hero is introduced to horror, usually identified within myth as the mythic underworld, it serves to force the hero to face death in all of its terrifying morbidity, and this was precisely what the Buddha endured in his own psychological underworld. The Buddha was psychologically visited by the most terrifying beings imaginable, and then by the threat of his own death and loss of individual identity, which came to him in the form of Kama-Mara, the god of desire and death:

> The dangerous god appeared mounted on an elephant and carrying weapons in his thousand hands. He was surrounded by his army.... The Future Buddha remained unmoved beneath the Tree. And the god then assailed him, seeking to break his concentration. Whirlwind, rocks, thunder, and flame ... bringing coals, hot ashes, boiling mud ... and fourfold darkness ... but the missiles were all transformed into celestial flowers [Campbell, *Hero*, 41].

The Buddha's ability to transform the harsh natural elements presented to him by Kama-Mara into flowers, another natural element, signals the thin layer between defining something natural as positive or negative; the Buddha's simple transformation of natural forms, while immersed within what is depicted as a psychological quest, shows that it is human perception that defines the elements of nature as good or bad, and that the natural elements themselves, even if they appear terrifying, need not be feared by the botanical hero who learns to define all aspects of life as natural.

Next, Kama-Mara unleashes his daughters, "Desire, Pining, and Lust" (Campbell, *Hero*, 32), to the forefront of the Buddha's psyche. It is interesting that Kama-Mara is presented as the god of both death and desire, as this myth identifies death and all types of desire as illusions connected to self-importance. If one grasps too firmly onto a fear of death, one will not be able to seek unification back into the natural whole of the universe in nirvāna; similarly, if one holds too resolutely to the desires of life, then one also remains bound to definitions of selfhood as individually important. When Desire, Pining, and Lust appear to the Buddha, he experiences mythically what all humans must contend with while alive. The three daughters tried to entice the Buddha in every way fathomable, but the Buddha merely sat beneath the Bo Tree and faced this assault for what it was—illusory desire to maintain identity. In not being enticed into succumbing to the elements of desire, the Buddha, as a botanical hero signals to audiences that he has willingly lost his selfhood. The three daughters do not only tempt the Buddha sexually; they tempt him in a similar way that Kama-Mara's tempted him. Kama-Mara attempted to terrify the Buddha into wanting to run from death, to shelter himself, to cling to life, but because the Buddha remained unafraid of Kama-Mara's onslaught, this shows his willingness to shed his identity by accepting death as naturally unimportant. And similarily, in not falling for desire, in all of her forms, as presented in this myth, he equally does not succumb to the desires associated with life: lust, love, acclaim, identity, and even continued life.

This stage of losing the illusion of self-importance, or the desire to believe in the separate immortality of the soul, is crucial in the botanical heroic quest because it ties the botanical hero to the patterns of nature and forces him or her to realize his or her own insignificance in a spiritual context. This letting go of the fear of death, as well as the loss of one's desire to maintain selfhood is the final key point that makes a hero a botanical hero, because a state of psychological transformation has occurred, where the botanical hero has become one with the indifferent and yet precisely perfect world of nature, and can therefore easily be reborn into ceaseless natural elements. In heroic myths from India and East Asia, "the ego concept is both expanded and annihilated, so that one's self in not identified with the temporal phenomenon here and now, but with the reincarnating principle" (Campbell, *Myths of Light*, 61). Therefore, to attain apotheosis of the botanical hero, that the Buddha attained, one must not seek popular recognition, but annihilation of self. Even the concept of reincarnation within Buddhism must cease for one to achieve enlightenment, as maintaining selfhood through consistent reincarnations still places importance upon the self. To reach nirvāna, one must also see the necessity of letting go of an autonomous selfhood, as well as conceptions that a distinct soul/essence lives on after death.

Once the Buddha was able to move past his own fear of his inevitable death and his longing to live holding onto the disillusioned belief that his autonomy was important, as a result of his psychological underworld experience, then he was said to press the palm of his hand onto the earth as a clear representation that he aligned himself with the natural world, and thus attained apotheosis. Nature is again connected to the Buddha's moment of enlightenment, as when the Buddha reached apotheosis, he "bid the goddess Earth bear witness to his right to be sitting where he was. She did so with a hundred, a thousand, a hundred thousand roars" (*Hero*, 32). Hearing this natural proclamation from the earth itself, the rest of nature also responds, as the tale depicts even Kama-Mara's battle elephant kneeling in obeisance. The natural acknowledgement of nature to the enlightenment of the Buddha makes it clear that the knowledge he has obtained is the wisdom of life as it is—the wisdom of nature. Nature's validation of the Buddha in this scene further legitimizes him as a botanical hero.

The legend of the Buddha makes him different from contemporary, popular renditions of many heroes because his tale clearly showcases all the archetypes presented in the heroic journey, but does so in a distinctly psychological way that makes it apparent to audiences that the heroic journey can indeed all be done within one's own psyche; "It is significant that the Buddha should receive his divine sign by gradual observation. Where the careers of ... most heroes involve violence and war, the Buddha's greatness is achieved through contemplation" (Leeming 54). The Buddha is also not presented as seeking acclaim for his enlightenment, though he was given it by devotees later; instead, his legend states that he merely was said to have gotten up from the Bo Tree and simply lived his life spreading a message of compassion towards others, as well as his method of release from worldly suffering through the natural cessation of self.

Later, upon the Buddha's death after many years, the Buddha is said to have told his congregation of priests that he was finally tired and wished to lie down. He was made comfortable between two sal-trees, where he lay upon his side. Dying a physical death, the Buddha declared to the priests around him: "'And now, O priests, I take my leave of you; all the constituents of being are transitory; work your salvation with diligence'" (Campbell, *Hero*, 363). The moment of death for the Buddha is once again depicted alongside natural imagery, which additionally connects him to botanical heroism by showing that his death is to be viewed as natural and thus transitory; "Now at that time the twin sal-trees had completely burst forth into bloom, though it was not the flowering season; and the blossoms scattered themselves over the body" (Campbell, *Hero*, 361). The Buddha, then, was said to pass into nirvāna.

It is critical that the Buddha does not tell precisely how his followers should seek their own enlightenment; instead, he tells them to continue to strive using their own means. Stories of botanical heroes must always portray their process towards enlightenment as an individual, psychological process towards spiritual apotheosis. Therefore, the story of the Buddha is one that speaks towards audiences because of its individualized, psychological message that asks others to partake on their own similar journeys. Pivotal to the philosophy of Buddhism is the concept that the Buddha was only a mortal, and that his enlightenment was something that any person can also achieve. It is this component of the lesson of the Buddha that makes him a true botanical hero because his message of letting go and becoming nature has the potential to be reborn countless times in myriad believers.

Guan Yin—Representative of Nature as Sacred

The Chinese myth of the goddess Guan Yin shows another myth of rebirth in a botanical hero after the experience of death.[1] The myth portrays Guan Yin as a beautiful, young maiden who refuses to marry despite her father's orders. Guan Yin, instead of marriage to a husband who would only control her autonomy, wished to renounce the world and become a Buddhist nun. This break from the confines of societal expectation immediately defines Guan Yin as upon a heroic journey.

Her father, Miao Zhuang, at first consents to Guan Yin's choice, but sneakily tries to give Guan Yin impossible and grievous labors while in the nunnery she entered, so as to thwart her renunciation of worldly affairs. All of nature, though, is portrayed as helping Guan Yin accomplish her father's tormented tasks, which initially signals Guan Yin as a botanical hero. But overwhelmed by his daughter's rebellious resistance, Miao Zhuang orders her nunnery to be burnt to the ground, with Guan Yin inside it. Again, nature intervenes, and rain extinguishes the flames. Miao Zhuang, infuriated, orders servants to cut off Guan Yin's head for her insolence and disobedience, but when this gruesome task is attempted, the sword shatters. Servants then try to stab Guan Yin a fatal blow, but the lance also will not penetrate her skin. Finally, her father takes the matter into his own hands and strangles her. Because Guan Yin has already renounced the world, she is mythically portrayed as being initially impenetrable from harm, yet Guan Yin does die when her father chooses to end his own daughter's life.

The myth states that at "the moment that her soul left her body a huge tiger appeared from nowhere and carried off the corpse to a nearby pine forest" (Allan & Phillips 125). This natural representation within the myth is key to its message. The tiger often appears in Chinese mythology, sometimes as a thing to fear, but here the myth shows the tiger as merely taking Guan Yin to a remote wilderness filled with evergreen trees. It is this scene within the myth that conveys its message of rebirth. In this natural scene, Guan Yin, as apparent prey to her father and also the patriarchal system in place, is like the evergreen trees of the forest she is placed within, as her death is portrayed as only a period of dormancy.

As in most heroic journeys, Guan Yin too descends into the mythic underworld, but having already renounced life, and having actually died a physical death, she is undeterred by the fearsome elements the underworld holds, which is again usually the fear of death for the protagonist. In the myth of Guan Yin, the underworld, therefore, holds no power against her. Also as previously discussed, the underworld can psychologically be a place where the hero must face the elements that holds him or her back in life, described as Campbell's stage of "Atonement of the Father," but again this myth portrays Guan Yin's actual father as attempting to hold power over Guan Yin, but ultimately failing at this. So the underworld is represented within this myth in the same way as Guan Yin's struggle with her father; it is portrayed as anti-climactic. Instead, Guan Yin's presence in the underworld merely shows that it is not a place to fear, as Guan Yin actually transforms the underworld into "a veritable Paradise" (Allan & Phillips 125)—an act seldom related in myth.

Guan Yin's remarkable ability to transform the underworld into a paradise is similar to the Buddha's action of turning Kama-Mara's harsh natural elements, like fire and burning mud, into flowers. This ability to transform what most fear into something that has been stripped of fear, points to a psychological component of the message of Guan Yin's heroic quest, and decidedly marks her as a true botanical hero.

Because Guan Yin has proven that she already superseded death in transforming the underworld into a paradise, the king of the underworld makes Guan Yin ascend back to earth, sending a mythic message that is in firm connection to myths of botanical heroism where there appears to be little difference between life and death. The myth shows that Guan Yin is ordered to reenter her corpse that has been lying within the forest, and like the evergreen trees' ability to remain green throughout the season of winter when most other botanical agents appear to die, her body does not decay even in death, which again signals her as a botanical hero, as Guan Yin once again embodies a mythic message that all stages of life and death are transitory. A botanical hero not only accepts death, but easily shows the possibility of rebirth for all living beings. It is the mythic element of rebirth that sends a message that life follows a trend of continuity; therefore, death, when viewed in natural terms, loses its stigma, and life dominates, as the natural cycle is always focused on predominantly life in its incessant demand of renewal. Guan Yin seamlessly renters life as easily as she entered death. She is then transported to a secluded island, where she "practiced meditation and self-discipline until she attained perfection as a bodhisattva or future Buddha" (Allan & Phillips 125).

The myth continues to show that Guan Yin's father is close to death, and his ministers, wanting to take over power once he dies, find out that Guan Yin is still living, so they seek her out and send a servant to cut off her hands and gouge out her eyes. However, the servant upon seeing her knows that she is holy, so he begs her to flee, but he is astonished to hear that Guan Yin orders him to do as instructed. Full of remorse the servant does as he is told, but Guan Yin merely takes the mutilated remnants of her body and transforms them into an ointment that she tells the servant to take back and give to her ailing father. The man does so, and Guan Yin's father is instantly healed. Finally Miao Zhuang regrets his treatment of his daughter and goes to see her on her island; seeing Guan Yin in her mutilated form, Miao Zhuang realizes the holiness of his daughter and renounces his throne to live with her. After this, Guan Yin serves as an embodiment of botanical rebirth when she instantaneously, like nature is able to do each season, transforms her body back to its original form. This final act of again accepting sacrifice with ease shows once more that Guan Yin is an ideal botanical hero as she reveals that after her physical affliction, she can easily regenerate the injured portions of herself as a plant would. Again, concepts of rebirth, reincarnation, and regeneration portrayed mythically with apparent ease portrays the most significant quality of the botanical hero.

After Guan Yin regenerates the injured portions of her body in yet another portrayal of renewal, as she did with the underworld by turning it into a paradise, and as she did in evading decomposition in death, her myth portrays her as choosing to live on her remote and overtly natural island; it was "a place of solitude and peace where she could chant for both the living and the dead and bring to those who prayed for her song, comfort in the continuing cycle of troubles that afflict all beings in the gyre of time" (Leeming & Page, *Goddess*, 128). Guan Yin's portrayal at the end of her myth shows her as a true botanical hero immersed within nature in imagery that signals her as essentially becoming a part of the environment; it is this aspect of the myth, like the flower petals that cover the Buddha's body upon his physical death, which allows Guan Yin to serve as a mythic figure who can educate and comfort others upon their own journeys towards botanical apotheosis.

Cúchulainn Becomes an Element of Nature

The *Táin Bo Cuailgne* ("The Cattle Raid of Cooley"), one of Ireland's most important mythological texts that is set in the 1st century CE but recorded in various sources in approximately the 11th–12th centuries, displays many elements that tie the characters within the text to natural associations. As has been stated, nature was a critical component in all aspects of Celtic life, and ideas of death and rebirth were associated directly with natural explanations, such as the druidic teachings of the immortality of the soul and the possibility of a soul being reborn after death into the body of any number of species. These Celtic tenets appear throughout the *Tain* showcasing the protagonist, Cúchulainn, as the sole character who must save the people of Ulster; this solitary focus on Cúchulainn readily marks him as one partaking on the heroic quest, and subsequent elements of this quest portray him as a botanical hero.

Many myths explain the background that leads up to the story of the *Tain*; one such myth is of Cúchulainn's birth. Cúchulainn's mother, Deichtine, is sometimes described as King Conchobar's sister and sometimes his daughter. In the *Compert C(h)on Culainn*, "The Conception of Cúchulainn," Deichtine is depicted as accompanying a hunting expedition where the Ulstermen go into the woods seeking a flock of mystical birds. Soon, the men are caught in a snowstorm, so they seek shelter in a nearby home. While enjoying refuge in this home, they discover that the host's wife suddenly goes into labor, so Deichtine helps the mother in delivering her son. While the baby boy is born, two colts are also birthed. After everyone within the house falls asleep for the night, Deichtine and the Ulstermen awaken to find that they are no longer in the quaint abode they fell asleep in the night before; instead, they learn that they are now within Newgrange, the Neolithic passage tomb of the Boyne Valley in Ireland. Though the small house, the host, and his wife have all disappeared, the baby boy and the two colts remain. Seeing significance in the recent mystical happenings, Deichtine decides to take the baby boy back with her to raise him as her own, but the boy soon dies of illness. As Deichtine is distraught by this loss, she happens to drink from a cup and swallows what the text describes as "a tiny creature" (*Tain* 23). That night she dreams that the god Lug appears to her and reveals that the host from the mysterious abode in the wilderness was none other than himself, and that he impregnated Deichtine with Sétanta while she was there. After this dream, Deichtine finds that she is indeed pregnant, but not yet married, she is ashamed to have sex with her new husband, Sualdam mac Roich, on their wedding night in her condition. She finds that on her wedding night, she vomits when she lies beside her new husband, and "the living thing spilled away in the sickness, and so she was made virgin and whole and went to her husband. She grew pregnant again and bore a son, and called him Sétanta" (*Tain* 23).

This account of Sétanta's miraculous birth serves to show his connection to botanical heroism. The natural events that result in Sétanta's birth, such as the magical birds, the sudden snowstorm leading the Ulstermen to the shelter in the woods, and the twin colts born at the moment of the birth of the first child, reveals that Sétanta will be a hero who is connected to the elements of the environment. Also, the fact that the natural elements of his birth are related to concepts of birth, death, and rebirth, through the birth of the first baby boy who must die, the swallowing of the second divine child who must be vomited up so that Deichtine can later give birth to Sétanta, foreshadows botanical concepts that Sétanta/Cúchulainn will need to embrace later in his saga. In addition, the mysterious incorporation of the Neolithic Newgrange into the myth also might point to elements of death and rebirth that are implicit in the makeup of Sétanta/Cúchulainn, as Newgrange was long believed, as discussed early within this text, to be in some way connected to such aspects of death and regeneration as found in nature.

In his childhood, Sétanta remains connected to elements within the natural world. As a child, he is said to have watched as King Conchobar's retinue of young men trained to be warriors, and he greatly desired to go and train with them, but Deichtine refused stating that he was too young to take part in such vigorous training. Sétanta went anyway, and while fighting, he entered into a "berserk" state; this state was often valued by Celtic warriors, as in this condition they were thought to be in such a heightened state of battle frenzy that no element could harm them. The young men who were training, as well as King Conchobar, saw the sheer ferocity of Sétanta, in this altered animalistic state, so they came to understand Sétanta's effectiveness in feats associated with battle, and at this young age he was brought into the sacred fighting regime of the kingdom of Ulster. Sétanta was said to be able to easily enter into this berserk state of battle frenzy "during which his hair stood on end, his muscles bulged and his body rotated within its skin. One eye protruded from his head, the other sank into his skull and his battle-cry drove people insane" (Fleming & Husain 59); this ability to tap into his own animalistic nature defines him as a hero, like Beowulf, who must remain connected to his natural, animalistic abilities in order to succeed upon his quest. However, precisely because of Sétanta's "wildness," as stated by Dooley, he often proved difficult to contain as "control of the young hero's aggression against the boy troop ... [was] achieved only with difficulty and ... [was] always in danger of breaking down" (110). In addition, "even the basic and natural function of sleep must be renegotiated for a hero who possesses such innate and natural wildness," as Sétanta is portrayed as not being able to sleep "until a verisimilitude of wildness and the hard life of a wild raider, the flat stone bed, is brought indoors and his volatile humours balanced" (Dooley 111).

Sétanta's natural, animalistic attributes, which remained with him from his birth into his childhood, marks him initially as a botanical hero because he is connected firmly with the natural world. His animalistic side even earns him his adult name, Cúchulainn, as one day King Conchobar is said to have invited Sétanta to a feast at the smith's, Culann's, compound. Once King Conchobar arrived and was asked by Culann if any other guests were coming, King

Conchobar forget that he invited Sétanta, and so Culann released his infamously ferocious hound to guard his property. Sétanta, though, was said to easily kill the hound, and since Culann was distraught at losing his guard dog, Sétanta vowed to serve in its place, until Culann could secure another fitting guard dog, thus Sétanta's name became Cúchulainn, which means "Culann's hound." His new name further aligns him as a natural representative, thus also signaling his botanical heroism.

Later, Cúchulainn leaves to study the art of war from the best teacher known to exist, the Scottish female warrior Scáthach. As discussed in previous chapters, often the connection to a female mythic character, as well as a retreat to a forest environment early in the life of a hero, serve as elements towards the education of botanical heroism. In many ways Scáthach serves as a reminder of the reverence for the female goddesses of Celtic literature whose connection to the deep wilderness helps to often transform the hero; Matthews supports this view by contending that Scáthach is a portrayal of "the eponymous goddess of the Isle of Skye" (75). Scáthach's residence is portrayed as imparting necessary elements towards the development of Cúchulainn, and again the components she imparts to him are connected with his own innate animalistic, and thus natural, abilities. Even upon entering Scáthach's compound, he is portrayed as having to leap over an insurmountable ravine, like a "salmon," in order to land in her abode; "Three times Cúchulainn tried to cross the bridge but his best efforts failed, and the men jeered him. Then he went and gave his war spasm. He stepped on the head of the bridge and gave his hero's salmon-leap onto the middle. He reached the far end of the bridge so quickly that it had no time to fly up at him. Then he sprang off onto the solid ground of the island" (*Tain* 29). This leaping like a fish is symbolic of Cúchulainn's need to trust his animalistic abilities in order to cross over into the home of this goddess representative. Also, it is important that Scáthach's home is almost inaccessible as it lies so deep within the concealment of nature, which makes it meet the requirements of the mythic otherworld to Cúchulainn. While residing with Scáthach, she fine-tunes Cúchulainn's fighting skills and teaches him to be among the best warriors in Ireland precisely because she introduces him to elements that appear otherworldly as they force him to contend with the realities of nature, such as a scene where he must kill his own son, presumably to face the fact of mortality, as so many botanical heroes must do. Therefore, these initial otherworldly scenes serve to necessarily test and confuse him, and his introduction to the first Earth Goddess representative within his life saga, Scáthach, also helps to propel Cúchulainn closer to becoming an actualized botanical hero, but first his must face the mythic underworld and emerge from it reborn.

Another significant story that provides background towards the plot of the *Tain* presents the character Fergus, who was an Ulsterman, as supposed to marry his brother's widow Nessa. She agreed if her son Conchobar could be king for a year. After the year, however, the people of Ulster loved Conchobar and wanted him to maintain his royal post, which he is seen as holding in the *Tain*. King Conchobar wanted to marry a woman named Deirdre, but she eloped with another man, and it came to pass that King Conchobar ordered all attendants who were traveling with Deirdre, as she went to her betrothed, to be killed, so that King Conchobar could have her for himself. This is how Fergus' son, Fiacha, ended up being slain. Fergus learned of what happened and abandoned Ulster to join forces with Connacht, taking his own formidable fighting abilities, as well as three thousand of Ulster's best warriors, with him.

Also important to the text is the back story of the men of Ulster. It is said that a man from Ulster, Crunnchru, married Macha, a divine queen, who appeared to him as a young mortal woman. She became pregnant, and before she gave birth, heavily pregnant now, Crunnchru boasted to the men of Ulster that Macha could outrun the king's horses. Macha tried to resist entering the race and vowed to run after she gave birth, but King Conchobar, insisted. Macha entered the race and beat the king's horses, but after she crossed the finish line, she gave birth to her twins, and then she died. To punish the men of Ulster, she made them experience the pangs of childbirth for nine days annually, only exempting the women and children of Ulster, so that the Ulstermen would commiserate with the ordeal women must go through in childbirth. This aspect of the mythological background of the *Tain* is essential because it shows another natural aspect to the myth. It suggests that the men of the epic, most specifically Cúchulainn as he is the protagonist of the text, must experience both sides of existence, that of a man and that of a woman, in order to achieve apotheosis; this mythic aspect also references the cost of natural regeneration that Cúchulainn will have to internalize.

The *Tain* presents the kingdom of Ulster as being under attack, but the Ulstermen cannot come to the aid of their kingdom because they are experiencing the curse of their birthing pains, so the sole protector, Cúchulainn, must stand alone to try and defend Ulster. Mythically Cúchulainn, at the age of seventeen, is able to defend Ulster because he is the child of the god Lug, so he is not by blood an Ulsterman and is not under the threat of Macha's curse. The birthing pangs of all the men of Ulster also reveal the power of the women characters within the *Tain*, as the roles of the females in this text "highlight the matrilineal nature of Celtic society: the power of women is often presented not only as equal to that of men, but ... exceeding it" (Leeming & Husain 56). Similar to the representation of Scáthach, there are many Earth Goddess portrayals within the *Tain*, and it is precisely their interaction with Cúchulainn that mark him as a botanical hero, propelling the message of nature's cycles.

The *Tain* begins with Queen Medb, of the kingdom of Connaught, lying in bed with her husband, King Áilill. Medb discusses her desire to own the prized Brown Bull of Cooley in addition to Áilill's sacred White Horned Bull of Ai. The background of the bulls within the *Tain* is central to an understanding of the myth and its message of botanical heroism because they are also clear representations of nature and point to agrarian values. In addition, Queen Medb's status as a powerful queen is important. Medb matter-of-factly, because of her desire to own the bull, declares that she would like to invade Ulster and attempt to steal the bull, even though she fully knows that it will start an epic battle. As Fleming & Husain state "In origin Medb was probably a goddess of fertility and sovereignty. She was a formidable woman—a strong leader and brave fighter with a ravenous sexual appetite" (60). As a possible representation of a Celtic Earth Goddess, Medb is portrayed as quite strong and independent. She is depicted as superseding all males within the text, except for a time, Cúchulainn, as her husband, King Áilill, merely bows down to all of her desires, many of which involve her openly having affairs with other men. Matthews states of Medb that "the strength of her sovereignty appears to derive from the land itself" (33), and because of this, it appears that her role within the myth is to aid Cúchulainn in becoming a botanical hero, as many mythic female characters, discussed in myriad myths thus far, have done. It is important to note that scholars, like Dooley,[2] have projected doubt onto the role of women within this narrative; she comments that this text, written after the introduction of Christianity to Ireland, undoubtedly shows conflict between Celtic and Christian ideologies. Still, most Irish mythological critics have long interpreted the role of characters like Medb, and later the Morrígan, as purposeful attempts to either revere or demonize the Celtic beliefs in sovereign Earth Goddesses (Dooley 158). This contradictory nature of the female characters within the text is evidenced, as discussed, in many world myths, when portraying Earth Goddesses, as the lessons they teach in heroic myth are often harsh with a focus on the necessary acceptance of death.

Battle ensues with only Cúchulainn facing and defeating hundreds of combatants because of his ability to enter into his animalistic, berserk state. Medb continues to send a seemingly endless number of reinforcements to combat Cúchulainn. The fact that Cúchulainn consistently fights hundreds of formidable opponents and defeats them single-handedly signals that he is on a heroic quest because he must solely depend upon his own faculties. The onslaught of constant warfare that he alone must endure easily puts Cúchulainn in scenes that could be described as the mythic underworld, as he ceaselessly must face the deaths of hundreds of men, as well as the constant possibility of his own demise. In addition, the incessant battles of the *Tain,* in which the lone Cúchulainn must endure, could also be defined as symbolic episodes that propel the psychological growth of Cúchulainn as a botanical hero, as Homer's *Iliad* exemplified with the portrayal of Achilles' psychological underworld as one where he alone must fight against elements within his own psyche. The fighting culminates in an important scene where Cúchulainn must fight his best friend and foster-brother, Lóch, even though both don't wish to fight one another, as both see the battle as meaningless. Dooley discusses this crucial scene as the culmination of a psychic underworld for Cúchulainn; "The whole context of Cúchulainn's predicament is his fear of collapsing into the terror of the liminal unknown" as he is forced to face the "disconcerting psychic confusion of having to fight his magically endowed double, his foster brother, Lóch" (139). This is a significant moment to the botanical heroic process because here Cúchulainn begins to see all life as set in a greater process, and he must resign to the fact that he is merely an insignificant part of this cycle, as again central to the quest of the botanical hero is the realization that one's selfhood is unimportant when viewed in accordance to the greater reality of nature; this lesson will further be realized by Cúchulainn through his meeting of the Morrígan.

The Morrígan, the goddess of war, but also of fertility, appears to Cúchulainn at a critical moment of his solitary fighting; Dooley also notes this moment as serving to thrust Cúchulainn further into his psychic underworld, as he if forced to face the Morrígan, with her connection to the inevitability of death (139). The appearance of the Morrígan in the *Tain* serves to propel Cúchulainn in his heroic quest towards becoming a botanical hero because she reveals to him, what also Queen Medb exposes, and what many Earth Goddesses are portrayed as revealing to botanical heroes—that death is inevitable and natural. As another representative Earth Goddess, the Morrígan is not only a goddess connected to demise though; she is also a goddess of fertility; as Matthews states of the Morrígan, she "stems from an early, pre–Celtic tradition of the Cailleach, the dark and foreboding figure who is at once the genesis and nemesis of life" (37). Her name "derives from the Celtic 'Great Queen'" (Matthews 37). So, the Morrígan serves to remind Cúchulainn that only with death can renewal be possible, thus solidifying him as upon the path of a botanical hero who must learn that rebirth results from demise.

The Morrígan appears to Cúchulainn in the form of a maiden and tells him that she reveres his talents thus far, but the myth fast changes to show her representation of maidenhood as only signifying one part of the developmental level of Cúchulainn, as he thus far is meeting only one part of the life cycle. When she comes as a maiden, Cúchulainn is only portrayed as one dimensional, full of mythic life and vigor, but the Morrígan's role in the myth suggests Cúchulainn's need to move beyond this one aspect of the life cycle. Her youth, in the form of her maiden self, praising him for his strength and valor, is a test, and his subsequent misidentification and rejection of her true identity is vital for his realization of the cycles of life. After being sent away from him and insulted, presumably because Cúchulainn doesn't recognize her, the Morrígan comes back to Cúchulainn and hinders his battle goals, but it is her intervention, like the obstacles presented by Medb, that helps Cúchulainn to understand and embrace his own mortality. The Morrígan returns to Cúchulainn in animalistic guises, first in the form of an eel, then a "she-wolf," and finally a "hornless red heifer" (*Tain* 136–7) and battles Cúchulainn in these forms. These animal representations, which now replace the Morrígan's maiden form, allow Cúchulainn to psychically evolve, as his interaction with each of them helps him to gain an understanding of his connection to the cycles of the natural world. With each animal Cúchulainn battles and finally injures, he grows weaker, something that has rarely happened in the text thus far when he has battled human opponents; this weakening of Cúchulainn forces him to admit that one day he too will succumb to the same fate as the animals he fights.

The Morrígan then comes back, now in the form of an old woman, to appear to Cúchulainn when he is depleted of his confident prowess and is filled with a "great weariness" (*Tain* 137). The text depicts her as a very old woman who wears the same injuries obtained as her three animal forms. And interestingly, here it is only Cúchulainn who can heal her:

> The Morrígan appeared to him in the shape of a squint-eyed old woman milking a cow with three tits. He asked her for a drink and she gave him milk from the first tit. 'Good health to the giver!' Cúchulainn said. 'The blessing of God and man on you.' And her head was healed and made whole. She gave him milk from the second tit and her eye was made whole. She gave him milk from the third tit and her legs were made whole. 'You said you would never heal me,' the Morrígan said [*Tain* 137].

This scene finally shows Cúchulainn's realization of what the Morrígan, in all of her forms, represents. Instead of shunning her now, like he did when she appeared in her maiden form, audiences see in his willingness to converse with her, a psychological transformation in Cúchulainn.

The Morrígan provides an experience for Cúchulainn that enables him to internalize the inevitability of his own death and loss of selfhood that is often associated in mythic scenes of the psychic underworld, but she also shows Cúchulainn that the natural cycle is one that always renews itself. After appearing to him as a maiden, and being unappreciated for her vital role as such, Cúchulainn literally fights against nature when he battles the Morrígan in her animal forms. Cúchulainn's subsequent exhaustion at fighting against nature, reveals to him the futility of such a fight; instead, he is forced to concede that as a mortal, not a vigorous hero who can defeat any adversary, as the text thus far has only portrayed him, he will weaken, grow old, and finally die. Cúchulainn's internalization of this is acknowledged when the Morrígan appears to him in the form of an old, injured woman, and he, instead of shunning her, shows her compassion. The scene reveals that when Cúchulainn converses with the old woman, drinking the milk she offers him, he is able to heal her; though this scene appears odd, it signifies the psychic transformation that has occurred within Cúchulainn.

In Cúchulainn healing the Morrígan, the true message of Cúchulainn's heroic quest in the form of his solitary battle is confirmed. The textual shift in the *Tain* reveals that Cúchulainn was thus far not fighting with myriad opponents from Connaught, but was fighting against himself and his unwillingness to face the laws of nature that call for the demise of all living beings. Like Achilles, Beowulf, and Gilgamesh, Cúchulainn had to learn that he cannot maintain the current state of his youthful vigour forever; instead, like the Buddha, Cúchulainn must embrace the loss of his identity, and this is precisely what happens while in his psychological underworld with the visit from the Morrígan. The Morrígan reduces Cúchulainn to facing the reality of his own mortality, and once he does this, he is able to receive her wisdom. As a quintessential Earth Goddess, the Morrígan shows Cúchulainn the lesson of botanical heroism—that after old age and death, one can be renewed. Like Guan Yin's regeneration, Cúchulainn drinks from the milk the Morrígan offers him and sees the power of regeneration after injury, old age, and even death.

His participation in the act of healing the Morrígan in the form of an old woman mythically presents Cúchulainn as spiritually transformed into a botanical hero. In each of the interactions with the Morrígan, Cúchulainn has displayed the stages of his own psychic development. When the Morrígan was a maiden, he believed he was invincible, but when he fought each animal form, he relented to the power of nature, and now facing old age and frailty, he learned too that this was merely a fleeting stage in the cycle of life—once having internalized this, the botanical hero, like Cúchulainn is able to do here, can mythically supersede the transitory nature of any life stage, often presented, as it is here, by miraculously healing wounds or resurrecting from death. The Morrígan helps Cúchulainn to connect the natural fact of death to nature's cycles of rebirth. Cúchulainn, as the story of his birth reflected, with its message of birth, death, and rebirth, is portrayed in this scene as finally attaining the wisdom of these natural cycles, which allows him to transform into a botanical hero.

After the Morrígan's visit, Cúchulainn's transformation is further confirmed, as he soon becomes so wounded that he must finally rest outside of battle. It is at this moment where the Ulstermen begin to stop experiencing their pangs of labor and can join in the war. Because Cúchulainn arguably has transformed past his former definition of selfhood, as that of indestructible warrior, he can now only watch the fight. Cúchulainn sees Fergus pulling back Medb's troops, as he promised Cúchulainn he would, which results in the Ulstermen forcing Medb and her soldiers to retreat. This conclusion of the *Tain* happens so fast and simply that it supports the idea that the battle was always meant to be a symbolic, mythic account dependent upon the evolution of Cúchulainn's character; this is further supported by the scene where Queen Medb is finally overtaken. Cúchulainn, having regained enough strength to join his fellow Ulstermen in the last moments of the battle, alone catches Medb off guard, because the text states that she was contending with the start of her monthly menstruation; "Then Medb got her gush of blood" (*Tain* 250). The text states that Medb tells Fergus that she has to relieve herself, and Fergus chastises her for choosing a bad time, as they are in the midst of the last stages of battle, but she states, "'I can't help it…. I'll die if I can't do it…. [So] Medb relieved herself. It dug three great channels each big enough to take a household" (*Tain* 250). Coming upon Medb in this state, the text presents Cúchulainn as deciding to let her live. This scene arguably connects Medb as again a symbolic representation of nature and its cycles.

Medb's ability to alter nature with the functioning of her body suggests, as discussed earlier, her portrayal as a representational Earth Goddess; Dooley states that scholars have connected this scene to similar scenes found in the Scandinavian *Edda* where incidents of divine women whose act of urination or menstruation alters nature (178). The Ulstermen throughout the text have experienced the pangs of childbirth, rendering them inept, which allowed Medb to threaten their territory, but when they are finished in their symbolic birthing process, the cycle is viewed as continuing through the Earth Goddess representation of Medb, as it is this precise moment that she resumes menstruation. The myth purposely moves from the birthing process to the stage of ready fertility once more, as it has all along portrayed themes that are in correlation with the cycles of nature, such as in the story of Cúchulainn's birth and the scene between the Morrígan and Cúchulainn. One may ask, what then did the Ulstermen give symbolic birth to? It appears that what is between their pangs of labor and Medb's cycle of fertility is two things—countless deaths and Cúchulainn. Therefore, again one must look to Cúchulainn to find meaning. The text's parallel portrayal of symbolic birth, presented by the Ulstermens' birthing pains, at precisely a time of tremendous death at the hands of Cúchulainn, indicates that Cúchulainn's solitary battle with an insurmountable foe is for purposes of birthing his own spiritual evolution. When Cúchulainn gains the wisdom presented to him by the Morrígan, Medb regains her period, thus solidifying the cycles of nature in this story of this botanical hero.

The *Tain* ends portraying the Brown Bull of Cuailnge spreading the remains of the bull Finnbennach, the White-Horned Bull, throughout the land of Ireland. The focus on the bulls at the end of the text shows that the message of the text again is tied to the laws of nature. The *Tain* showcases its focused battle as being one that is without cause; it was simply started to try to win the possession of a bull. In addition the text does not end in a clear and defined victory; instead, the text makes it clear that this victory is short-lived, as peace is only negotiated for seven years, and that this whole process was only part of an unending cyclical process that will assuredly repeatedly occur. As Dooley states "a positive outcome is to be understood as temporizing, and no hero can rest secure in his fame. This kind of end is never simply the end: it remains permanently locked into the open-endedness of what will happen next time" (186). This cyclical promise of the heroic saga shows that nothing really was overcome; instead, Cúchulainn learns to let go of his selfhood throughout the myth, and just like the White-Horned Bull, Finnbennach, whose remains will directly replenish Irish soil, so too does Cúchulainn now know that he too will one day succumb to the same fate, allowing him to resurrect, not as a revered, societal hero, but as an element of nature.

In a later myth involving Cúchulainn, he is further confirmed as a botanical hero because of his experience in the Celtic otherworld, which allows him to continue his journey towards losing his desire for selfhood. In this myth, Cúchulainn falls in love with a goddess of the otherworld, Fand, wife of the god of the oceans, Manannan Mac Lir, though Cúchulainn is happily married to Emer. His tale recounts Cúchulainn entering into a state of deep sleep, where no one can entirely rouse him, as he is held within the otherworld. Fand and Cúchulainn fall in love, but Cúchulainn eventually remembers his life with Emer and wishes to go back home. Ultimately, though, the reunion between husband and wife is not as expected; Cúchulainn upon realizing that he has lost Fand and left the otherworld, cries out in grief and seeks solace alone in the mountains where he does not sleep or drink. His near death causes Emer to seek the assistance of the druids to make him forget Fand and his time in the otherworld; he does forget and reunites with his wife in his former life, but the myth describes Cúchulainn as forever sad; "Cúchulainn had no memory of his passions but there lingered in him a deep sorrow, the reason for which he could not recall" (Ellis 96). Cúchulainn's otherworld tale shows that the heroic spiritual quest is a confusing one; he never can come to terms with what is morally right or wrong; he loves both women, but rather than only seeing this as a love triangle; instead, the myth suggests Cúchulainn's inability to live happily in either his earthly or otherworldly realm. Once glimpsing the other-world with its love of the goddess Fand, he was no longer suitable for the world of his former identity. His depression at the end of the myth further signals his eventual letting go of his need to maintain identity in either world.

Cúchulainn's death comes to him seven years after his experience in the *Tain*. Queen Medb again plots his death using the help of six sorcerers who were the children of one of the druids Cúchulainn killed in the *Tain*. Here again, the downfall of Cúchulainn is viewed as a necessary event that is aided by the Earth Goddess representation of Medb. King Conchobar is said to have known of the coming onslaught of powerful magic directed at Cúchulainn; he tried to save Cúchulainn, but the sorcerers convinced Cúchulainn that a battle had begun that threatened Ulster again. Soon knowing that this battle would lead to his death, Cúchulainn tied his body to a rock and fought the onslaught of warriors. A raven, a symbol of the Morrígan, landed on his shoulder, and it was then that Cúchulainn conceded to his death. The use of natural imagery again showcases Cúchulainn as a botanical hero, as he chooses to willing accept his demise as natural. After his death, his physical remains also legitimize his connection to nature, as Conall Cernach is said to have retrieved the severed head of Cúchulainn and placed it upon a rock, "but such [was] its power that it split the stone, burying itself deep within it: a symbolic restoration of the hero into the bosom of the engendering earth" (Matthews 38). This last scene shows that Cúchulainn does not resurrect while maintaining identity, but still he is depicted as returning into the earth, so that he is displayed as a symbolic representation of resurrection, as his willingness to accept his own death and loss of identity, allows the remains of his body to mythically propel itself into the earth to be reborn as a natural element. Thus, Cúchulainn is portrayed as being reborn as nature itself, making him a prime example of a botanical hero who has reached apotheosis.

Herakles' Natural Resurrection from Death

The Greek hero Herakles also provides an example of a botanical hero who attains apotheosis. Many Greek and Roman writers, from Pindar, Euripides, Apollodorus, Ovid and Seneca, have portrayed Herakles as an epic hero, though his portrayals have varied from comic to tragic. It is true that Herakles is often known primarily for his brute strength and bravery, but when one looks at his mythic story, there are elements that also align this legendary hero to botanical heroism. In some of Herakles' representations, such as Hesiod's *Theogony*, Herakles appears to be "a beneficent, regulatory force that fights against the disorderly and abnormal forces of a nature" (Galinsky 16), but in other versions, like Pindar's, he becomes a figure who "fights against enemies who flout a general, universal 'order' or 'law,' which has become the generally accepted norm or way of life for both men and gods" (Galinsky 35), but oftentimes are portrayed as unnatural. Therefore, when viewing Herakles in botanical terms, he most often appears as an agent who reminds audiences of the necessity of the natural elements within life, as he is most well known as the "archetypal 'man of nature'" (Galinsky 69).

K. Armstrong discusses Herakles as a relic of the Paleolithic hunter; "he even dresses in animal skins, like a caveman, and carries a club" (*Short History*, 38); K. Armstrong also contends that Herakles "is a shaman, famous for his skill with animals; he visits the underworld, seeks the fruit of immortality, and ascends to the realms of the gods on Mount Olympus" (*Short History*, 38). It is this shamanic aspect of Herakles that exposes him as holding wisdom that may be in line with more traditional, nature-dependent belief systems and helps him, arguably, achieve botanical heroism. However, the myths of Herakles also present aspects similar to other Greek myths, like "Jason and Golden Fleece" or the *Odyssey*, that seemingly portray cultural conflict over the centuries of shifting belief systems in Greece. Some scholars, like Barnes, portray Herakles as only a patriarchal symbol meant to eradicate matriarchal belief systems, as evidenced in mythological characters like Perseus and Theseus. Whether Herakles is a relic of the Paleolithic period or a classical attempt to justify patriarchal power structures is difficult to prove; however, he is a hero who seems to have endured because he represents at least a clash between two cultural extremes, and more often than not, his myths do indeed impart messages that are aligned with tenets of botanical heroism.

Herakles is known for being able to overcome almost every impediment that is placed before him, but many of his myths depict him as being forced to lose his bravado. Herakles, always hated by Hera for being the illegitimate son of her husband Zeus and a mortal woman, Alcmene, was persecuted by the goddess. Famously, Hera tried to kill the infant Herakles by sending two venomous vipers to bite him, but being the son of Zeus, he easily strangled the snakes. Much of his youth is then spent evading Hera's wrathful designs, until finally happily married with kids, Hera forces Herakles to commit a task that makes him desire his own demise. Hera causes Herakles to experience temporary insanity, so that he murders his own wife and children. Upon awakening and seeing what he did, Herakles goes to the Oracle at Delphi to inquire how to heal himself psychologically, and after hearing the Oracle's prophecy, which must seem to him to spell certain death, he takes it upon himself to seek out the evil King Eurystheus, so that he may be assigned twelve impossible labors.

It is this component of his myth that marks Herakles not on a quest to achieve fame or prove his brute strength, but on a heroic quest to heal his psyche, which is a proper quest for a botanical hero.

Herakles' twelve labors are portrayed as tasks that are continuously connected to nature. His first labor is to kill the Nemean lion, which according to some myths would appear in the form of a woman to lure over-confident warriors into a cave; once inside, the maiden's true form would be revealed, spelling immediate death for the warriors. The symbolism of both female and animal being tied to the death of young males within a cave is revealing, as it may again reflect a more traditional, earth-based ideology in Greece; however, Herakles does not appear to only be another representation of the male hero defeating traditional Earth Goddesses. He indeed does kill the Nemean lion, but he seems to also learn essential components of the botanical heroic quest that allow him to continue upon his psychological journey from this episode. Herakles, in quintessential heroic measure, knows that the only way to defeat the lion is to enter into its lair. Herakles blocks the entrance of the cave, so he and the lion are trapped inside to meet their fates; this willing acceptance to enter into this clear underworld environment, facing the terror of his own death, marks Herakles early on as a different type of hero than Perseus for instance who accomplishes his task of killing Medusa with ease through the help of mystical agents. Herakles defeats the Nemean lion with only his club and his bare hands, as he hits it upon the head to stun it, and then strangles it, knowing that no weapon was capable of penetrating its skin, a task that is similar to Beowulf's killing of Grendel, and as with Beowulf, signals the success of Herakles being tied to his natural abilities, as opposed to his relying upon manufactured materials. Furthermore, this death of the Nemean lion is also significant as it carries with it a new identity for Herakles. In most artistic portrayals of Herakles, he is depicted wearing the skin of the Nemean lion, as protection certainly, but also as evidence that he is taking the power of the lion within himself, becoming both man and animal. Just as the shamans of many nature-based communities often wear animal skins to perform their sacred ceremonies, so too does Herakles' depiction wearing the lion skin make him identifiable as a spiritual intermediary between the realm of human beings and the secrets of the animal kingdom.

Next Herakles goes on to defeat another mythological creature that is overtly connected with nature, only now instead of him being forced to contend with nature's animalistic side, he now must face a representation of nature's botanical elements. The Hydra, a ferocious dragon with many heads, does not appear overtly botanical, until Herakles attempts to cut off one of its heads with a harvesting sickle, a clear connection to the Hydra as a vegetative symbol.

Herakles quickly finds that decapitating each of the heads is not the way to defeat the Hydra, as each wound produces two heads where there was one, making the Hydra even more of a formidable opponent. The symbolism of the Hydra suggests that Herakles can only defeat it in similar ways that he did the Nemean lion—by fully facing it and taking part of it within his psyche. By observing the Hydra, he learns to finally cauterize the wounds after he decapitates the heads of the creature, thus preventing new heads from emerging, but the lesson of first having to learn from the Hydra how to defeat it through observation teaches Herakles the power of the resilience of the botanical environment, and it is a lesson that will remain with him as he finishes his other labors. Herakles is only able to complete his impossible tasks by respecting nature's power, not trying to manfully overpower the elements of the environment. This is seen in his third labor with Artemis.

Herakles was next ordered to steal Artemis' Golden Hind, but he knows that the only way to obtain this treasured creature, loved by the goddess of the wilderness, Artemis, is to ask her permission. It is clear here that his respect for Artemis, a clear representation of nature in the form of an Earth Goddess, allows him to accomplish his task with ease. Herakles goes on to accomplish his other labors by also consistently showing that he works with nature instead of against it, like when he was assigned the task of cleaning out the infamously dirty Augean Stables in a mere day. Instead of painstakingly cleaning the stables by hand, he uses natural elements to accomplish his task, as he reroutes the nearby rivers, Alpheus and Peneus, to naturally wash the stables clean. His command of nature is revealing here, as it shows that as his labors continue, his knowledge of the workings of nature also expands. In another labor, Herakles is tasked to retrieve the belt of Hippolyta, Queen of the Amazons, again a possible representation of an early Earth Goddess or priestess. Here too Herakles instead of trying to defeat Hippolyta, shows his respect for her, and simply again asks for her belt, of which Hippolyta is readily willing to give him. However, Hera is said to intervene by sowing distrust in Hippolyta's army of Amazon women, so battle ensues, and Herakles, to his horror, finds that he accidently kills Hippolyta, something he had no intention of doing and is devastated by. Again, as often stated, the archetypal heroic quest serves to psychologically confound heroes, so they may shed their former personas and reach apotheosis. Herakles is evidenced as embracing this confusion as he learns the laws of nature throughout his long journey to accomplish his twelve impossible tasks; the main lesson he must learn, though, is that of his own mortality and loss of selfhood in order to achieve botanical heroism.

In Herakles' eleventh labor he is commanded to steal the golden apples of the Hesperides. Again, the imagery of the serpent Ladon guarding the golden apples of immortality is distinctly suggestive of older belief systems in Greece. Barnes states that it is significant that Herakles kills the serpent and takes the apples to the "new patriarch in Mycenae," and by doing this he "terminated, the gift of golden fruit of immortality, which was the most cherished inheritance from Mother Earth" (86). This scene can be interpreted as a gross disrespect for the ideology of nature worship. Killing the serpent and taking the apples may portray the eradication of matriarchal belief systems by a male hero in a time of flux in Greece, or it might suggest more. As discussed in the introduction, the evolution of many civilizations away from predominant nature-dependence often produced tales of mythic heroes who became less identifiable as agents who readily succumbed to nature's power; instead many heroes developed into representatives of new cultural values, such as a shift in the perception of time as linear and the heightened importance of one individual life. Often life became mythically portrayed through heroic legend as something that should be cherished on an individual level, but the important thing to consider is that many of these myths still recorded a belief that an individual life, identity, and even legacy, are things that cannot last indefinitely. Oftentimes, hero myths, like the one of Herakles, remind audiences that even though new ideologies suggest time as linear and the life of a singular individual as important, they repeatedly continue to embrace traditional, nature-dependent belief systems, reminding audiences that no matter what, humans are in fact a part of nature, and it is to nature that all human beings will return, regardless of the adopted ideology dominant at any historical moment. Therefore, perhaps Herakles stealing the apples of the Hesperides and bringing them back to Mycenae imparts a mythic message that immortality is impossible for any mortal. By bringing the apples back to the patriarchal Mycenae, Herakles is thus bringing with him the lessons of the matriarchal cultures' reverence for the cycles of nature, which demands individual death in its promise of natural immortality. This is further represented by Herakles' final labor to the realm of death, Hades.

For his final labor Herakles must journey into Hades to retrieve Cerberus, the three-headed dog that guards the underworld, and as this crucial heroic archetype usually signals the hero needing to face his or her worst fears, mainly of death, in order to achieve self-actualization, with Herakles, it seems that he may have already learned the botanical lesson of the underworld upon his previous labors. Herakles, instead of depending upon his bravado, relies on his newfound wisdom of nature; he enters Hades and takes Cerberus with every intention of returning the animal unharmed to its rightful place within the underworld. It is significant that Herakles does not attempt to harm Cerberus, but treats this ferocious being with the respect he treated Artemis' Hind; this signals that Herakles fully accepts what Cerberus represents—death.

The ease of which Herakles enters and exits Hades further connects him with shamanic attributes that some scholars, like K. Armstrong, associate with Herakles. As discussed throughout this book, shamans within Paleolithic and hunter/gather communities were often presented as entering representative underworlds in order to educate the community on the functioning of nature to spiritually revitalize them. The ability of shamans to voyage in and out of the physical world mythically showed the tribe that life and death are but parts of an endless, natural cycle. An indication that Herakles has fully embraced his own death, and serves a mythic role of shaman, is the mythological depiction of him first going to Eleusis to be initiated in the Eleusinian Mysteries, depicted artistically on a frieze now housed at the Naples National Archeological Museum in Italy. As stated, Eleusis and its Eleusinian Mysteries held for initiates the sacred guidance of the myth of Demeter and Persephone. Initiates who endured the consecrated Mysteries were said to fully face the fact of their own mortality through components of terror. Herakles undergoing this act, that explicitly ties him again to a respect of nature and its representatives, the Earth Goddesses Demeter and Persephone, shows that he is a hero who does not attempt to defeat nature but has come to understand and respect the workings of nature's cycles.

Once his labors are accomplished, contrary to expectations for an archetypal hero's return from a successful heroic mission, Herakles is merely depicted as going to Thebes to resume a normal life. He gets married to another woman, Deianira, and has many children with her, signaling that the goal of his journey, psychological healing past the trauma and guilt of the murder of his family, may have been partially accomplished. However, Deianira one day doubts Herakles' love for her, and falling for the deceit of a centaur killed by Herakles, Deianira gives Herakles a robe with the centaur's blood upon it because she was fooled into thinking the blood was a love potion. However, the blood produces the means to kill Herakles, as it actually acted like acid and began to eat away at his flesh once he put the robe on. The portrayal of the natural element of blood finally killing Herakles is significant because it shows the power of nature in killing one of the most revered heroes of Greek mythology.

Herakles is depicted as dying in agony. His physical death is quite significant in marking him as a botanical hero as it serves to portray him as not superior to other people, but equal to them; in dying, he is also not specifically marked for his partial divinity. Herakles' death scene sends a mythic message that Herakles, although semi-divine, is indeed mortal and must die a physical death through the means of a natural element. Further marking Herakles as a botanical hero who has been psychologically transformed because of his heroic quest, he shows that he fully embraces his death, even though it is painful.

Herakles' final act is to cut down the trees that will be used for his own funeral pyre, and once he climbs upon it, he readily faces his demise in the fire that he lit. Seemingly because of the acceptance of the loss of his life, and the fact that he willingly aids his own process of death, he is mythically elevated to spiritual immortality; "now, at the point of death, with burnt and withered flesh, Hercules grew calm again. On top of the pyre, he spread the skin of the Nemean lion. He rested his head on his club as on a pillow, and lay down among the flames with a peaceful face" (Leeming 250). The peaceful demeanor of Herakles upon the moment of his death explicitly portrays him as an enlightened hero. He is not depicted as crying out when his death approaches, or chastising Deianira, but as aiding his death along, and peacefully accepting it. The mythic image of Herakles atop of his self-constructed funeral pyre burning away his physical body, while at peace, sends audiences a message about the necessary acceptance of mortal death; it also mythically reveals a spiritual transformation on the part of Herakles that emulates the enlightenment attained by the Buddha.

It is seemingly because of the spiritual wisdom Herakles obtained throughout his quest that enabled him to readily accept his own death, as well as be mythically resurrected. The Olympic Pantheon is said to have seen Herakles' final act and conceded that he belonged with them for all eternity, so after his mortal body burned away, they gave Herakles divine immortality. This divinity and ascension to Mount Olympus after his death signals Herakles as a botanical hero because it symbolizes the natural archetype of death and rebirth. Like the Buddha, Guan Yin, and Cúchulainn, Herakles learned upon his heroic quest to shed his conceptions of self as superior; instead, he learned to slowly shed his desire for individual importance. After losing love when he lost his family, he mythically learned to systematically let go of his own desires that tied him singularly to life, like the Buddha did when he faced the desirous daughters of Kama-Mara and like Cúchulainn did when he let go of his longing for the goddess Fand when he left the otherworld.

It should be stated that the point of such myths as this is not to showcase the necessity of only accepting death, so much so that one shuns the gift of life. Myths, such as this one, or the tale of the Buddha, do not advocate a wish for death in an abhorrence of the desires associated with life; instead, in shedding desire for a belief that one is singularly important, a botanical hero gains a knowledge that more readily aligns him or her with the natural world. The Buddha after having attained enlightenment did not simply kill himself, as Herakles did not commit suicide after his return from Hades; both heroes instead went on to live their lives with perhaps more awareness of the beauty of the natural world, more compassion for the beings of the earth, and more certainty of the continuous patterns of nature, so that when their time came to die, they embraced it for what it was—only a stage in a recursive cycle. Herakles, therefore, left Hades and married again; he also did not spew hateful utterances at Deianira for falling for the centaur's trick; he simply faced his death with an assurance that he would experience a natural rebirth.

In Herakles' realization and acceptance that his own life was fleeting, he also, like the Buddha and Cúchulainn, gained an understanding in something that provided him with timeless certainty—the laws of nature. The body of the Buddha upon death became covered with flowers, Cúchulainn's head was absorbed back into the earth, and Herakles' remains became ashes that were whisked away by the wind. Herakles' mythic resurrection to Mount Olympus does not make him singularly important, like a depiction of Christ's resurrection is often interpreted; instead, Herakles' resurrection is depicted as natural. Herakles' resurrection, or rebirth, happens because he embraces not his superiority or his semi-divinity, but his mortality. In dying as an average mortal, he, as a botanical hero, shows audiences the promise that resurrection, too, is average when depicted in terms of nature.

Hera's role within the myth is hard to be interpreted as anything but cruel, but, like Medb served to educate Cúchulainn about the necessity of accepting death through her harsh lessons, perhaps Hera can be interpreted in a similar way. Hera consistently served a purpose for Herakles to face death; her mythic tragedies of killing the people Herakles held most dear, his family, Hippolyta, and finally himself, readily prepared Herakles to finally experience the spiritual ascension that he does. Hera upon Herakles' death is depicted as serving a central role in allowing Herakles to enter Mount Olympus, as she undergoes a ritual where she mimics the birthing process and then formally adopts Herakles; she is said by Diodorus to then "'cherish him with a mother's love'" (qtd. in Scott 36). Upon this ending of Herakles' myth, that clearly shows him as being mythically reborn with the help of the Earth Goddess representative, Hera, it becomes clear why Herakles is named as such; Herakles is a derivative of Hera, signaling all along that the two serve a united mythic goal of aiding audiences in seeing the monumental importance of connecting the simple patterns of nature to the lives of human beings in order to see the certainty of natural rebirth for all.

Orpheus' Botanical Journey

The Greek Orpheus is perhaps one of the best examples of a botanical hero. The early myths of Orpheus' life present him as a carefree youth, excelling in his musical talent of playing the lyre. He also is depicted as having traveled with Jason as one of the Argonauts, though his exploits with the Argonauts do not define him as heroic in botanical terms. Instead, Orpheus' myth of his attempting to bring his wife, Eurydice, back from the dead presents a tale that appears odd when held against other heroic myths of Greece, because it clearly shows Orpheus failing his quest but achieving spiritual wisdom. Orpheus is a mythic character who is "firmly entrenched in Greek heroic myth and yet set apart from other heroes" precisely because he returned from Hades and moreover, he proceeded to "set down the knowledge he attained in the underworld for the benefit of those who came later" (Graf and Johnston 175). In this myth of Orpheus and Eurydice, they were said to fall in love instantaneously, but upon their wedding day, Eurydice was bitten by a snake and died. Orpheus, devastated by not being able to begin his new life with his wife, attempted to defy death by retrieving Eurydice back from Hades.

Like Ishtar who demanded to enter the underworld to face her sister Ershkigal, Orpheus, with overt confidence, set a plan in motion to enter the underworld, play his lyre, and successfully save his wife from the clutches of death. In the beginning of his myth, Orpheus believes that he can overcome the natural processes of life; he wrongly assumes that his individual talents will supersede the laws of nature, but his experience within the underworld teaches him that he must shed his desire for his own individual happiness, mythically sending a message that he must discard his conception of his own singular identity in order to achieve botanical apotheosis. In Hades, seeing the spirits of the dead all around him and witnessing the partnership of the god Hades and his wife Persephone, who is clearly tied to vegetative cycles, Orpheus rightly learns to let go of his former, pompous aspirations of living a singularly happy life while married to Eurydice. The underworld teaches Orpheus a lesson of natural mortality, as it did in the similar myths of the Zuni husband trying to save his wife from death and the Pawnee father attempting to retrieve his deceased son.

In the underworld, Orpheus plays his lyre for the god Hades and Persephone, and they are moved enough to allow Orpheus a chance to retrieve his former life ambition. They allow him to attempt to take Eurydice out of Hades if he agrees to never look back in order to assure that she is following him. However, Orpheus, having successfully walked past sights that no living mortal should ever witness, does look back when he is almost out of Hades and loses Eurydice forever. In his glance backward, he is symbolically letting go of not only her, but also his own identity, similar to when Gilgamesh fell asleep upon securing his goal, the flower that would have provided him with eternal youth, thus losing it forever. Botanical heroes must concede that any mission they sought while starting their quest was conceived with the knowledge they held before they obtained the natural wisdom of the underworld; therefore, as discussed in the previous two chapters of this book, their initial goals must be relinquished as a symbolic concession of the loss of their individual identity. In losing Eurydice forever to death, Orpheus learns to let go of his former persona with his longing for singular happiness, but he also glimpses the natural cycle of life and death which initiates his spiritual enlightenment.

Orpheus, again alone, ascends from the underworld, having failed his mission. The myth does not showcase Orpheus as being revered by anyone for having accomplished his impossible deed of traversing to the realm of death; instead, the myth continues to show the psychological aspect of Orpheus' journey that leads to his portrayal as a botanical hero. Upon ascending from the underworld, the myth portrays Orpheus as spiritually reborn. He emerges from the symbolic womb of the earth, having witnessed the terror of the death of others, most significantly the death of his beloved wife, but moreover, the myth presents him as also symbolically dying in Hades, as all of what defined his life before his journey has now been lost.

When Orpheus emerges out of the underworld, the myth explicitly presents him as a changed person, reborn as a result of obtaining spiritual knowledge. Upon ascension, Orpheus is often depicted wandering alone in the wilderness, as the recesses of secluded nature now appeal to him in his transformed state. After his ascension from Hades, he is portrayed as often sitting in nature and playing such mysterious songs upon his lyre that the animals and the plants of the forest pause to listen to him. The mythic portrayal of Orpheus' rebirth is essential towards understanding the myths of botanical heroism, as Orpheus is not depicted as climbing out of Hades, forever distraught that he failed his mission and will not be reunited with Eurydice to live the life he conceived for himself; instead, he is portrayed as renewed upon his sorrowful loss. This mythic portrayal of him is full of life, not fatalism or defeat, and this is vital. The songs that he is now able to play symbolically show that Orpheus has been reborn with a deeper outlook on life. He now takes the time to sit and play his lyre for all of nature to listen and enjoy, not only for human audiences who can give him praise, and moreover, nature is mythically presented as responding to his songs; "On the top of a certain hill there was a level stretch of open ground…. There was no shelter from the sun, but when the … poet seated himself there and struck his melodious strings, shady trees moved to the spot" (Leeming, *World*, 294–5).

The response that Orpheus' music induces in the environment around him mythically signals that the knowledge he received in the underworld was tied to the secrets of nature. Orpheus, after witnessing the necessity of death and the underworld, serves as a mythic example of the patterns of life for all living beings, as from his symbolic death, he is mythically reborn. Orpheus, thus, resurrects with a renewed embrace of life as it is, sorrowful, but also fantastically beautiful and full of vibrancy, and his music reflects this. This mythic portrayal of Orpheus reveals the message of botanical heroism—that by embracing the laws of nature, one gains a renewed perspective of life.

Orpheus' music also presents his expedition as similar to the shamanic journeys displayed in many myths thus far, as he has obtained wisdom on the workings of nature because of his transgression into the underworld. Again, like the myth of the American Indian Zuni man who also attempted to retrieve his wife from death, Orpheus has learned the same botanical lesson about the timelessness of nature that the Zuni husband learned in his quest. The squirrel taught the Zuni husband this lesson by showing him that death could be transgressed easily by simply planting a seed, which caused a tree to instantly grow, providing the man the means to cross the chasm that he initially perceived was impossibly separating him from life and death. The squirrel, then, showed the man that death and life are but momentary stages of a never-ending cyclical pattern, and when one reaches botanical apotheosis, the cycle is revealed without beginnings or endings, but with timeless wholeness. Similarly, because Orpheus journeyed into and out of the underworld, as a shaman is often depicted as doing in order to receive spiritual knowledge, Orpheus witnessed the ceaseless natural cycles of the earth, which eradicated his former limited view that life and death are singular events. When botanical heroes realize the ceaseless patterns of nature, they are often presented as spiritual guides to their people; again like shamans are often portrayed as passing on this wisdom through sacred ritual, the botanical hero often passes on this lesson by mythic example to audiences of the myth.

Graf and Johnston state that by the Classical period in Greece "Orpheus ... was ... a teacher of rituals" (50); in this light, he was often associated as bringing many mystery cults to Greece (173), largely because "Orpheus ... [was] an extraordinarily apt figure to stand behind" (Graf and Johnston 186). The myth of Orpheus was regarded in ancient Greece and Thrace as replete with sacred knowledge; therefore, Orphic mystery cults became numerous. The Orphics used Orpheus as their model because "Orpheus was a man of peace, whose inspired poetry tamed wild beasts, calmed the waves, and made men forget their quarrels" (K. Armstrong, *Great Transformations*, 223). Orphism promoted an ideology that proscribed to a belief in the transmigration of the soul after death into another natural life form, showing that the perception of the myth always carried with it an embrace of the role of nature in the spiritual lives of its devotees. Orphics often believed in separating themselves from society, in an embrace of a more natural lifestyle, where all living beings were viewed as possessing a spirit that was equal to the Orphics' identity, as inherent in Orphism was the belief that human beings have and would again reincarnate into myriad animal and botanical agents. From the myth of Orpheus, Orphics adopted a view that all living beings were equal, but also they viewed life, because of the mythic example of Orpheus, as following a cyclical, natural pattern that had no definitive beginning and no end. Therefore, the adopted belief systems of ancient times helps one understand the spiritual significance of Orpheus' mythological quest.

In many ancient, artistic renditions of Orpheus, he is often depicted after his ascension from Hades, sitting isolated within the wilderness, surrounded by an abundance of botanical elements, where animals of every kind encircle him; predators even sit next to their common prey, in an apparent momentary pause of the natural cycle. Significantly, Orpheus is repeatedly portrayed as sitting calmly in the middle of this paused natural scene. These artistic representations, similar to many artistic depictions of the Buddha or Christ, signal the ancient belief that Orpheus was a hero, not because of strength, talent, bravery, semi-divinity, etc., but because he attained spiritual knowledge. These myriad artistic depictions of Orpheus playing his lyre while surrounded by animals and plants show him sitting at the center of the cycles of nature. His portrayal as center is not to be confused as him serving to control the powers of nature; it is instead a representation to show that he is aware that he is part of the environment. Just as the depiction of the Hindu conception of karma is often circular, or the Greek conception of the universe is in the shape of a giant serpent consuming its own tail, the Ouroboros, so too is Orpheus depicted as a cognizant part of this cyclical wholeness. Both the Buddha and Orpheus are signaled as enlightened because they sit in the center of the natural cycle of life, seeing time as illusory.

In some sources, like the Roman Ovid's *Metamorphosis*, Orpheus is depicted later in life as shunning the presence of women, which is sometimes described as the cause for his physical death. Under this telling of the myth, Dionysus' maenads enter into such a frenzy while Orpheus sits alone playing his music that they tear Orpheus' body to pieces out of rage that he spurned them all by not returning the love they felt for him. This interpretation, though, seems to lessen the magnitude of the act that enables Orpheus' physical death. As previously discussed, the maenads represent an acceptance of nature in its many forms; they appear in their myths as unruly and sometimes terrifying, but they appear this way only to societal perception. The maenads instead serve to show that nature, to the perception of humans, seems harsh and unforgiving, similar to how the Hindu Shiva or the Egyptian Sêt are often portrayed, but that these aspects are crucial for the preservation of nature's renewal. Therefore, when the maenads dismember Orpheus, it seems more likely that they are conducting the same symbolic act witnessed in the myths of the Neolithic Earth Goddess, where the male consort is often dismembered to show that death is essential for initiating renewal. In this myth of Orpheus, the pieces of his body are spread throughout the land, and again, like the many other myths that portray this archetype, the myths of Baal and Osiris for example, it is clear here that Orpheus' physical death mythically is meant to portray a message that serves to educate audiences of nature's cycles, as after the maenads tear Orpheus's body to pieces, a maenad was said to have found his head floating in a nearby river, and when she held it, it continued to emit the music he played upon his spiritual enlightenment. Therefore, Orpheus' myth shows that he mythically resurrects, not only once from Hades upon losing Eurydice, but twice, after his own physical death.

The end of Orpheus' myth appears odd, but it documents the goal of apotheosis for the botanical hero quite well. Orpheus is physically sacrificed, in a sense, by the maenads. Central to myths of botanical heroism, Orpheus openly accepts his sacrifice because this action, like the acceptance of Herakles at his own death, shows a mythic character willingly giving himself over to the natural order of life. But, Orpheus' myth does not end with simply his acceptance of the loss of his selfhood and death; instead, the myth presents an undeniable message of continuation after death, and it is this point that marks this myth as an exceptional example of botanical heroism. Orpheus dies in his myth, but, like Herakles, his myth shows his death as an illusion. Instead, Orpheus' body, spread throughout the land, will directly serve to replenish the wilderness and thus create new life; therefore, his death is not mythically presented as an end at all. The continuation of Orpheus' song after his dismemberment serves as a mythic lesson to teach others about the continuous cycles of life, quite similar to the American Indian Cherokee myth of the Corn Mother. The myth symbolically shows that Orpheus will always live on, as will all living beings in nature's ceaseless patterns. Through Orpheus' mythic sacrifice of self, he revealed to all human beings the harsh but regenerating promise of the cycles of nature—that death is inevitable, but it is also only temporary, making rebirth just as inevitable. This spiritual realization allows audiences to strive towards the serenity Orpheus maintained upon his ascension from the underworld, so that audiences too learn to cherish the beauty and vitality of the natural world while one is permitted to live.

Nature Teaches Tavgytsy About Cyclical Time— Life, Death, Rebirth

The Siberian Samoyed people also have a myth of the hero Tavgytsy[3] that exemplifies his status of shaman to his people because of a journey that is directly tied to him gaining an understanding of his own connection to the botanical process. The myth begins with Tavgytsy lying in bed near death; his people start to prepare for his demise, but as he lies in his weakened state, he hears a voice call to him telling him that he must undergo a quest to attain a new name, or identity. The myth makes it clear that Tavgytsy remains physically on his death bed while he psychologically undergoes his heroic journey towards symbolic rebirth.

Tavgytsy begins his quest in primordial water; in a scene that is reminiscent of the beginning of creation itself, he struggles to leave the water and emerge onto land. Once he is able to pull his body out of this primordial water, like the first land-dwelling beings, he proceeds to painstakingly climb atop of a nearby mountain, where he finds a naked woman, the Lady of the Water, "on whose undulating breast he suckled hungrily. 'You are my child,' soothed the Lady of the Water'" (Leeming & Page, *God*, 18). Tavgytsy's portrayal as first undergoing what seems to be a symbolic evolutionary process to emerge out of primordial waters onto land, and then being portrayed in an infant-like state signals that he is beginning his journey in a stage of innocence where he will need to be systematically educated in order to fulfill his quest. The fact that he receives nourishment directly from the land, as represented by the Lady of the Water, serves to reveal that his heroic journey will need to incorporate him taking nature within his being, just as Herakles merged with the Nemean lion. It is also important that nature, through the representation of the Lady of the Water, is explicitly revealed to him as a nurturing mother, as it also showcases Tavgytsy as cognizant that he is a being created directly from nature.

Ready to begin the next stage of his journey, Tavgytsy meets the Lady of the Water's husband, the Lord of the Underworld, along with what will be Tavgytsy's guides throughout the remainder of his journey, the ermine and mouse. The portrayal of the Lord of the Underworld being married to the Lady of the Water ties these two natural elements together with clear regenerative qualities; also this environmental reference of the marriage between earth and water serves to mythically reveal the underworld as a place of growth, not a place to fear. Moreover because Tavgytsy meets these two environmental necessities suggests that to continue his heroic journey he will have to be reborn as a plant would, by first entering the underworld of the earth as a seed. His animal guides also serve to psychologically enable Tavgytsy to concede the he is inextricably connected with the natural world, not superior to it, as he must rely upon the ermine and mouse to guide him through the geography of his spiritual quest.

While atop of the Lady of the Water's mountain, Tavgytsy journeys on to a series of tents where each represents the different aspects of life that are associated with illness, death, and decay. Tavgytsy enters one tent to find "the denizens of the underworld and sickness who received him into their midst by tearing the heart from his chest and throwing it gleefully into a pot" (Lemming & Page, *God*, 18–9), and then he enters another tent to experience madness and "all other human disorders" (Leeming & Page, *God*, 19). It is essential that Tavgytsy experience each of these stages, just as Ishtar was forced to suffer the pains associated with illness and death for mortals. These stages clearly signal that Tavgytsy is psychologically within the mythic underworld, where he must contend with his own death and lose his former identity, as all botanical heroes must.

Tavgytsy is then led by his animal guides to the "Land of the Shamanesses," where he knows without needing to be told the importance of the "Tree of the Lord of the Earth." The myth describes this Tree as being full of splendor for Tavgytsy. The Tree of the Lord of the Earth is surrounded by the ancestors of all the plants on earth. He continues his journey, visiting myriad places, such as all of the seas of the earth, but he always returns to the Tree of the Lord of the Earth. The Tree is clearly identified as being the center of the universe, like the Norse Yggdrasil. In this myth, the Tree is distinguished as being the creator of humanity; this signals the interconnected botanical cycle of life, clearly identifying all humans as inextricably tied to the natural world and its seasonal laws. The fact that Tavgytsy knows the Tree's importance without being told and repeatedly returns to it signals that his spiritual progression within the myth is explicitly tied to his veneration for nature

Finally, one day while Tavgytsy sits in the Tree's branches, he is able to see all the people of the earth. He is then instructed by "the Lord of the Tree" to make a drum from its branches; "'I am the Tree that gives all life to men'" (Leeming & Page, *God*, 19). Tavgytsy eventually comes to understand upon hearing the message of the Tree that he, as a result of his long and arduous journey, is now capable of being a shaman who will be able to physically and spiritually heal his people.

This myth is again vital in showing the botanical heroic quest as similar to the shamanic journey, as Tavgytsy, as shaman apprentice, is experiencing the same archetypes the botanical hero must face. Corelyn also agrees with K. Armstrong's discussion of the hero as shaman, as discussed earlier within this chapter, in that the hero's quest and the shamanic journey are related in their archetypal patterns, but also in their goal of providing spiritual knowledge to the community. Mythically relating the botanical hero's journey in a similar way to the experiences of the spiritual shaman from many nature-dependent cultures exposes significant information about the role of the botanical hero within many ancient cultures. If the botanical heroic quest often mimics the shamanic journey, then the botanical hero is revered with similar sacred reverence as the shaman, thus making the tales of botanical heroes serve as examples of spiritual guidance for the community.

A vital difference, though, between the shaman and the botanical hero is that often the shaman, as the spiritual guide of the people, undertakes his or her quest internally, often keeping the tenets of the journey secret from the community, so that his or her role as spiritual adviser or healer can be maintained with authority. If spiritual guides of the community do not publically reveal the stages of their quests to the community, then they run the risk of being held up as superior, making the shamanic quest seem separate from the abilities of the common people. This is the same risk that comes from misunderstanding the mythic botanical hero, as often he or she is inaccurately portrayed in contemporary times as a superior human specimen, distinctly better than the common person. This is a misrepresentation of the botanical hero because again the botanical hero's journey must serve a spiritually transformative role within the community, and the main message of the botanical heroic quest is that anyone can undergo this same process towards apotheosis. The botanical heroic quest provides audiences of the myth with a step-by-step guide on how to transgress the same spiritual geography that the shaman voyaged; the fictionalized heroic journey then serves to teach audiences the same spiritual knowledge that the spiritual guides of the community possess, making botanical heroes of each audience member. This myth of Tavgytsy is unique because it presents the shamanic quest in terms of a myth, connecting both the heroic journey with the voyage of the shaman, making it a tale that can educate all audience members towards botanical enlightenment.

Once Tavgytsy acknowledges the necessity of the natural stages of the life cycle, like a plant, he is able to begin to symbolically grow again. Though Tavgytsy has learned that he is to be a shaman, the myth still presents him as having more to learn. Therefore, he mythically leaves the Tree of the Lord of the Earth and enters a cave, again another symbolic underworld, where two naked women proceed to give birth to reindeer; it is made clear in the myth that these animals are to be the food that nourishes the people. Here, Tavgytsy explicitly learns the cycle of nature. Like many botanical heroes before him, Tavgytsy sees, through the birth of these reindeer, that life and death are only a part of an endless natural process. The reindeer will be sacrificed to provide sustenance to the next generation, but will assuredly also return as part of the natural cycle to begin a new life. Therefore, he sees that the belief in a life as singularly important is only an illusion when viewed in terms of the natural order of life and death. Also, the reindeer, birthed by human mothers, again relays the myth's message of the interconnectedness of all living beings.

Tavgytsy mythically moves on to another cave, where this time a naked man sits tending a cauldron over a fire. The repeated tenet of Tavgytsy discovering nude people within caves suggests the belief that all life emerges from the womb of the earth. The man in the cave grabs Tavgytsy, "before Tavgytsy could think of his own death" (Leeming & Page, *God*, 20) and cuts his head off, chops his corpse into many pieces and throws them into his cauldron. As discussed with Orpheus, this theme of mythic dismemberment is common. Tavgytsy, to finally be a spiritual shaman, and also a prime example of a botanical hero, must concede that he is no different than the reindeer who are born to seemingly die for the nourishment of the ecosystem. This realization allows the botanical hero, like it does for Tavgytsy, to accept that his or her individual identity is only an illusion based primarily on the fear of death as a distinct end of identity. Tavgytsy, as a botanical hero, shows that one must let go of the need to believe one is distinctly important and embrace one's natural role that connects human beings to all the other living beings of the world. Tavgytsy's willingness to embrace his rightful place in the natural order of the universe opens the door to his enlightenment, as he learns the botanical lesson that though death and loss of identity are inevitable, they reflect only a brief blip in an endless and everlasting cycle that eradicates life and death as singular. This is mythically related by the fact that Tavgytsy has fully experienced death, but again, his physical body remains intact and quite alive back home in his bed.

After years within the mythical man's cauldron, the man constructs Tavgytsy's body anew, and Tavgytsy is ready to return to his people as a new shaman with his new identity of "the Diver" (Leeming & Page, *God*, 21). Tavgytsy's psychological, shamanic journey presented in mythic form, reveals to audiences the steps of the botanical heroic journey, which openly adopts the understanding that life for all mortals is irrevocably tied to the demands of the botanical cycle. As a seed, Tavgytsy entered into the earth, experiencing dismemberment, but also like a seedling he emerged again from the earth with spiritual knowledge that allowed him to teach his community how to embrace the same laws of nature in order to secure botanical apotheosis.

Aadja's Shamanic Lesson of Everlasting Life

The Turkic Yakut's also have a legend about a shaman, Aadja,[4] who dies of illness as another man at the age of twenty, and because of his journey he is reborn as a botanical hero. Though he lay dead, the man who would become Aadja, could still hear the noises around him. He felt as if he was in a deep sleep, but found that he could not move his body. He could only lie immobile and wait for his family to bury him. He felt the experience of being placed in a coffin, having dirt shoveled on top of him, and then lying still, but conscious within the earth. He began to cry, but then he heard the sound of someone digging him out. He thought it must be his older brother, but he was shocked to see four men lift him out of his coffin and stand him up so that he could see his own house.

Far beneath the earth, the man felt that he could hear what sounded like "the bellowing of a bull," and the earth began to tremble; "From the bottom of the grave the bull emerged. It was completely black and its horns were close together. The animal took the man, sitting between its horns, and went down again through the opening from which it had just emerged" (Campbell, *Primitive*, 259). The bull carried the man far into the earth, until they reached a house where an old man welcomed him and held him within his withered hand, estimating his weight, but to the man's surprise, the old man stated "'Take him back! His fate predestines him to be reborn up there!'" (Campbell, *Primitive*, 259). So, the man found that he was ascending once more from the earth.

Once on earth again, the "living corpse" felt a raven come between his standing legs and swoop him high into the air. The man felt himself arrive in the cosmos next to the sun and moon, where people lived with the heads of ravens. Again, the man arrived in the palm of an old man who now stated that he should be taken down to earth and placed within the highest tree. The man then was carried to a nest in the highest of trees where a winged white reindeer came and nursed him, similar to the depiction of Tavgytsy being nursed by the Lady of the Water.

For three years the man lay in his nest, being nursed by the reindeer, until he found that his body had become indescribably small. One day, he heard again the voice of the old man who lived with the raven-headed people tell his seven sons to descend to earth and bring back a wife, which they proceeded to do. The man in the nest heard them secure the woman and lock her away in a barn, but suddenly the man also heard another faint and enticing sound—a drum. He recognized it as a shaman's song; "these sounds gradually grew, coming nearer—nearer—till finally, from below, there appeared ... a head, and from the nest could then be seen a man .... Hardly had he fully appeared, however, when ... he was immediately transformed into a bull with a single horn that grew forward from the middle of his forehead. The bull shattered with a single blow the door of the barn in which the woman was locked and galloped off with her, down, and away" (Campbell, *Primitive*, 260). The man in the nest knew that the bull man who appeared was a shaman rescuing the soul of a deceased woman from his tribe.

The man saw many more similar episodes happen as he waited within his nest, but one day he again heard the old man speak, telling him that his time was up; he was to be reborn as another person and named Aadja. The seven sons of the old man flung him to earth where the man lost consciousness; he was reincarnated, but had lost all memory of his past. But, when Aadja reached the age of five, he suddenly remembered his entire history; he knew that he had lived before as a man, died, and witnessed the workings of a shaman in the otherworld.

When Aadja turned seven, he found that he was seized "by the spirits, forced to sing, and cut to pieces," but despite this, he still grew stronger; at eight he began to shamanize; at nine he was famous, and at twelve he was considered one of the best shamans to exist (Campbell, *Primitive*, 262). Aadja then traveled back to his old family from his previous life, but they did not recognize him. While there, he saw the shaman he saw while in the nest, and immediately, the shaman recognized him; "'when I once was helping another shaman recover a soul of a sick woman, I saw you in the nest on the ninth, the uppermost, bough, sucking the teats of your animal mother. You were looking out of the nest'" (Campbell, *Primitive*, 262). To this, Aadja became furious at the old shaman for revealing the facts of his birth, but the old shaman simply told Aadja that he too was raised on the eighth bough of the same tree, and that he too will be reborn once more and nurtured in the same fashion under the guidance of the Great Father Raven. The old shaman told Aadja to kill and eat him, which Aadja proceeded to do; "the shaman spirit swallowed him and thus committed him to death—and no one saw" (Campbell, *Primitive*, 263).

Alexeyev Ivan stated that "'it is said ... that the really good shamans are cut up three times in their life, the poor only once. The spirit of an exceptional shaman is born again after his death. They say that great shamans are reborn three times'" (qtd. in Campbell 267). This legend recounts the binding together of the human and natural world. Aadja must die and return into the earth to begin his spiritual journey. He also must join with his animal brethren, as in the legend the animals are clearly equal to Aadja, since they are crucial to his survival and education. What is more, the legend of Aadja teaches listeners about death in a natural way; he dies, but remains alive. He, like a botanical element, returns within the earth, but is let out to grow among the highest tree. He is explicitly nurtured by nature in the form of his animal mother. When ready, he is simply reborn. In every way, he is a botanical hero, parlaying the cycles of life, death, and rebirth as mundane cycles in an endless pattern. He becomes a shaman because he learns that this process strips him of his need for an autonomous existence and propels him into a spiritual existence that is connected to a greater nature. This is why at the close of the myth, Aadja easily kills and eats the other shaman who invites him to do so, as they both know, having attained apotheosis, that, botanically, death only initiates new life.

There Is No Death in Nature—The Bear Man

The American Indian Cherokee legend of the Bear Man[5] also provides an ideal example of a botanical hero. In this myth a hunter is out looking for bears to hunt, so that he may provide sustenance for his people; alone in the deep wilderness, the hunter spots a bear, but he is shocked by what happens next. The bear speaks to the hunter and invites him into his den to learn his ways. Within the den, the man initially distrusts the bear, thinking that he might have been lured there so the bear can attack him, but the bear, as well as holding the ability to speak, can also read minds, so it knows the fear that possesses the man. The bear tells the man not to worry, that he only wants to teach the hunter the ways of the bears.

Soon the hunter comes to love and respect the bear. But after a year passes, the bear reads the worried thoughts of the hunter and knows that the hunter is concerned because his own people will soon come and kill the bear in their annual bear hunt each winter. The bear again shocks the man by speaking of the very thing that had recently consumed his thoughts. The bear tells the man that when his people come, he is to go with them, but he is also to turn back and look at the bear moments after it has been killed when no one else is looking.

The hunter, as the bear foretold, is found by his people within the cave of the bear, and just as the bear said, the people kill the bear, without the bear showing any resistance, and cut it into pieces to carry away to their camp. After killing the bear, the people think that the man hiding in the back of the cave is also another bear, as his appearance has become so transformed that he looks wild; this is significant in addressing the hunter as a botanical hero as his experience within the womb of the earth, the bear's cave, so transformed him in merely a year that he looks to his community like a bear. It is the myth's final scene, though, that truly identifies the quest of the hunter as a botanical quest.

Upon leaving the bear's cave and reuniting with his community, the hunter looks back as instructed by the bear before his death and sees "the bear rise up out of the leaves, shake himself, and go back into the woods" (Leeming 231). The message of this myth is also reflected in a prayer of the indigenous Ainu people of Japan, "To the bear: 'Precious little divinity ... please come to us again and we shall again do you the honor of a sacrifice'" (Campbell, *Primitive Mythology*, 348). As discussed, American Indian hunters often believed that "the immortal souls of their prey would return to their villages for reincarnation" (Lowenstein & Vitebsky 68). Significantly, the myth here, and the belief of the immortality of the soul of the animal, reflects the botanical concept that there is no death, only a natural transference of matter.

This myth presents the hunter as a botanical hero because he meets the archetypes required of the hero. He enters alone into the wilderness, where he steps into what is to him an otherworld where the bear speaks to him. Also, the man's journey into the bear's cave is symbolic of the underworld, as it is within the earth, and it eventually serves to reveal to the man the lessons of mortality that often come from the hero's experience in the underworld. The man is elevated to a botanical hero because of his behavior towards the bear. The man comes to first trust and then love the bear, so much so that he fears for its life. Then the man's appearance is so transformed that he comes to resemble a bear, which indicates that he has been psychologically altered into realizing his clear connection with nature as a result of his journey. Furthermore, the man, because of his willingness to lose his former identity as human, is mythically permitted to witness the law of nature's cycles.

When the man sees his friend, the bear, killed, he is permitted, as the bear instructed him to do, to turn backwards and see what no other member of his tribe can see—that there is no death in nature, as the bear, reduced to a pool of blood, simply rises up again, shakes himself off, and continues to live. This spiritual wisdom that comes to the man because of his heroic journey signals that he is a botanical hero who has reached apotheosis; this is further realized by the conclusion of the myth that presents the man going back into his community. However, when the man enters his village, the people know that he is not in a state of a human being, but in a sacred bear state. They realize that they must separate the man alone for seven days and nights, "until the bear nature had left him and he became like a man again" ("The Bear Man"). But the myth states that the man's wife could not resist seeing her husband again after his long disappearance, so she finds him and brings him back to live in their home, but she is horrified to find that he dies within a few days.

The man's death signals his spiritual transformation. Like the myth of Orpheus, whose death and dismemberment after his ascent from the underworld signals his apotheosis, the Bear Man also must mythically die to remind audiences that he cannot simply shed his newfound "bear nature," as his people assume, because it is this nature that signals his enlightenment. The man, therefore, mythically dies just as the bear willingly died, to show his community, and the audience of the myth, the same lesson that the bear showed him—that again death is but a fleeting, and necessary, moment of a continuous cycle.

One American Indian Skidi Pawnee myth, "The Man Who Lived with

Bears,"[6] also tells of a hunter who came upon a young bear cub near death, and instead of killing the cub, the man tied a bundle of tobacco around its neck as an offering. He went home, recounted the story of the cub to his pregnant wife, and when she gave birth, their son felt closely tied to all bears. In time, the boy grew to be a man, but one day he was killed and dismembered by a neighboring war party. A male and female bear found the remains of the man, collected them together, and resurrected him. The man, after his rebirth lived for a long while with the bears, and in this time "he came to revere bears as the greatest and wisest of beings, with the most powerful souls. The bears, however, reminded him of their place in the order of things" (Lowenstein & Vitebsky 99).

In time, the man knew that he must leave the bears to return to his people. The male bear, upon hearing this, embraced the man, "pressed its mouth to the man's lips, and rubbed him with its paws and fur. The touch of the fur gave the man power. He became a great warrior and established the Bear Dance among his people" (Lowenstein & Vitebsky 99). Again, this myth, like the Cherokee myth of the Bear Man, speaks towards a message that life is cyclical. The bears, as the man learns, understands this as "their place in the order of things," and seemingly this is the lesson that they give to the man. Again mythically presenting the man cut up, as a butchered bear would be after the hunt, and then easily revived, like the bear in the Cherokee myth, and like many other botanical heroes, presents a message that when viewed in terms of nature's cycles, there is no ultimate end.

The Lesson Is Not About Death, but Always About Life— The Wonderful Lifetimes of Tuan

The Celtic myth of Tuan Mac Cairill[7] also exceedingly exemplifies what is perhaps the best example of a botanical hero. The myth discusses a transformation of the mythic protagonist, Tuan, into various aspects of nature as an indicator of spirituality. The myth states that after a great flood, all of Tuan's people within his kingdom of Ulster perished, leaving him utterly alone. Seeing himself as the sole survivor of his kingdom filled him with loneliness, despair, and fear. He began to feel as though all the wild beasts of this new wilderness sensed that he was now alone; once a brave warrior, he now flinched at every sound, as even a twig snapping made him jump like a rabbit into hiding. He soon found that indeed the animals of the forest did know that he was now all alone, but to his great surprise, they did not attack him; instead, they came to him and offered him the chance to live among them, so that they may teach him the skills needed to survive in his new life.

Over time Tuan became as the animals; he could run as fast as a deer and hear as good as a wolf. He lived in this way for many years, until his body began to age, and then he found a cave deep in the earth and fell fast asleep. The myth, showcasing him completely isolated and finding a cave at the end of his life reveals the lesson of this myth. Tuan's isolation keys the audience towards a spiritual journey; his new life indicates that he is on a physical journey but also a psychological one. His life lived according to the ways of the animal kingdom, and the fact that at the end of his life he retreats into the symbolic womb of the earth, again mythically referred to as a cave, shows his understanding of the seasonal cycles of life. The myth continues to solidify this natural message.

Tuan as an old man asleep within his cave dreams that he has been transformed into a stag. He wakes from the dream and finds that he has been given a young and healthy body that is indeed in the form of a stag. And instead of panicking, he revels in this new state, enjoying what it feels like to experience life as a deer:

> "I stood awhile stamping upon a rock, with my bristling head swung high, breathing through wide nostrils all the savor of the world. For.... I had writhed from the bonds of age and was young again. I smelled the turf and knew for the first time how sweet that smelled.... How the world was new!" ["The Story of Tuan"].

Next, Tuan after living a whole lifetime as a stag, reenters the same cave and falls into another deep sleep, and again he dreams, only this time he awakens transformed into a young and ferocious boar. He again embraces this transformation, reveling in living a lifetime as an animal bigger and stronger than all of the other animals of the forest. As a boar, he earns the respect of the other animals, but again when he finally ages after many years, he returns to his cave to slumber.

Tuan next dreams he has become an eagle, and then awakens again to find that indeed he is now able to experience life in this new form. Life as an eagle shows him the limitations of all of the other life forms he experienced thus far, as he is now able to soar through the air, feel the breeze upon his body, and see the earth from a perspective he could never before imagine; "'I left the ground.... I soared, I swooped.... I lived in joy and slept in peace, and had my fill of the sweetness of life'" ("The Story of Tuan"). In the form of an eagle, Tuan learned every curve of each hill and every stretch of coastline in the land of Ireland. But after a lifetime as an eagle, he again grows old and retreats back to his cave to slumber.

Next Tuan dreams that he transformed into a salmon; in his dream the waters of the sea rose high enough to cover him in safety, and when he awakens, he finds that this is true. Upon realizing that he is a salmon, he again experiences the awe he felt with his previous transformations; as a fish, he now cannot imagine how encumbered he was in his other life forms. As a man, stag, and boar, he always was aware of his body, needing to fold his limbs beneath him when he slept; as an eagle, he also had to always be aware of his solid environment, making sure he didn't fly into a tree for instance. But now as a salmon, he marvels at his new streamlined body:

> In all my changes I had joy and fullness of life. But in the water joy lay deeper, life pulsed deeper.... The fish has but one piece from his nose to his tail. He is complete, single and unencumbered.... How I flew through the soft element: how I joyed in the country where there is no harshness: in the element ... which caresses and lets go, and will not let you fall ["The Story of Tuan"].

He vastly enjoys this new existence, as he did all the rest, until one day, he feels compelled, not to return to his cave, but to return to the land in which he was king—Ulster.

The myth's odd portrayal of what appears to be in part the devolution of Tuan is vitally important. Tuan enjoys each life form he gets to experience, and though, in an evolutionary sense he may appear to be devolving, his internal sense is of relief at each transformation, as he realizes how encumbered he was in his previous existences. His realization of how burdened he used to be is highly symbolic of his spiritual transformation, that is again in direct correlation to his understanding of the natural world. As he is a salmon, he is depicted as enjoying the final shedding of not only a body that is often viewed as a superior life form than that of a fish, but also an enjoyment of shedding the confines of living in a fixed physicality of life on solid ground. His embrace of an anonymous fish is crucial to the myth's message of botanical heroism.

Feeling compelled to return to Ulster, Tuan undertakes an arduous journey, as he must struggle through wave after wave pushing him away from his goal:

> "And then, far away in the sea, I remembered Ulster, and there came on me an instant, uncontrollable anguish to be there ... through days and nights I swam tirelessly ... with ... a whisper through my being that I must reach Ireland or die.... The waves held me back and held me back.... Only the unconquerable heart of the salmon could brave that end of toil" ["The Story of Tuan"].

Near death, Tuan, as a salmon, perseveres. He returns to Ulster to now see that there are people living there again. Soon, the people spot this massive salmon and try again and again to capture it, but Tuan knows their tactics and evades being captured. Finally, though, the new king of Ulster is able to catch him, and though Tuan resists, pushing the net back into the water with all of his might, he is astonished to see that the king is able to simply lift the net out of the water and bring about Tuan's death. Tuan now must finally experience what it feels like to die as he gulps for oxygen, reminiscent of the hero's symbolic death in the underworld, though it is significant now that Tuan is actually depicted as dying. The new king of Ulster, proud that he has finally caught this renowned fish, does not want to eat him, but when he brings Tuan home, the queen of Ulster insists that they fry the fish and eat it for dinner. Tuan endures the heat of the frying pan and finally physically dies. Yet, Tuan also is still able to feel the pieces of his body going into the body of the pregnant queen, and soon she gives birth to a boy. Tuan is then depicted as being reborn in the body of the newborn prince.

Tuan, instead of being depicted as full of remorse that he must endure constant transformations into animal forms, is filled with awe and respect for each of the life forms he consciously is allowed to experience. He does not value any one life that he lived as superior to any other; though some may define certain species as inferior, Tuan openly embraces all of his existences. This mythic representation of Tuan enjoying and openly accepting his metamorphoses sends two messages inherent to the quest of the botanical hero: first, that all living beings are interrelated, and second that death is only an illusion when viewed in terms of the natural life cycle.

The role Tuan's reincarnations play within the myth demonstrably point towards his acceptance of the cycles of nature. Each slumber and awakening as a new species is revealed as a rebirth for Tuan, as he is depicted as living a lifetime as a man, stag, boar, eagle, and salmon, before he is reborn again as a human being. The portrayal of him going into the cave each time he is to be "reborn" suggests that he is going within the womb of the earth to emerge as a new species. This portrayal of mythic reincarnation is in correlation with Celtic belief; its inclusion in this myth sends audiences a message that the life of a human being is only a singular part of a much more complex natural system. Because Tuan embraces his transformations into various animals with exuberance, most of his deaths are mythically ignored. Tuan is repeatedly depicted as not really dying; instead, he is mythically portrayed as simply continuing to live in a succession of different, yet equally valuable lifetimes. In the mythic presentation of Tuan as merely retreating to a cave and slumbering, not dying, the indication of death as a fearful, or even significant, event within the myth is intentionally avoided, signaling a cultural belief system that is in line with botanical heroism.

Often the botanical heroic journey showcases a hero who symbolically dies so that he or she may find a renewed sense of life upon symbolically resurrecting, but here, Tuan is an exceptional example of a botanical hero because he physically dies many times, but ignores this moment, and solely focuses on the vibrant experiences of his renewed life into different natural forms. This is precisely the goal of the botanical hero's journey—that though death and loss of selfhood are crucial for the botanical hero to accept, there is no great tragedy in this acceptance, as nature provides the botanical hero ceaseless life in its ever recurrent patterns. Again, at the core of the botanical heroic quest is the focus upon everlasting life, where death can be viewed as momentary.

The myth does show Tuan finally, cognitively, experiencing the full pain of a physical death, but even this moment is portrayed as fleeting, as he is mythically depicted as simply being reborn once again as a human being. This mythic representation of Tuan physically dying in what appears to be a harsh manner—being cooked, cut up, and consumed, only to be reborn—connects him to other botanical heroes of many nature-dependent communities, such as the Penobscot Corn Mother or the Cherokee bear. Tuan's physical death, when it is explicitly related, is mythically portrayed as anticlimactic, like the Corn Mother's or the bear's death, because the myth's central message, as it has repeatedly shown in Tuan's other metamorphoses, is that death is not a finality in nature, so instead, a botanical hero must focus on the glory of ceaseless life.

The close of the myth details Tuan, as an old king again, recounting this story to a visiting priest. The priest of the new faith of Christianity that has spread into Ireland, upon listening to this strange, and to his faith, blasphemous tale, simply pauses, and then tells Tuan that he will enable him to be born again as a Christian convert. To this, Tuan merely sighs and tells the priest that he knew this day would one day come and that it would put an end to his people and their belief systems. Tuan denies conversion, asks the priest to leave, and then is fabled to live on forever continuing to live and enjoy lifetime after lifetime, and in this way he is said to preserve the beliefs of the Celts, so that he may be repeatedly reborn, serving always as an example of an exemplar botanical hero in the generations to come.

The Botanical Hero's Journey Is Our Own Journey

The American Indians, Aboriginal Australians, Africans, Greeks, Celts, and many other cultures discussed within this book venerated nature as divine because nature provided humankind with everything they needed to survive, physically and psychologically. As civilizations emerged and became more technologically dependent, human beings throughout history often began to imagine themselves superior to nature, but in looking at the myths, or at least the archetypes that have been preserved from the initial myths of nature-dependent communities, one sees wisdom in embracing nature and its cycles as inescapably dominant. Myths of the botanical hero, often found in ancient sources but also arguably apparent in myths throughout many eras, allow audiences a chance to internalize the harsh, sometimes terrifying, laws of nature and mortality, and in doing this, botanical heroes reveal the means towards apotheosis for the audience. The botanical hero was thus created to show audiences that apotheosis is attainable by all.

Once one psychologically acknowledges the patterns of the most ancient of quests, undertaken by shamans, mythic male consorts, mythological divine beings, and botanical heroes alike, one sees that death is a necessary and natural part of life, but also that apotheosis is as natural as death. Apotheosis then is merely conceding that one is nature, and like all aspects of nature, human beings must follow nature's regenerative cycles.

Conclusion

"Forget not that the earth delights to feel your bare feet and the winds long to play with your hair."—Khalil Gibran

"Live in each season as it passes; breathe the air, drink the drink, taste the fruit, and resign yourself to the influence of the earth."—Henry David Thoreau

The Botanical Heroic Journey and Everlasting Life

It is not easy to embrace the lessons of the botanical hero, when the message of these myths, most succinctly stated, is that each human must concede to the fact that he or she is in fact no different or more important than any other living being upon the earth. Humans, with their active abstract mental capacities and abilities to perceive their identity as autonomously significant, often want to believe that upon their deaths they will maintain some sense of selfhood and continue on in alternative realms. But myths of the botanical hero repeatedly present characters who buffer the shock of the myths' ultimate message by showcasing heroes who bravely face the process of accepting both physical death and the annihilation of selfhood. Botanical heroes charter unknown territories and embrace the horror, confusion, and fatalism that often comes from a full realization of mortality. However, botanical heroes offer a reminder to audiences about the importance of correctly aligning oneself to the natural world, so that he or she may gain the spiritual wisdom that enables one to fully embrace life while alive and also to seek peace in the fact that after death, a greater natural cycle will always preserve a part of us all.

Cultures still show an inherent need to understand the lives of mortals through mythic and heroic portrayals, as evidenced by the various filmic versions of heroic archetypes. Myths, therefore, are not merely strange tales of bygone cultures; instead, they should be embraced as sacred examples of human beings attempting to explain the cycles of life. And myths of the hero's journey should especially be revered for their regenerative messages for each individual audience member, as "The journey of the hero is about the courage to seek the depths; the image of creative rebirth; the eternal cycle of change within us; the uncanny discovery that the seeker is the mystery which the seeker seeks to know" (Cousineau xix). Yet, contemporary popular culture has lost sight of what a hero should be. Quite often contemporary books, films, and television shows present heroes in terms that serve to disconnect them from audiences. Popular heroes of contemporary culture are most often represented as super-human beings with extraordinary physical and mental powers who mask their identity and easily, usually through violence, kill off clearly "evil" adversaries. This representation of a hero is detrimental to audiences who come to view the heroic quest with such associations—if the hero is better than the average audience member because of his or her superhuman powers, than the audience member does not associate him or herself as capable of accomplishing his or her own heroic quest. Popular contemporary heroes are often beloved by the people they help to protect, and this too is an odd concept for the hero, as it places the hero again on a pedestal that makes his or her accomplishments unattainable to the common person. If the contemporary hero is viewed as needed by the people in order to protect them, then this immediately demotes the capabilities of the average person to protect him or herself, and more succinctly to journey upon his or her own quest.

What does the contemporary heroic quest really teach its viewers then? The contemporary popular heroic quest lacks the tenets that define most mythic heroic journeys. Contemporary heroes most distinctly lack the psychological components that serve to educate audiences of myth about timeless human struggles, most specifically about the meaning of life and death. Without the quest serving to psychologically better the hero, then no spiritual awakening can occur, which often presents the contemporary hero as void of substantial meaning for the audience. Botanical heroes, like the Buddha or the Bear Man, teach audiences that they can begin to face the psychological components that terrify themselves the most, so that they can choose to embrace themselves as natural beings who will one day die and lose all identity. This realization allows audiences to gain the spiritual wisdom that enables them to live on forever in the everlasting regeneration of nature.

The Khoi of Southwest Africa relate a myth of humankind's misunderstanding of nature's cyclical promise. The myth states that the Moon once instructed an insect to give a message to mankind: "'Go to men and tell them, as I die, and dying live; so you shall also die, and dying live'" (qtd. in Ford 193).

The insect went to earth but was stalled by Hare. Hare told the insect that he was faster than the insect and could therefore reach mankind quicker, so the insect related the correct message to Hare. But Hare upon reaching humans messed the message up, saying "'I am sent by Moon to tell you, as I die and dying perish, in the same manner you also shall die and come wholly to an end'" (qtd. in Ford 193). Hare then, proud of his accomplishment, returned fast to Moon and related what he told mankind. Moon sadly realized then that mankind would always misrepresent death and would be unable to see it as part of a never-ending natural process that eradicates the finality of death.

    Without more botanical heroes represented in contemporary popular culture, society becomes complacent with an expectation that they need to be saved by an idealized superior hero, which of course rarely happens in the real world. As Campbell states:

> One may invent a false finally unjustified image of oneself as an exceptional phenomenon in the world.... Such self-righteousness leads to a misunderstanding, not only of oneself, but of the nature of both Man and the Cosmos. The goal of the myth is to dispel the need for such life-ignorance by affecting a reconciliation of the individual consciousness with the universal will [*Hero*, 205–6].

    Once a belief system has been adopted that attempts to place the individual as superior to the natural world, the view of a singular life well-lived becomes of the utmost importance and the invention of an identity-driven immortality that is perceived as coming through fame for one's deeds in life or through the envisioning of an afterlife takes precedence, but with this adoption, the price to pay is the loss of natural immortality. Brown and Cousins state that many contemporary religions have lost sight of the sacred quality of nature; "While the awareness of this sacrility was certainly present at the origins of the Judeo-Christian tradition, it has now been forgotten, and, in its absence, our society continues to abuse the natural environment" (85). Therefore, the earth is now often viewed as a commodity instead of sacred.

    In our contemporary era, we have come to such a state of environmental jeopardy that we may not be able to correct the destruction we have caused. Like the myths of botanical heroes who die and resurrect, countless myths relate the end of life on earth as inevitable, but their portrayals of the demise of the known world present this destruction too as a necessary stage that will result in the rebirth of a new world. In Hinduism, for example, the world must continuously succumb to a never-ending cycle of creation, destruction, and recreation. The Norse also believed that the loss of life for all beings at Ragnarok was vital to secure a new and revitalized world. The Babylonians, Greeks, Hebrews, Chinese, Mayas, etc., all believed that the earth had to experience a great flood that resulted in massive destruction, so that a renewed world could emerge. However, we as a people have come to an unprecedented time where we may have done irreparable damage to the earth's ability to maintain its cycles. We may have so thoroughly destroyed the environment and its natural resources that we might have thwarted its promise of everlasting regeneration. Still, we must strive to treat nature with the respect it deserves in order to try to maintain its vital and sacred cycles of continuality, or else we as a people may destroy all opportunities for rebirth, even for ourselves.

In our contemporary society, with our state of rampant environmental destruction and overall unwillingness to face the reality of life for all living beings upon this earth, we have lost sight of the meaning behind quests of botanical heroism, and so they have become a forgotten endeavor. As human beings we often try to escape the harsh realities of nature that call for aging, death, and decay, but if we run away from these natural facts, we run away from who we really are. As this book has tried to portray, there is serenity in internalizing the truth of our existence. If we embrace ourselves as natural beings, we are promised a natural immortality not articulated in religious doctrine, but promised nonetheless each moment of every day just beyond our windows and doors. In accepting the proper place of human beings within the ecosystem, as not elevated but equal to all living beings, one gains humility. And perhaps it is humility that is needed today to at least try to heal the damage we have done in forgetting our duty to take part in our own botanical heroic quests.

Therefore, let us all remember that which we came from, that where we will inevitably go, and that which we inherently are—nature—the source of all myths and heroes alike.

Chapter Notes

Introduction

1. Many critics have questioned the validity of Riane Eisler's *The Chalice and the Blade*. Though some of the conclusions in the book may be contested, David Loye's statement in *The New York Times*, November 1, 1987, speaks towards the merit of Eisler's scholarship.

2. Alan Dundes, *Sacred Narratives* (Berkeley: University of California Press, 1984); Walter Gulick, "The Thousand and First Face," in *Paths to the Power of Myth*, ed. Daniel C. Noel (New York: Crossroad, 1990); Marc Manganaro, *Myth, Rhetoric, and the Voice of Authority* (New Haven: Yale University Press, 1992); Robert Ellwood, *The Politics of Myth* (Albany: State University of New York Press, 1999).

Chapter 1

1. Henry R. Schoolcraft, *Myth of Hiawatha and Other Oral Legends* [1856] (Marquette, MI: Avery, 1997), 25–51.

2. Joseph Campbell, *Hero with a Thousand Faces* (Princeton: Princeton University Press, 1949).

3. Tony Allan, Charles Phillips, and Michael Kerrigan, *Artic Myths: Spirits of the Snow* (London: Duncan Baird, 1999), 77.

4. Charles Phillips and Michael Kerrigan, *Slavic Myth: Forests of the Vampire* (London: Duncan Baird Publishing, 1999), 34.

Chapter 2

1. Qtd. in Richard Buxton, *Forms of Astonishment: Greek Myths of Metamorphosis* (Oxford: Oxford University Press, 2009), 126–7.

2. Michael Kerrigan, Alan Lothian, and Piers Vitebsky, *Middle Eastern Myth: Epics of Early Civilization* (London: Duncan Baird Publishing, 1998), 46–47.

3. David Lemming and Jake Page, *The Mythology of Native North America* (Norman: University of Oklahoma Press, 1998).

4. Ibid, 203–204.

Chapter 3

1. Robert M. Torrance, *Encompassing Nature* (Washington, D.C.: Counterpoint, 1999), 64–5.

2. Karen Armstrong, *The Great Transformation: The Beginning of Our Religious Traditions* (New York: Anchor Books, 2007), 93.

3. Joseph Campbell, *Hero with a Thousand Faces* (Princeton: Princeton University Press, 1949); David Leeming, *Mythology: The Voyage of the Hero* (Oxford: Oxford University Press, 1998).

4. Leeming points to the works of James Frazer and Carl Jung in connecting the mythology of the dying god to the symbol of the tree.

5. Probably a more recent addition with the arrival of Christianity, as the text of the *Popul Vuh* was recorded after the arrival of the Spanish.

6. Donna Rosenberg, *World Mythology* (New York: McGraw-Hill, 1999), 604–6.

7. Cheryl Humphrey, *The Haunted Garden* (New York: Self-Published, 2012), 63–6.

8. Ibid., 67–8.

9. Ibid.

10. J. F. Bierlein, *Parallel Myths* (New York: Random House Publishing Group, 1994), 109–10.

11. Henry R. Schoolcraft, *The Myth of Hiawatha* (Marquette, MI: Avery, 1997), 88–91.

12. Joseph Campbell, *Primitive Mythology* (New York: Penguin, 1959), 221.

Chapter 4

1. Tony Allan and Charles Phillips, *Chinese Myth: Land of the Dragon* (London: Duncan Baird Publishers, 1999), 124–5.

2. Ann Dooley, *Playing the Hero: Reading the Irish Saga Táin Bó Cúailnge* (Toronto: University of Toronto Press, 2006), 158–9.

3. David Leeming and Jake Page, *God: Myths of the Male Divine God* (New York: Oxford, 1996), 18–21.

4. Joseph Campbell, *Primitive Mythology* (1959) (New York: Penguin, 1991), 258–60.

5. "The Bear Man, a Cherokee Legend," *First People—The Legends*. Web.

6. Tom Lowenstein and Piers Vitebsky, *Native American Myth: Mother Earth, Father Sky* (London, Duncan Baird Publishers, 1997), 99.

7. "The Story of Tuan Mac Cairill" *Sacred Texts*. Web.

Bibliography

Allan, Tony, and Charles Phillips. *Chinese Myth: Land of the Dragon*. (London: Duncan Baird Publishers, 1999.
_____. *World Myth: The Great Themes*. London, Duncan Baird Publishing, 2000.
_____, and Michael Kerrigan. *Artic Myths: Spirits of the Snow*. London: Duncan Baird, 1999.
Allan, Tony, Clifford Bishop, and Charles Phillips. *South American Myth: Lost Realms of Gold*. London: Duncan Baird Publishers, 1998.
Allan, Tony, Fergus Fleming, and Charles Phillips. *African Myth: Voices of the Ancestors*. London: Duncan and Baird Publishers, 1999.
Allan, Tony, Fergus Fleming, and Michael Kerrigan. *Oceanian Myth: Journeys Through Dreamtime*. London: Duncan Baird Publishing, 1999.
Allan, Tony, and Michael Kerrigan. *Japanese Myth: Realm of the Sun*. London: Duncan Baird Publishers, 2000.
Allan, Tony, and Sara Maitland. *Greek and Roman Myth: Titans and Olympians*. London: Duncan Baird Publishers, 1997.
Allan, Tony, and Tom Lowenstein. *Aztec and Maya Myth: Gods of Sun and Sacrifice*. London: Duncan Baird Publishers, 1997.
"Anguish of Rebirth." In *Encompassing Nature: A Sourcebook—Nature and Culture from Ancient Times to the Modern World*, ed. Robert M. Torrance. Washington, D.C.: Counterpoint, 1999.
Apollonius of Rhodes. *The Argonautica*. Trans. E. V. Rieu. New York: Penguin, 1972.
Armstrong, Karen. *The Great Transformation: The Beginning of Our Religious Traditions*. New York: Anchor Books, 2007.
_____. *A Short History of Myth*. Edinburgh: Canongate, 2005.
Armstrong, Rebecca. *Cretan Women: Pasiphae, Ariadne, and Phaedra in Latin Poetry*. Oxford: Oxford University Press, 2006.
Asaka, Yoshiko, and Simona Alias. "An Analysis of Nature in *Beowulf*: From the Perspective of its Relation to Man." *The Bulletin of the Japanese Association for Studies in the History of the English Language*, 2008, 1–10.
Auerbach, Loren, and Jacqueline Simpson. *Viking and German Myth: Sagas of the Norsemen*. London: Duncan Baird Publishers, 1997.
Baggs, Sydney, and Joan Baggs. *The Underworld in Myth, Magic, and Mystery*. North Charleston, SC: Bowker's Books, 2003.
Barnes, Craig S. *In Search of the Lost Feminine: Decoding the Myths That Radically Reshaped Civilization*. Golden, CO: Folcrum Publishing, 2006.
Barron, Patrick. "The Separation of Wild Animal Nature and Human Nature in Gilgamesh: Roots of a Contemporary Theme." *Papers on Language and Literature*, 38.4 (Fall 2002): 377–94.

"The Bear Man, a Cherokee Legend." *First People—The Legends.* Web. http://www.firstpeople. us/FP-Html-Legends/TheBearMan-Cherokee.html.

Beowulf. Trans. by Kevin Crossley-Holland. Suffolk: Phobe Phillips Editions, 1987.

Berndt, Ronald M., and Catherine H. Berndt. *The Speaking Land: Myth and Story in Aboriginal Australia.* Rochester, VT: Inner Traditions International, 1994.

"Bhagavad-Gita." Translated by William Quan Judge. The Theosophical University Press Online Edition. Web. http://www.theosociety.org/pasadena/gita/bg-eg-hp.htm.

Bierlein, J. F. *Parallel Myths.* New York: Random House Publishing Group, 1994.

"Book of Sermons." *Encompassing Nature: A Sourcebook—Nature and Culture from Ancient Times to the Modern World.* Ed. by Robert M. Torrance. Washington, D.C.: Counterpoint, 1999.

Brown, Joseph Epes, and Emily Cousins. *Teaching Spirits: Understanding Native American Religious Traditions.* Oxford: Oxford University Press, 2001.

Buxton, Richard. *Forms of Astonishment: Greek Myths of Metamorphosis.* Oxford: Oxford University Press, 2009.

Campbell, Joseph. *Goddesses: Mysteries of the Feminine Divine.* Novato, CA: New World Library, 2013.

_____. *Hero with a Thousand Faces.* Princeton: Princeton University Press (1949).

_____. "Hinduism." *Hindu Wisdom.* Initially posted on *The Joseph Campbell Foundation Website,* 2001. Web. http://www.hinduwisdom.info/articles_hinduism/12.htm.

_____. *Myths of Light: Eastern Metaphors of the Eternal.* New York: New World Library, 2012.

_____. *Myths to Live By* (1972). New York: Penguin, 1993.

_____. *Occidental Mythology: The Masks of God.* New York: Penguin Books, 1968.

_____. *Oriental Mythology: The Masks of God.* New York: Penguin Books, 1962.

_____. *Primitive Mythology: The Masks of God.* New York: Penguin Books, 1959.

Cauvin, Jacques. *The Birth of the Gods and the Origins of Agriculture.* Trans. Trevor Watkins. Cambridge: Cambridge University Press, 2000.

Chambers, R.W. *Beowulf: An Introduction to the Study of the Poem with a Discussion of the Stories of Offa and Finn.* Cambridge, UK: Cambridge University Press, 1967.

Chāndogya Upanishad. Encompassing Nature: A Sourcebook—Nature and Culture from Ancient Times to the Modern World. Edited by Robert M. Torrance. Washington, D.C.: Counterpoint, 1999.

Clasby, Nancy Tenfelde. "'Manabozho': A Native American Resurrection Myth." *Studies in Short Fiction,* 30.4 (Fall 1993): 583–94.

Clauss, James L. *The Best of the Argonauts: The Redefinition of the Epic Hero in Book 1 of Apollonius's Argonautica.* Berkley: University of California Press, 1993.

Conway, John. "The Significance of the Bull in the Minoan Religion." Synonym. Web. http:// classroom.synonym.com/significance-bull-minoan-religion-6916.html.

Corelyn, Senn F. "Journeying as Religious Education: The Shaman, the Hero, the Pilgrim, and the Labyrinth Walker." *Journal of Religious Education,* 97 (2), Web. http://www.tand fonline.com/doi/abs/10.1080/00344080290060897.

Cousineau, Phil. "Preface." *Joseph Campbell: The Hero's Journey.* Novato, CA: New World Library, 1990.

"Creation Cycle." In *World Mythology: An Anthology of the Great Myths and Epics,* ed. Donna Rosenberg. Chicago: NTC/Contemporary Publishing Group, 1999.

Crossley-Holland, Kevin. "Introduction." *Beowulf.* Trans. Kevin Crossley-Holland. Suffolk: Phobe Phillips Editions, 1987.

Dawson, Terence. "The Orpheus Complex." *Journal of Analytical Psychology.* Vol. 45 (2000). 245–266.

Dooley, Ann. *Playing the Hero: Reading the Irish Saga Táin Bó Cúailnge.* Toronto: University of Toronto Press, 2006.

Dougherty, Carol. *The Raft of Odysseus: The Ethnographic Imagination of Homer's Odyssey.* Oxford: Oxford University Press, 2001.

Downing, Christine. "Journeys to the Underworld." *Mythosphere*. Vol. 1, Issue 2 (1999). 175–193.

Egeler, Matthias. *Celtic Influences in Germanic Religion*. Munchen: Utz, 2013.

Eisler, Riane. *The Chalice and the Blade: Our History, Our Future*. San Francisco: Harper and Row, 1987.

Ellis, Peter Berresford. *Celtic Myths and Legends*. New York: Carroll and Graf Publishers, 2002.

Ellis Davidson, H. R. *Gods and Myths of Northern Europe* [1964]. New York: Penguin, 1988.

Fleming, Fergus, and Alan Lothian. *Egyptian Myth: The Way to Eternity*. London: Duncan Baird Publishers, 1997.

Fleming, Fergus, and Sharukh Husain. *Celtic Myth: Heroes of the Dawn*. London: Duncan Baird Publishers, 1996.

Frazer, James G. *The Golden Bough: The Roots of Religion and Folklore* [1890]. New York: Avenel Books, 1981.

Frothingham, A. L. "Medusa, Apollo, and the Great Mother." *American Journal of Archeology* 15 (3) (July 1911), pp. 349–377.

Galinsky, G. Karl. *The Herakles Theme: The Adaptations of the Hero in Literature from Homer to the Twentieth Century*. Oxford: Basil Blackwell, 1972.

"Gilgamesh." In *World Mythology*, ed. Donna Rosenberg. New York: McGraw-Hill, 1999.

Gimbutas, Marija. *The Gods and Goddesses of Old Europe: 7000–3500 B.C. Myths Legends and Cult Images*. Berkeley: University of California Press, 1974.

Goldsmith, Margaret E. *The Mode and Meaning of "Beowulf."* London: Athlone Press, 1970.

Graf, Fritz, and Sarah Iles Johnston. *Ritual Texts for the Afterlife: Orpheus and the Bacchic Gold Tablets* (2007). New York: Routledge, 2013.

Gwara, Scott. *Heroic Identity in the World of Beowulf*. Leiden: Bill Publishers, 2008.

Hahn, Thomas, editor. "The Wedding of Sir Gawain and Ragnelle." *Sir Gawain: Eleven Romances and Tales*. Web. http://d.lib.rochester.edu/teams/text/hahn-sir-gawain-wedding-of-sir-gawain-and-dame-ragnelle-introduction.

Heiden, Bruce. *Homer's Cosmic Fabrication: Choice and Design in the Iliad*. Oxford: Oxford University Press, 2008.

Herbert, Marie. "Transmutations of an Irish Goddess." In *The Concept of the Goddess*, ed. Miranda Green and Sandra Billington. New York: Taylor and Francis, 2002.

Hinds, Katherine. *Ancient Celts*. New York: Marshall Cavendish, 2010.

Homer. *Homeric Hymns*. Trans. Sarah Ruden. Indianapolis: Hackett Publishing, 2005.

———. *Iliad*. Translated by Robert Fagles. New York: Penguin, 1998.

———. *The Odyssey*. Translated by Robert Fagles. New York: Penguin, 1996.

"Jason and the Golden Fleece." In *World Mythology: An Anthology of the Great Myths and Epics*, ed. Donna Rosenberg. Chicago: NTC/Contemporary Publishing Group, 1999.

Johnston Staver, Ruth. *A Companion to Beowulf*. Westport, CT: Greenwood Publishers, 2005.

Kalsched, Donald, and Alan Jones. "Myth and Psyche: the Evolution of Consciousness." C.C. Jung Foundation, for Analytical Psychology, Inc. 1986. Web. http://www.cgjungny.org/d/d_mythpsyche.html.

Katha Upanishad. Encompassing Nature: A Sourcebook—Nature and Culture from Ancient Times to the Modern World. Ed. by Robert M. Torrance. Washington, D.C.: Counterpoint, 1999.

Kerrigan, Michael, Alan Lothian, and Piers Vitebsky. *Middle Eastern Myth: Epics of Early Civilization*. London: Duncan Baird Publishing, 1998, 46–7.

Krzyszkowska, Olga. *Mycenaean Seminar, 1998–1999*. Bristol: Institute of Classical Studies, 1999.

Leader, Carol. "The Odyssey—A Jungian Perspective," *British Journal of Psychotherapy* 25.4 (2009): 501–520.

Leeming, David Adams. *Mythology: The Voyage of the Hero*. New York: Oxford University Press, 1998.

Leeming, David Adams, and Jake Page. *God: Myths of the Male Divine*. New York: Oxford, 1996.

_____. *Goddess: Myths of the Female Divine*. New York: Oxford, 1994.

_____. *The Mythology of Native North America*. Norman: Oklahoma University Press, 1998.

Lefkowitz, Mary. "The Myth of Joseph Campbell," *American Scholar* 59.3 (1990): 429–442.

Leland, Charles G. *Algonquin Legends* [1884]. New York: Dover, 1992.

_____. *The World of Myth: An Anthology*. New York: Oxford University Press, 1990.

Lengers, L. "The Death of Beowulf" E-Thesis. Web. http://www.ethesis.net/beowulf/beowulf.htm.

Lev Kenaan, Vered. *Pandora's Secrets: The Feminine Character of the Ancient Text*. Madison: University of Wisconsin Press, 2008.

"Little Water Ceremony." In *Encompassing Nature: A Sourcebook—Nature and Culture from Ancient Times to the Modern World*, ed. Robert M. Torrance. Washington, D.C.: Counterpoint, 1999.

Loomis, Roger Sherman. *Celtic Myth and Arthurian Romance*. New York: Columbia University Press, 1926.

Lowenstein, Tom, and Piers Vitebsky. *Native American Myth: Mother Earth, Father Sky*. London: Duncan Baird Publishers, 1997.

Lusching, C. A. E. *Granddaughter of the Sun: A Study of Euripides' Medea*. Leiden: Brill Publishers, 2007.

Luthra, Rashmi. "Clearing Sacred Ground: Women-Centered Interpretations of the Indian Epics." *Feminist Formations*, 26.2 (Summer 2014): 135–161.

The Mabinogion. Trans. Sioned Davies. New York: Oxford University Press, 2007.

MacLeod, Sharon Paice. *Celtic Myth and Religion*. Jefferson, NC: McFarland, 2012.

Magoulik, Mary. "Quotes from Scholars of Myth." *On Heroism and Myth Throughout History and in Today's World*, 106.

Matthews, Caitlin. *The Celtic Tradition*. Shaftesbury, Dorset: Element Books Limited, 1995.

McCoppin, Rachel. *The Lessons of Nature in Mythology*. Jefferson, NC: McFarland, 2015.

McCoy, Dan. "Berserkers and Other Shamanic Warriors." *Norse Mythology for Smart People*. Web. http://norse-mythology.org/gods-and-creatures/others/berserkers-and-other-shamanic-warriors/.

McGrath, Kevin. *The Sanskrit Hero*. Boston: Brill Publishers, 2004.

McKie, Robin. "Prehistoric Cave Art in the Dordogne." *The Observer* (May 25, 2013), Web. https://www.theguardian.com/travel/2013/may/26/prehistoric-cave-art-dordogne.

Molloy, Barry P. C. "Martial Minoans: War as Social Process, Practice and Event in Bronze Age Crete." *The Annual of the British School of Athens*, 107 (2012) 87–142.

Montiglio, Silvia. *From Villain to Hero: Odysseus in Ancient Thought*. Ann Arbor: University of MI Press, 2014.

Mountford, Charles P. *The Dreamtime: Australian Aboriginal Myths*. Perth: Rigby Publications, 1965.

Moyes, Holly. *Sacred Darkness: A Global Perspective on the Ritual Use of Caves*. Boulder: University Press of Colorado, 2012.

"Ness of Brodgar Excavations: Revealing a Prehistoric Complex in the Heart of Neolithic Orkney." 2015. Web. http://www.orkneyjar.com/archaeology/nessofbrodgar/excavation-background-2/.

"Newgrange." *World Heritage Ireland*. Web. http://www.worldheritageireland.ie/bru-na-boinne/built-heritage/newgrange/.

"Ninhursag." In *Primal Myths: Creation Myths around the World* (1971), trans. Barbara C. Sproul. New York: HarperCollins, 1991.

Nixon, Lucia. "Changing Views of Minoan Society" in *Minoan Society*, ed. O. Krzyszkowska and Lucia Nixon. Bristol: Bristol Classical Press, 1983.

Norman, Dorothy. *The Hero: Myth/Image/Symbol*. New York: World Publishing Company, 1969.

Oelschlaeger, Max. *The Idea of Wilderness: From Prehistory to the Age of Ecology.* New Haven: Yale University Press, 1991.

O'Hare-Lavin, Mary Ellen. "Finding a 'Lower, Deeper Power' for Women in Recovery." *Counseling and Values,* 44.3 (Apr. 2000): 200.

Olson, Jess. "Celtic Influence on Arthurian Legend: Particularly in 'Sir Gawain and the Green Knight.'" 2013. Web. http://hubpages.com/literature/Celtic-Influence-on-Arthurian-Legend-Particularly-in-Sir-Gawain-and-the-Green-Knight.

Ovid. *Metamorphosis.* Trans. David Raeburn. New York: Penguin, 2004.

Pearson, Michael Parker. *Bronze Age Britain.* London: Batsford Publishers, 2003.

Pharo, Lars Kirkhusmo. "A Methodology for the Deconstruction and Reconstruction of the Concepts of 'Shaman' and 'Shamanism.'" *Numen: International Review for the History of Religions,* 58 (1), 2011, 6–70.

Phillips, Charles, and Michael Kerrigan. *Slavic Myth: Forests of the Vampire.* London, Duncan Baird Publishing, 1999.

_____, and David Gould. *Indian Myth: The Eternal Cycle.* London: Duncan Baird Publishing, 1998.

Plato. *Timaeus* (c. 360 BCE). Translated by Benjamin Jowett. Web. http://classics.mit.edu/Plato/timaeus.html.

Platon, Nicholas. *Crete.* Geneva: Nagel Publishers, 1966.

Popul Vuh: The Definitive Edition of the Mayan Book of the Dawn of Life and the Glories of the Gods and Kings. Trans. Dennis Tedlock. New York: Touchstone, 1985.

Porter, Anne M., and Glenn M. Schwartz. "The Archeology of Sacrifice in the Ancient Near East." *Academia.* Web. http://www.academia.edu/1651773/Sacred_Killing_The_Archaeology_of_Sacrifice_in_the_Ancient_Near_East.

"Purusha." In *Hindu Mythology, Vedic and Puranic* (1900). Trans. by W. J. Wilkins. Web. http://www.sacred-texts.com/hin/hmvp/hmvp36.htm.

"Quetzalcoatl." In *World Mythology: An Anthology of the Great Myths and Epics.* Ed. by Donna Rosenberg. Chicago: NTC/Contemporary Publishing Group, 1999.

Raglan, Lord. *The Hero: A Study in Tradition, Myth, and Drama* (1956). Westport, CT: Greenwood Press, 1975.

Ramsey, Jarold. *Reading the Fire: Essays in the Traditional Indian Literatures of the Far West.* Lincoln: University of Nebraska Press, 1983.

Rank, Otto, Lord Raglan, Alan Dundes, and Robert A. Segal. *In Quest of the Hero.* Princeton: Princeton University Press, 1990.

Redfield, James M. *Nature and Culture in the Iliad: The Tragedy of Hector.* Durham: Duke University Press, 1994.

Rig Veda. Primal Myths: Creation Myths Around the World (1971). Trans. by Barbara C. Sproul. New York: HarperCollins, 1991.

Rosenberg, Donna. *World Mythology: An Anthology of the Great Myths and Epics.* Chicago: NTC/Contemporary Publishing Group, 1999.

Schoolcraft, Henry R. *The Myth of Hiawatha and Other Oral Legends* [1856]. Marquette, MI: Avery, 1997.

Scott, James M. *Adoption as Sons of God.* Tübingen: Mohr, 1992.

"Sedna and the Fulmars." In *Encompassing Nature: A Sourcebook—Nature and Culture from Ancient Times to the Modern World,* ed. Robert M. Torrance. Washington, D.C.: Counterpoint, 1999.

"Sigurd the Volsung." In *World Mythology: An Anthology of the Great Myths and Epics,* ed. Donna Rosenberg. Chicago: NTC/Contemporary Publishing Group, 1999.

Sir Gawain and the Green Knight. Trans. W. S. Merwin. New York: Alfred A. Knopf, 2002.

Srinivasa Iyengar, K. R. *Sitayana: Epic of the Earth Born.* Madras: Samata Books, 1987.

Sturluson, Snorri. *The Prose Edda: Norse Mythology.* Trans. Jesse L. Byock. New York: Penguin, 2005.

Stone, Merlin. *When God was a Woman*. New York: Harvest/Harcourt Brace, 1976.

"The Story of Tuan Mac Cairill." *Sacred Texts*. Web. http://www.sacred-texts.com/neu/celt/ift/ift01.htm.

Swan, James A. *The Sacred Art of Hunting: Myths, Legends, and the Modern Mythos*. Minocqua, WI: Willow Creek Press, 1999.

Tacitus. *The Agricola and the Germania*. New York: Penguin, 1970.

The Táin: From the Irish Epic the Táin Bó Cuailnge. Trans. Thomas Kinsella. New York: Oxford University Press, 2002.

"Theoi Greek Mythology: Exploring Mythology in Classical Literature and Art." Web. http://www.theoi.com/Retrieved November 4, 2014.

Torrance, Robert M. *Encompassing Nature: A Sourcebook—Nature and Culture from Ancient Times to the Modern World*. Washington, D.C.: Counterpoint, 1999.

Trckova-Flamee, Alena. "Ariadne." *Encyclopedia Mythica*. November 2006. Web. http://www.pantheon.org/articles/a/ariadne.html.

Trubshaw, Bob. "An Overview of Mythological Theory." *Mythology, Cultural Studies and Related Disciplines*, 1–17.

Tun-yi, Chou. "The Great Ultimate." *T'ai-chi-t'u-shuo*. In *Encompassing Nature: A Sourcebook—Nature and Culture from Ancient Times to the Modern World*, Ed. Robert M. Torrance. Washington, D.C.: Counterpoint, 1999.

Tzu, Lao. *Tao Te Ching*. "Wisdom of the Lao Tzu." Web. http://www.poetryintranslation.com/PITBR/Chinese/TaoTeChing.htm. Retrieved November 6, 2014.

Valmiki. *The Ramayana*. Trans. by R. C. Dutt. Web. http://www.sacred-texts.com/hin/dutt/.

Van Nortwick, Thomas. *Somewhere I Have Never Travelled: The Hero's Journey*. New York: Oxford University Press, 1996.

_____. *The Unknown Odysseus: Alternate World's in Homer's Odyssey*. Ann Arbor: University of Michigan Press, 2011.

Vitebsky, Piers. *The Shaman: Voyages of the Soul Trance, Ecstasy and Healing from Siberia to the Amazon* (1995). London: Duncan Baird Publishers, 2008.

Webb, Eugene. "Rene Girard and the Symbolism of the Religious Sacrifice." *Anthropoetics 11* (1) (Spring/Summer 2005). Web. http://www.anthropoetics.ucla.edu/ap1101/webb.htm.

Wessing, Robert. "Sri and Sedana and Sita and Rama: Myths of Fertility and Generation." *Asian Folklore Studies*, 49 (2) (1990), 235–57.

Wilk, Stephen R. *Medusa: Solving the Mystery of the Gorgon*. New York: Oxford University Press, 2000.

Wilkinson, Philip. *Myths and Legends: An Illustrated Guide to Their Origins and Meanings*. New York: Metro Books, 2009.

Wood, Juliette. *The Celts: Life, Myth, and Art*. London: Watkins, 1998.

Zabriskie, Beverly. "Orpheus and Eurydice: A Creative Agony." *Journal of Analytical Psychology*. Vol. 45 (2000). 427–447.

Zimmerman, Larry J. *American Indians, The First Nations: Life, Myth, and Art*. London: Watkins, 2003.

Index